THE FIRST VOYAGE AROUND THE WORLD

ANTONIO PIGAFETTA

The First Voyage around the World 1519–1522

An Account of Magellan's Expedition

Edited by
Theodore J. Cachey Jr

UNIVERSITY OF TORONTO PRESS
Toronto Buffalo London

© University of Toronto Press 2007
Toronto Buffalo London
Printed in Canada

ISBN 978-0-8020-9370-7

The Lorenzo Da Ponte Italian Library

Printed on acid-free paper

Libraries and Archives Canada Cataloguing in Publication

Pigafetta, Antonio, ca. 1480/91–ca. 1534
The first voyage around the world, 1519–1522: an account of Magellan's expedition /
Antonio Pigafetta; edited and introduced by Theodore J. Cachey Jr.

(Lorenzo Da Ponte Italian library series)
Includes bibliographical references and index.
ISBN 978-0-8020-9370-7

1. Magalhães, Fernão de, d. 1521 – Travel. 2. Pigafetta, Antonio,
ca. 1480/91–ca. 1534 – Travel. 3. Voyages around the world – Early works to 1800.
I. Cachey, T.J. (Theodore J.) Jr. II. Title. III. Series.

G420.M2P63 2007   910.4'109031   C2007-906270-9

This volume is published under the aegis and with financial assistance of:
Fondazione Cassamarca, Treviso; Ministero degli Affari Esteri, Direzione Generale per
la Promozione e la Cooperazione Culturale; Ministero per i Beni e le Attività Culturali,
Direzione Generale per i Beni Librari e gli Istituti Culturali, Servizio
per la promozione del libro e della lettura.

Publication of this volume is assisted by the Istituto Italiano
di Cultura, Toronto.

University of Toronto Press acknowledges the financial assistance to its
publishing program of the Canada Council for the Arts and the
Ontario Arts Council.

University of Toronto Press acknowledges the financial support for its
publishing activities of the Government of Canada through the Book
Publishing Industry Development Program (BPIDP).

For Eleanor

Contents

Introduction

1. ' ... *to gain some renown with posterity*'

The Colombian novelist Gabriel García Márquez provided a memorable introduction to Antonio Pigafetta's *First Voyage around the World* (*Viaggio attorno al mondo*) when he evoked, at the beginning of his 1982 Nobel Lecture, the Renaissance traveller 'who went with Magellan on the first voyage around the world' and wrote 'a strictly accurate account that nonetheless resembles a venture into fantasy.' In the words of the Colombian novelist, the Italian witnessed 'hogs with navels on their haunches, clawless birds whose hens laid eggs on the backs of their mates, and others still, resembling tongueless pelicans, with beaks like spoons. He wrote of having seen a misbegotten creature with the head and ears of a mule, a camel's body, the legs of a deer and the whinny of a horse. He described how the first native encountered in Patagonia was confronted with a mirror, whereupon that impassioned giant lost his senses to the terror of his own image.'[1]

In effect, for García Márquez, Pigafetta's 'short and fascinating book ... even then contained the seeds of our present-day novels.' He acknowledged in Pigafetta a genealogical source for the 'marvellous' realism (more familiar perhaps as 'magical realism') that one has come to associate with the novelist's own fictions as well as those of other prominent Latin American authors. The political implications of these Renaissance origins were not lost on the Latin American Nobel Laureate. Indeed, the rhetorical category of the 'marvellous' that characterized Renaissance literature of discovery and exploration was often employed to veil an act of power and to gloss over real conflict by evoking 'a sense of the marvelous that in effect fills up the

emptiness at the center of the maimed rite of possession.'² Towards
the end of his address, the Colombian novelist pointedly isolated the
literary category of the 'marvellous,' synonymous with so much European 'Americanist' writing, and turned it back against the Old World.
For García Márquez the contemporary novelist's report of Latin
America's incredible political reality – the incessant upheavals, the military coups and massacres, the continents surreal political melodrama
– was 'strictly accurate' but nonetheless resembled 'a venture into
fantasy.' Exploiting another trope of European Americanist writing,
the commonplace of the New World's immense proportions when
compared with those of the Old World, García Márquez observed
that the number of *desaparecidos*, at that time 120,000, was equivalent
to all the inhabitants of Uppsala, Sweden, being unaccounted for. He
noted that the death toll from civil strife in Central America of one
hundred thousand in four years was proportionally equivalent to
1.6 million violent deaths in the United States. Europe's 'marvellous'
dream of possession had become Latin America's incredible night-
mare of war and massacre, of exile and forced emigration.

García Márquez's citation of Antonio Pigafetta's *First Voyage around
the World* is among the more recent and resonant of a long line of
prestigious literary responses to this Italian travel narrative. If
Pigafetta undertook his voyage, as he says, 'so that I might be able to
gain some renown with posterity' (2), he can be said to have succeeded brilliantly. The author's desire for fame, for the extension of
the self in space and time, was in fact a prominent motive for both
undertaking the journey and writing the narrative in the first place.
Pigafetta's account of the circumnavigation originally expressed a
desire for the circumvention of death that is at the heart of travel literature itself, which has always sought to 'fix and perpetuate something as transient and impermanent as human action and mobility.'³

William Shakespeare's use of Pigafetta's *libretto* (or 'little book,' as
the author terms it) in *The Tempest* is perhaps the best known manifes-
tation of Pigafetta's literary fame during the Renaissance:

> Caliban [*Aside*]: I must obey – his art is of such power,
> It would control my Dam's god, Setebos,
> And make a vassal of him. (1.2. 372–4)

And later,

> Caliban: Oh Setebos, these be brave spirits indeed!
> How fine my master is! I am afraid
> He will chastise me. (5.1. 261–3)

Shakespeare's 'Setebos' derived from his reading of Richard Eden's 1555 Tudor English translation of Pigafetta's narrative. Pigafetta had first introduced the Tuhuelche name into European circulation when he described a pair of Patagonian giants who, upon realizing Magellan had them placed in irons through subterfuge, 'raged like bulls, calling loudly for Setebos to aid them' (148); later, in one of his native word lists, Pigafetta defined 'Setebos' as 'their big devil' (231).[4] García Márquez, for his part, borrows from Pigafetta another moment from the same 'marvellous' anthropological encounter with the Patagonians that had inspired Shakespeare. The giant described by García Márquez, who confronts a mirror and is rendered senseless in terror at his own image, has a distinctively Shakespearean or Calibanic resonance. That Shakespeare was a possible mediator of García Márquez's perspective on Pigafetta is suggested by an allusion to Shakespeare made in an earlier meditation on the difference between New and Old World language and poetics, where the Colombian author first expressed his appreciation for Pigafetta's *First Voyage* (calling it there 'uno de mis libros favoritos de siempre'). Intriguingly, to illustrate the untranslatability of the Latin American experience, García Márquez used the example of the word *tempestad*: 'When we write the word *tempestad*, the Europeans think of thunder and lightning, but it is not easy for them to conceive of the same phenomenon which we are seeking to represent.'[5]

Shakespeare was not the earliest Renaissance poet to find inspiration in Pigafetta's *First Voyage*. A preliminary draft of canto 15 of Torquato Tasso's *Gerusalemme liberata* was largely based upon the American portion of Pigafetta's narrative. While most of the episode was suppressed in the poem's final version, it nevertheless represents an important moment both for the history of the elaboration of Tasso's poem and for the history of Italian Renaissance 'Americanism' in general.[6] According to Tasso's original plan, the extra-Mediterranean portion of Carlo and

Ubaldo's marvellous voyage to Armida's island followed a radically different itinerary from the one familiar to readers of the *Gerusalemme liberata*. Rather than pass directly to the Fortunate Islands, the 'barca avventurosa' set out upon the Ocean Sea bound for the New World. Tasso's heroes coasted a lengthy tract of South American *terra ferma* identified as the land of the 'inospitali Antropofagi,' and sighted along the shore the incredible 'Patagon giganti' made famous by Antonio Pigafetta's narrative. The literary quality of Pigafetta's book strongly stimulated the imagination of the Italian epic poet, especially its 'marvellous' treatment of the voyage. Tasso created a gallery of poetic marvels in a series of octaves based directly upon Pigafetta's prose account. Pigafetta's literary reception therefore, stretching from Torquato Tasso to Gabriel García Márquez, suggests intriguing lines of continuity, especially as regards the literary category of the marvellous, from the High Renaissance travel narrative, to High-Renaissance poetics of the marvellous (practised and expounded upon at length by Tasso and other High-Renaissance literary theorists), to contemporary Latin American magical realism.[7]

2. The Book of a Courtier

The prestigious literary circulation enjoyed by Pigafetta's book is due only in part to the heroic dimensions of its incredible historical subject – the Magellan-Elcano circumnavigation of the globe of 1519–22. In fact, if the return of the *Victoria* and its few surviving crew represented the greatest and culminating feat of the Renaissance Age of Discovery, so too Pigafetta's account of that achievement, first published in manuscript between February and June 1525, represented the literary epitome of its genre.[8] One of the masterpieces produced by Italian courtier culture of the High Renaissance, Pigafetta's *First Voyage* belongs to the same generation, albeit in a minor generic key, as other more familiar Italian literary classics published in the first decades of the 16th century such as Sannazaro's *Arcadia*, Machiavelli's *The Prince*, Ariosto's *Orlando Furioso*, and Castiglione's *The Book of the Courtier*. Like these works, Pigafetta's *First Voyage* emerges from a period of deep political and cultural crisis in Italy that began with the initial French invasion of the peninsula in 1494 and reached its height in the Sack of Rome in 1527. The breakdown of the Italian court system under the pressures of French and Spanish incursions, the religious revolution set in motion by the Protestant Reformation, and the great oceanic discoveries all contributed to Italy's increasing marginalization within the context of early modern Western European history. From a literary and cultural point of view, the Italian High Renaissance therefore represented a kind of swansong, a brilliant culminating flourish. Like the better-known literary classics and artworks of the period, Pigafetta's *libreto* achieves a kind of fulfilment or realization in its genre within an Italian context. And in its own way, like other Italian cultural products of the period, Pigafetta's *First Voyage* went abroad and achieved an international reputation, beginning with at least three French illuminated manuscripts and the Simon de Colines *editio princeps* published in Paris circa 1525.[9] Pigafetta's *First Voyage* illustrates in its own way, even at the reputedly unexalted level of the travel narrative, both the mobility of the cosmopolitan courtier and the exportability of Italian courtier culture of the High Renaissance. At the same time that Italian culture enters a period of deep crisis and growing marginalization, the Italian courtier-traveller goes out into the world, pen in hand,[10] to assert a compensatory literary authority, in relation to European political hegemony established over the newly discovered lands by some of the same emerging European powers that were engaged in carving up the Italian peninsula.

The original Italian courtly derivation of the work merits further consideration, given that Pigafetta's *First Voyage* represents a particularly mature expression of courtly Italian Renaissance travel writing. Indeed, to speak of an Italian courtier extraction for the work is to locate it within the 'lingua e letteratura cortigiana' (courtly language and literature) that flourished briefly on the peninsula between the end of the fifteenth and the first decades of the sixteenth centuries, and produced the Italian High Renaissance. We can gain perspective on Pigafetta's literary and linguistic sensibility by considering his position in relation to the Italian 'Questione della lingua,' that is, as expressive of Italian cosmopolitan court culture in contrast to the vernacular humanist and municipal Florentine outlook on the Italian scene. As we will see, Pigafetta stands in suggestive counterpoint to the classicizing vernacular humanism canonized by Pietro Bembo's *Prose della volgar lingua* (first published, like Pigafetta's narrative, in 1525), which resurrected the fourteenth century language and style of Petrarch (for poetry) and Boccaccio (for prose) as the vernacular classicizing model for subsequent Italian literary history.[11]

But more particularly, it is important to appreciate how Pigafetta's book represents the culmination and at the same time the confluence of two particularly important subgenres of Italian Renaissance travel writing. In the first place, Pigafetta appears at the end of a distinguished line of Italian Americanist *auctores* (an Atlantic tradition, if you will, which goes back to Boccaccio's *De canaria* in the fourteenth century and Cadamosto's letters in the fifteenth). If Pigafetta's is indeed a first-hand account of the circumnavigation, he nevertheless shows himself time and again to be extremely self-conscious about writing in the literary tradition of Renaissance travel. In the dedicatory letter to his book, for example, Pigafetta mentions that he had been prepared for his participation in the voyage by 'having learned many things from many books that I had read' (2). And it is easy to imagine our author as a youth (he was born around 1492)[12] devouring one of the earliest collections of discovery voyages, published in his home town of Vicenza in 1507 by Enrico da Ca' Zeno: Fracanzio da Montalboddo's *I paesi novamente ritrovati et Novo Mondo da Americo Vespucio Florentino intitolato*, a volume that included the narratives of the voyages of Cadamosto, Columbus, and Cabral, besides Vespucci. The Vicentine appears to be especially indebted to the universally read (as More tells us)[13] Amerigo Vespucci; but he also displays affinities to other Italian Americanists, including, for example, Niccolò Scillacio (*De insulis*, 1494) and Michele Da Cuneo, whose letter to Hieronymo Annari (1495) represents a significant example of Italian courtly travel writing in its own right. Pigafetta's book, more or less contemporary with Verrazzano's 1524 letter to Francis I regarding his explorations of the North American coast, represents the culmination of the Italian *americanista* tradition, and recapitulates many of the salient characteristics of that tradition, such as a heroic ideological perspective, a relative detachment from national political and commercial interests, and a paradoxically legitimating utilization of the 'marvellous.' Girolamo Benzoni's *Historia del nuovo mondo* (1565), the last major Italian contribution to the tradition of Americanist travel writing, is, by comparison, merely a highly interesting epigone of that tradition, as well as a masterpiece of Americanist plagiarism.[14]

Pigafetta's book also represents the point of arrival for an important Orientalist subgenre of Italian Renaissance travel writing. The *isolario*, or Book of Islands genre might plausibly be termed 'Orientalist' since the earliest examples from the fifteenth century limited their coverage to the culturally mixed, and politically and commercially contested, archipelagos of the eastern Mediterranean.[15] The fifteenth century prototype of the Book of Islands genre, Crisotoforo Buondelmonti's *Liber insularum archipelagi*, circulated widely during the fifteenth and sixteenth centuries, and as a member of the Order of the 'Sea Knights' of Rhodes, Antonio Pigafetta would surely have been familiar with this work.[16] To recognize the *First Voyage's* affinity to the *isolario* tradition generally, and to Buondelmonti in particular, is to recover an important aspect of the work's original courtier Renaissance character, which has been lost on post-Enlightenment readers of the work.

3. Reading for Scholars and Princes

The book's courtly Americanist and Orientalist origins are conveniently signalled in the dedicatory letter: by the presence of Pigafetta's fellow Vicentine and patron, the powerful ecclesiastic and diplomat Francesco Chiericati, who first took Pigafetta with him to Spain; and by the dedication of the work to the Grand Master of the Knights of Rhodes, the French noble Philippe Villiers de l'Isle-Adam. Francesco Chiericati, with whom Pigafetta 'discussed the great and marvellous things of the Ocean Sea' (2) possessed impeccable Americanist credentials. He appears, for example, in the introduction to one of Matteo Bandello's *Novelle* (I, 34), at the court of Pandino upon his return from Portugal, recounting the marvels of the New World, and displaying 'golden objects, pearls, precious stones and other beautiful things brought back from those countries. He exhibited also certain idols marvelously fashioned in mosaic, that those people, who have by now for the most part become Christians, used to adore.'[17] Bandello has Chiericati go on to tell about the custom among some men in those new countries to vie for the honour of having their wives pass the night with foreign visitors, concluding that 'jealousy has no place among those simple and primitive people, nor does it cause them to take up arms.' An observation that leads, without fail, to a *novella* illustrating the negative effects of Old World jealousy. Beyond this literary representation, Chiericati's own travel writings, usually addressed to Isabella d'Este (to whom he recommended Pigafetta immediately following the return of the *Victoria*), include a fascinating account of a trip to Ireland,[18] and oscillate between the same poles of critical investigation and ingenuous enthusiasm for the marvellous that characterize Pigafetta's narrative.

As a member of the Order of the 'Sea Knights' of Rhodes, Pigafetta dedicates his *First Voyage* to Grand Master Villiers de l'Isle-Adam at a crucial historical moment. The Order of the Hospital of St John of Jerusalem had since the fourteenth century represented 'the bulwark of Christendom' in the Levant. The surrender of Rhodes and flight to Italy, which led to the Order's temporary settlement in Viterbo and later establishment in Malta, sent shock waves through Christian Europe. Clearly, no more dramatic period of crisis for the order, or of Christian power in the eastern Mediterranean, could be conjured up as a background for Magellan's circumnavigation. As we shall see in the next section, recognition of this 'Rhodian' context for Pigafetta's *First Voyage* suggests a strong connection between Pigafetta's book and the Book of Islands genre. For the moment, however, one can observe how Chiericati and the Grand Master provide a literary and ideological framework for a reading of the work.

The dedicatory letter also establishes the heroes of the narrative, for there are indeed two heroes of this epic – Magellan and Pigafetta – just as there are two heroic activities to be celebrated – exploration and narration. A recent Italian editor of Pigafetta's narrative has persuasively illuminated the care with which Pigafetta structured the text so as to celebrate the heroic figure of Magellan as 'bon pastore' (good shepherd) and as 'bon cavaliero' (good knight).[19] Magellan's death, in fact, occurs almost exactly at the midpoint of the narrative (699), and he emerges as a heroic figure worthy of the extraordinary geographical feat of the circumnavigation that he tragically did not live to see through to its end. But Pigafetta's treatment of Magellan should not obscure the extent to which the author stages himself as the hero of his own text, albeit in a quite subtle way. Pigafetta is careful to place his two heroes on the same social plane in the dedicatory letter, where they are described as members of prestigious religious-military orders setting out to discover 'the spicery in the islands of Molucca' (3); Pigafetta styles himself a 'patrician of Vicenza and Knight of Rhodes' (1) and Magellan 'a Portuguese gentleman, commendador of the Order of Santiago de le Spada' (3). Magellan's death, following his preaching and thaumaturgic display (594–610) in the Philippines (which leads to many conversions), is described by Pigafetta in terms of a religious martyrdom. Pigafetta's own near-death experience is no less resonant, from a literary perspective. Early on in the navigation among the islands of the Philippine archipelago, on the Feast Day of the Annunciation, Pigafetta writes,

> I went to the side of the ship to fish, and putting my feet upon a yard leading down into the storeroom, they slipped, for it was rainy, and consequently I fell into the sea, so that no one saw me, and when I was all but under, my left hand happened to catch hold of the clew-garnet of the mainsail, which was dangling in the water. I held on tightly, and began to cry out so lustily that I was rescued by the small boat. I was aided, not, I believe, indeed, through my merits, but through the mercy of that font of charity [the Virgin]. (334–6)

Here the emphasis is on Pigafetta's own travel as a heroic test, as a loss that brings about a gain of stature and certainty of self. Pigafetta survives this near-death experience, just as he had survived the crossing of the Pacific ['Nineteen men died twenty-five or thirty men fell sick. By the grace of God, I suffered no infirmity' (244–5)]. He survives the circumnavigation itself, acquiring in the process an increased stature among mortals, emerging as a worthy witness to

Magellan's martyrdom and the achievement of the circumnavigation. The narrative presents the account of a kind of fictional death and resurrection of Pigafetta, 'fictional rather than real because death is used as a context for the assertion of an essential and irreducible self; implicitly denied is the reality of death as a dissolution of form and a solvent of identity.'[20] Just as the circumnavigation is figured by Pigafetta as an escape from death, Pigafetta's book expresses at yet another level a heroic desire to circumvent death and to 'gain some renown with posterity.'

Without question, Pigafetta's experience and its writing are in their own ways celebrated as glorious and heroic. Besides 'the great and wonderful things' to report from 'my long and dangerous voyage,' Pigafetta's 'vigils, hardships, and wanderings' (5) recall the heroic vigils and sleepless nights of Amerigo Vespucci, canonized in the famous *Stradanus* engraving that portrays the Florentine sighting the stars during the middle of the night, while sailors lie slumped around him sleeping in a kind of New World Gethsemane. Like Vespucci, Pigafetta is careful to cite all the highly placed personages who legitimate his endeavour in one way or another – and what more appropriate patrons for a circumnavigation of the globe than the emperor and the pope. Pigafetta sailed in fact 'with the good grace of his Caesarean Majesty' (2), and upon his return was summoned by the pope to recount his adventures. The author's reference to his 'going to see his Holiness, Pope Clement' (4) alludes to just one key moment in the remarkable history of Pigafetta's peregrinations after his return (these are detailed in the bio-bibliographical treatment that follows this introduction). At one point, there was actually the promise of Pope Clement VII's sponsorship for the printing of Pigafetta's book.

From a rhetorical perspective, the legitimating strategy of evoking highly placed patrons for one's explorations was of course commonplace. It had already been masterfully practised by Vespucci: 'two [voyages] were by command of the exalted King of Castile Don Fernando VI, to go west over the depths of the Ocean Sea, and the other two were by the command of the mighty King Don Manuel of Portugal, to go south.'[21] Pigafetta adopts a similar strategy in both the dedicatory letter and in the work's concluding paragraph, which is more explicit in this regard, and which represents a kind of envoi to the work (a quintessentially courtly literary feature). The narrative, in fact, circles around like the voyage itself, and returns to the courtly context from which it had departed, with details concerning the courtly reception that awaited the author:

> Leaving Seville, I went to Valladolid, where I presented to his sacred Majesty, Don Carlo, neither gold nor silver, but things worthy to be very highly esteemed by such a sovereign. Among other things, I gave him a book, written by my hand, concerning all the matters that had occurred from day to day during our voyage. I left there as best I could and went to Portugal, where I spoke with King Dom João of what I had seen. Passing through Spain, I went to France, where I made a gift of certain things from the other hemisphere to the mother of the most Christian king, Don Francis, Madame the Regent. Then I came to Italy, where I devoted myself forever, and these my poor labours, to the famous and most illustrious lord Philippe Villiers de l'Isle-Adam, the most worthy Grand Master of Rhodes. (1352–6)

While Amerigo Vespucci reports in his letters that he had explored and discovered at the command of the kings of Spain and Portugal, Pigafetta records in a similar vein his post-circumnavigation tour, during which he was repeatedly called upon to recount his experiences at court. There had been an evident shift in emphasis since 1492, from the Genoese Columbus's claim to glory as 'inventor' of a New World (as an explorer first and a writer second), to Antonio Pigafetta's claim on 'some renown with posterity' based principally upon his having composed a book about the circumnavigation. Vespucci occupies a middle position between these two. While the Florentine's contributions in the literary 'invention' of America through the publication of the *Mundus Novus* and *Letter to Soderini* surpass and overshadow his contributions to geographical and navigational knowledge, the latter were nonetheless based upon some genuine expertise, given that Vespucci was appointed 'Pilot Major' by the king of Spain in 1508. Italy's role however as historical protagonist in the discoveries and explorations, exemplified by the Genoese Columbus and other Italians, came to an end after one generation. Pigafetta's role as simple witness some thirty years following the discovery of America reflects the general eclipse of Italy as the geographical, religious, and commercial centre located at the heart of the Mediterranean Old World, and its increasing marginalization as the New World of Atlantic colonial nation states emerged.[22] Moreover, the Italian Pigafetta's enduring fame as witness and scribe of a historic achievement effected by an Iberian power encapsulates the fundamentally humanistic and literary character of Renaissance Italy's response to foreign political domination and to its estrangement from 'modern' European history.[23] In other words, Italian Renaissance culture's commitment to writing and its belief in the enduring status of the written word are powerfully illustrated even by an ostensibly non-humanistic text like Pigafetta's *First Voyage*. On this point, Italian vernacular court culture was evidently no less imbued with the same ideal that inspired the vernacular humanists and contemporary Florentines in their literary endeavours.

Pigafetta's request in the dedicatory letter that the Grand Master deign to take up 'this little book when you will take some rest from your continual Rhodian cares' speaks specifically to the travel narrative's function within the courtly literary system. There is a direct parallel in Vespucci's *Letter to Soderini*, where the Florentine addressed the Gonfaloniere: 'continually occupied as Your Magnificence must be with public concerns, still you must reserve some hours for recreation, and spend a little time in trifling or delightful things; and just as fennel is customarily placed on top of delicious foods to improve them for digestion, so you will be able to escape from your many occupations, to have this letter of mine read, so that you may take refuge somewhat from the continual care and assiduous consideration of public matters.'[24] The precise echo of Vespucci's desire to assuage Soderini's 'assiduous consideration of public matters' in Pigafetta's offer to relieve the Grand Master's 'continual Rhodian cares' (5) underscores the analogous conceptions these authors had of the literary category in which they were writing. Travel is taken here as a recreative category of literature combining useful (particularly ethnographic and geographical) information, with delightful, 'marvellous' matters. Moreover, it makes ideal reading for princes and scholars for it serves 'to relax a little the intention of their thoughts, that they may be more apt and able to endure a continued course of study,' as Lucian put it in the preamble of the *True History*.[25]

This courtly literary context for Pigafetta's *First Voyage* explains in large measure the role of the 'marvellous' in Pigafetta's narrative, as well as much of the work's undeniable literary appeal. The narrative of the voyage more or less begins with a description of the miraculous tree of the waterless island of Hierro in the Canaries (on the threshold between the Old and New Worlds): 'the leaves and branches of which distil a quantity of water ... [and] the people living there, and the animals, both domestic and wild, fully satisfy themselves with this water and no other' (30). The first in a series of marvels that constitute Pigafetta's account of the outward passage, the miraculous tree of Hierro had, since Columbus, represented one of those classic Atlantic myths that served rhetorically to mark the passage from Old World to New. The tree's status as a literary commonplace seems paramount here, especially in light of the fact that the expedition did not stop at Hierro. The marvellous serves to establish the authority of Pigafetta's account with the contemporary courtly audience, which had come to expect such wonders from their travel narratives. Other marvels of crossing include tremendous storms and the repeated appearance of St Elmo's fire, sharks with terrible teeth, and those birds mentioned by García Márquez that 'make no nest because they have no feet, and the hen lays her eggs on the back of the cock, and hatches them.' The marvellous 'caccia de' pesci' with which our author highlights the passage through the Strait of Magellan (later poeticized by Tasso) represents yet another marvellous 'passage,' which serves both to establish the alterity of the new worlds encountered and, paradoxically, to legitimize the veracity of Pigafetta's account. Another related strategy employed by Pigafetta is exemplified by the stereotypical account of his first encounter with the natives of Brazil (49–86), based upon the authoritative descriptions of Columbus and Vespucci. In this regard Pigafetta continues in the line of Vespucci, who had imitated Columbus in a similar fashion. The 'inventor' Columbus not only discovered a continent but inaugurated a new Americanist sub-genre within the context of travel narrative, and thus became a model for imitation. After satisfying the readers' initial expectations, Pigafetta goes on to describe the famous encounters with the Patagonian giants, which can be seen as brilliant literary elaborations on a theme of American giants inaugurated by Amerigo Vespucci both in his first familiar letter and in the *Letter to Soderini*.

This kind of appreciation for the Italian courtly literary context for the *First Voyage* also casts light on the notorious problem presented by the fact that in this, the most important by far of the first-hand sources regarding Magellan's voyage, there is so little information about the dramatic episodes of mutiny and desertion that plagued the expedition from the start, and even this is garbled and oblique. Indeed, the expedition's internal politics, that have always fascinated historians of the voyage, are generally elided in favour of the 'marvels' of travel, the heroic stature of the captain-general, and the achievement of the circumnavigation. An initial incident in fact took place during the Atlantic crossing when Juan de Cartagena's insubordination led to his deposition as commander of the *S. Antonio* and his being placed in the stocks. As we have just seen, Pigafetta, during this part of the voyage, instead treats us to a gallery of transatlantic 'marvels.' Generally speaking, the 'marvellous' seems to expand and fill the narrative space in precisely those moments when trouble is afoot.

The mutiny that Pigafetta could not ignore took place at Port St Julian by Gaspar Quesada, Juan de Cartagena, and Juan Sebastian del Cano on 1–2 April 1519. The story is perhaps best told by Magellan's excellent biographer Guillemard, who based himself upon a collation of all the sources.[26] While Pigafetta is generally considered the most important source for the expedition's history, on these episodes he is no help at all. Indeed, according to Guillemard, his account is 'remarkable for its extraordinary inaccuracy' (174); it seemed 'incredible that an eyewitness – which [Pigafetta] undoubtedly was – should have failed to remember circumstances such as these, and the fact somewhat lessens the value of his book as a credible narrative' (174). For fuller and more accurate accounts of the mutiny,

Guillemard must turn instead to the official historiographers such as the Spaniard Herrera and the Portuguese Barros, who had competing national interests to safeguard in their respective histories. At this crucial point in his narrative, Pigafetta is more concerned with the description of the encounter with the Patagonian giants, which includes several well-developed episodes (107–62). He squeezes his account of the mutiny (176–9) between the encounter with the Patagonians (the one that made an impression on Shakespeare) and the discovery of the strait (180–230). Certainly, from a literary perspective, Pigafetta's 'marvellous' encounter with the Patagonian giants more than compensates for his lack of information about the mutiny. In any case, Pigafetta's intention to celebrate his hero Magellan did not require that he descend into the domestic details of who did what to whom, beyond the fact that Magellan won the day.

Pigafetta's remarkable detachment from the local political aspects of the voyage goes together with his emphasis on the 'marvellous' and the heroic celebration of Magellan. Pigafetta seeks to create a sense of the 'marvellous' in order to 'fill up the emptiness at the center of the maimed rite of possession,' to use Stephen Greenblatt's formula for Columbus's writing.[27] Columbus's claims of possession declared on the beach at San Salvador are no more plausible or legitimate than those made by European powers seeking to establish their hegemony over the Spice Islands. This was by means of a long tradition of legalistic fictions going back to the Papal bull *Inter caetera* (1493) and the Treaty of Tordesillas (1494), in which the entire globe was divided into Spanish and Portuguese spheres of influence. The competing colonial claims of these emerging powers upon the whole world and the commercially motivated extension of European power are masked to some extent by Pigafetta's literary program. Magellan is heroically and unproblematically figured as a Christian knight gone out to convert the heathen and subdue the infidel according to a broader supranationalist crusader ideal. Given the 'international' courtly audience for whom Pigafetta's narrative was intended, political disputes between European powers are naturally muted in favour of a general picture of Christian unity vis-à-vis the Gentile or Moorish peoples of the antipodes. Indeed, it is remarkable that, besides making occasional reference to the 'line of demarcation,' Pigafetta never explicitly discusses the political issue that the historians tell us constituted the motivating force behind the circumnavigation in the first place: to determine the true position of the Spice Islands (or Moluccas), and to establish that they were on the Spanish side of the line.

Pigafetta also exhibits a relatively neutral perspective on the commercial aspects of the expedition, which is what one would expect given both his courtier social background and his epic-heroic literary intentions. Vespucci had already belittled the achievement of the Portuguese Vasco da Gama for sailing for primarily commercial reasons, a motivation that detracted from the heroic virtue of discovery as an end in itself.[28] The voyage of discovery, in order to be the heroic object of epic celebration, must find a way around the commercial bourgeois motive for travel more appropriate to the literary category of romance.[29] Like Vespucci before him, Pigafetta apparently had little direct economic or political stake in the voyage. Instead, he is 'Antonio Lombardo' (Antonio of Lombardy), 'sobresaliente' (a supernumerary), as he is called in the expedition's roster. The detached perspective of the courtly observer is drawn to the 'marvellous' natural and anthropological world encountered, and celebrates both the heroic virtues of the captain-general (whose attributes of 'bon pastore' and 'bon cavaliero' are exalted beyond the realm of immediate political contingency), and the epic geographical achievement of the circumnavigation.

4. A Unity of Narrative and Cartography

It would be misleading to leave the impression that Pigafetta's narrative is a marvel-filled travel narrative and hagiographic text, although it presents characteristics of both these genres. Indeed, *The First Voyage* is much more: its remarkably accurate ethnographic and geographical account of the circumnavigation has guaranteed its elevated status among modern historiographers and students of the discoveries and earliest contacts between Europeans and the people of the East Indies. Recall that Gabriel García Márquez emphasized in his Nobel address the accuracy of Pigafetta's account 'that nonetheless resembles a venture into fantasy.' While we have just seen how, with respect to the political implications of the 'marvellous,' Pigafetta's procedure may constitute a diversion (which García Márquez took pains to rectify), the ethnographic and geographic truth value of Pigafetta's account is not finally undermined. Indeed, although it might seem something of a paradox, there is clearly a sense in which the marvellous aspects of the narrative serve rhetorically to authorize or enhance the truth value of the ethnographic and geographic evidence. The post-Enlightenment view of geography and ethnography as sciences distinct from the literary leads us to see them as exclusive of literary 'marvels,' when for Pigafetta and his Renaissance readers the 'marvellous' and the true could still be not only co-present but actually mutually reinforcing. In fact, structurally speaking, Pigafetta's 'marvellous' can be said to enclose the central experiences in the book regarding the expedition's encounters in the Philippines and Moluccas. The prominent place given to the marvellous natural and anthropological encounters in the New World, based as they are on recognizable literary stereotypes, and the Marco Polian encounters (second-hand reports) of India and China, which Pigafetta recounts before embarking on the return trip (1267–1322), serve as an authorizing frame for what's most new and most true in Pigafetta's narrative. Indeed, it is the extremely lucid and precise account of the time spent navigating the East Indian archipelagos of the Philippines and the Moluccas, including the repeated courtly negotiations with various indigenous groups, which constitutes, beyond the celebration of Magellan, one of the book's major interests.[30]

Two aspects of Pigafetta's account are particularly worthy of note in this regard. The first is Pigafetta's attention to the language of the peoples encountered, which results in wordlists or vocabularies, including extensive lists for the Philippine (160 words of what he calls 'the language of the heathen' to distinguish it from the Malay Muslims) and Malay languages respectively (this last made up of some 450 words). The second is Pigafetta's contribution to the cartography of the East Indies, which takes the form of twenty-three painted maps, featured in the earliest manuscripts of the book. Both aspects were already present in the previous tradition: in Columbus's and Peter Martyr's embryonic word lists of the Taino language, and in the close linking of narrative account to cartographic record by Columbus and Vespucci. Pigafetta, however, raises both the treatment of indigenous languages and cartography to a new level in his *First Voyage*, and, on both counts, again appears informed by the peculiarly Italian courtier context for his writing.

The Vicentine's remarkably acute linguistic sensibility is evidenced throughout the narrative, and his extreme attention to and remarkable ear for languages seems to reflect his formation as an Italian courtier. The linguistic character of Pigafetta's text itself is an eclectic, yet highly efficacious, mix of literary Tuscan, Venetisms, and Iberianisms. The cosmopolitan linguistic identikit of our author is informed by his experience in an Italian court society that was open to diverse linguistic and cultural influences from abroad. From the beginning of the narrative he gives numerous Spanish and Portuguese technical terms, often, unlike Vespucci, glossing them for his Italian reader. Pigafetta's accounts of diplomatic negotiations (in which he participated on occasion as European ambassador) are particularly compelling. At one point Pigafetta translates what has since been identified as a common Malay idiom, when he reports that the Malay king 'told us that he was like a child at the breast who knew his dear mother was departing and was leaving him alone' (1119). He even goes so far as to note that in the local language of Java, the name of the island is pronounced Jaoa, and not Java (1258). The accuracy of his transcriptions of place names is striking. The vast majority of Pigafetta's East Indian toponyms are easily matched to their modern equivalents. It is not surprising then if Pigafetta's record of indigenous toponyms, like his list of 450 words of Malay, have been described by competent scholars as extremely accurate. The Malay vocabulary is one of the oldest written specimens of the Malay language, the earliest surviving manuscripts being dated from around 1500–50. Pigafetta's Philippine and Malay word lists cumulatively constitute a kind of implicit anthropological portrait of the East Indian societies encountered.[31] Pigafetta's linguistic attitude presents a stark contrast to Pietro Bembo's classicizing vernacular humanism, which was establishing itself at the same time in Italy with the *Prose della volgar lingua* (1525). The Vicentine occupies the most avant-garde position within the courtly linguistic perspective on the Italian 'Questione della lingua'. Indeed, there appears to be a highly suggestive, even proportional inverse relation between the Italian vernacular humanist Bembo's turning inward and back in time to erect Boccaccio and Petrarch as literary and linguistic *auctores* for Italian eloquence, and, simultaneously, the Italian courtier Pigafetta's linguistic opening to other worlds at the farthest reaches of the globe. Pigafetta similarly redirects an Italian cartographic tradition and sensibility in his twenty-three charts depicting the East Indian archipelagos. But in order for its contribution to that tradition to be adequately appreciated, his book must first be restored, as in the present edition, to its earliest form as a synthesis of narrative and cartography. This unity, which characterized the work from its first appearance in the earliest manuscripts, was lost as soon as the book began to be printed; neither the humble setting of the Colines editio princeps (c. 1525) nor the nondescript 1536 Italian imprint anonymously published by Giambattista Ramusio include the twenty-three charts, which were an integral part of Pigafetta's original conception of the book (and neither did he later include them in his *Navigazioni e viaggi*). The separation of the maps from the narrative effected at the beginning of the editorial history has been continued by most editions, including, symptomatically, the recent and otherwise authoritative edition of the Italian text upon which the present edition is based.[32] The interpretive result of this dismemberment of the book has been the loss of a sense of Pigafetta's original conception of the book as a unity of narrative and cartography, and its generic relationship to the tradition of Renaissance *isolari*, and especially the most important *isolario* of the fifteenth century and the genre's *capostipite*, Cristoforo Buondelmonti's *Liber insularum Archipelagi* (*The Book of the Islands of the Archipelago*).[33]

Buondelmonti (born around 1380) is primarily known for the *Liber insularum* and the *Descriptio insulae Cretae* (*Description of Crete*), works authored during his travels in the Aegean, taking Rhodes as his base of operations, between 1415 and his death around 1431. A Florentine prelate and contemporary of Poggio Bracciolini, with contacts to the humanist circle of Niccolò Niccoli, Buondelmonti was one of the most significant figures of the fifteenth century Aegean world, which played host to a cosmopolitan and socially mixed culture with strong ties, through a dense network of diplomatic, ecclesiastic, and commercial relations, to the world of Italian humanism. As a travel writer, Buondelmonti's most significant innovation was to fuse the humanistic genre of geographical encyclopedic compendia (like Boccaccio's *De montibus*, Bandini's *Fons memorabilium universi*, and Da Silvestri's *De insulis et earum proprietatibus*) with that of contemporary sailing journals, charts, and portolans. Both the *Liber insularum* and the *Descriptio insulae Cretae* represent first-hand accounts of Buodelmonti's travels laced with antiquary commentary and accompanied by charts of the islands visited.

The original version of the *Liber insularum* was dedicated to the humanist bibliophile Cardinal Giordano Orsini and forwarded to him in Rome in 1420. Surviving in at least four redactions made during the Quattrocento, it was subsequently enlarged, altered, emended, and improved throughout the fifteenth century. It is known in sixty-four manuscripts, only thirteen fewer than Marco Polo's travels, and evidently had an immense success during the Renaissance not only throughout Italy and in the Aegean, but also in other Western European countries. Not less than three vernacular translations of the *Liber* were made in Italy during the Quattrocento. In addition, there was a translation in modern Greek in the fifteenth century, as well as one in English during the sixteenth century. The work's character as a historical and practical guide should be emphasized, as this explains its wide diffusion among those who had the occasion to travel or live in the Aegean. It should also be stressed that this diffusion was not limited to Italian humanists or other erudite Orientalists. In fact, its popular character is suggested by the several versions in various Italian vernaculars, as well as the one in modern Greek. It is natural and reasonable to suppose that the work enjoyed a particularly wide diffusion among members of the Order of St John of Jerusalem, based on Rhodes.

Compelling analogies between Pigafetta's and Buondelmonti's books include their island subject matter, their mode of literary treatment alternating between narrative and expository modes, their

first-person authorial perspective, and last but not least the complement of island charts. The charts serve especially to establish a
generic link between Pigafetta's *First Voyage* and Buondelmonti's *Liber
insularum*, the first and most important of Renaissance *isolari*. Both
works share the same unique manuscript typology characterized by
coloured maps of islands embedded within the narrative, displayed at
the appropriate moment, usually immediately after the relevant narrative regarding the island depicted.

The analogies in textual content, treatment, and manuscript typology suggest strongly that, when Antonio Pigafetta conceived of his *First
Voyage,* he did so with the 'Book of Islands' tradition, which would have
been very familiar to his Rhodian brethren, very much in mind. The
isolario format evidently would have presented itself to Pigafetta and his
readers, beginning with the Grand Master of the Order, as an ideal
means of representing the archipelagos of the East Indies.[34]

Each of the twenty-three charts is closely linked to a particular passage
or passages from the narrative; from the first depicting the Patagonian
strait at the end of a peninsular-shaped (perhaps suggesting an island
form) South American continent to the last representing two unidentified islets in the midst of 'Laut chidol, that is, the great sea.' A few charts
include charming iconographic features like the one that represents a
lateen-sailed catamaran and two bearded natives from 'the island of
thieves' (the Mariana Islands). All charts include scrolls identifying
island names, and sometimes topographical detail including hills and in
some cases clusters of native houses standing on poles indicating villages,
as well as other scrolls including allusions to noteworthy events related in
the text, such as the one that identifies Mactan: 'Here the Captain-
General died.' The relationship between narrative and cartography is
intriguingly interactive, and it would well repay further investigation.
The cartographic achievement of the twenty-three charts of Pigafetta's
East Indian *isolario* is not as insignificant or naive as it may at first appear.
The charts in fact present an impressive cartographic record of the voyage, experienced from the perspective of the traveller, according to the
structure of passage.[35] Carlo Amoretti, the discoverer of the Ambrosiana
manuscript, was even able to recompose them as a plausible synthetic
portrait of the East Indian archipelagos in his edition of 1800.

While an essential correlation between the 'Book of Islands' genre and Pigafetta's *First Voyage* has not been previously made, it nevertheless appears that Pigafetta has significant claim on the legacy of Buondelmonti's *Liber insularum* – at least as important as the better known *isolari* published during the fifteenth and sixteenth centuries by Bartolomeo da li Sonetti, Benedetto Bordone, and Tommaso Porcacchi.[36] It is not irrelevant to the history of the 'Book of Islands' genre that Pigafetta's manuscript book first appeared in the same years that marked the beginning of the sixteenth century editorial establishment of the genre, in the 'coffee-table book' form with which Renaissance scholars are most familiar.

It has recently been observed how, from a narrative perspective, the literary vitality had gone out of these printed *isolari* of the Cinquecento, a decline attributed to the commercialization of the genre in the age of print. The sixteenth century *isolario* is no longer connected with a first-hand travel narrative and becomes the mere compilation of already published materials (a process that was already underway in the fifteenth century in Bartolomeo da li Sonetti's incunable *Isolario*, which recapitulated in part material from Buondelmonti). By the time one arrives at Tommaso Porcacchi's *L'Isole più famose*, the genre is explicitly intended only for those interested in the maps, that is, for those who 'dello studio della geografia si dilettano' (delight in geographical studies). The commercial success of Bordone and Porcacchi 'alienated from the *isolario* the readers of Ariosto and Tasso,' for geography and travel narrative had in that genre been divorced.[37]

Thus the appearance of Pigafetta's *First Voyage*, the most vital achievement after Buondelmonti in both the literary and cartographic aspects that originally distinguished the genre, is contemporary with the literary decline of the 'Book of Islands' genre in the age of print, which was reduced to a mere compilation of maps and inert, for the most part borrowed, textual material. Indeed, the progressive decline in literary vigour of the Cinquecento *isolario* appears irreversible, and is accompanied by an increasingly narrow geographical orientation. Bordone's book, for example, has been termed 'veneziocentrico'[38] with its focus on the Mediterranean with Venice at its centre. Porcacchi's 1572 edition opens with a treatment of Venice and the islands of the archipelago as if to reinforce their centrality to the author's and his prospective readers' world view. Pigafetta's mapping of the East Indies, on the other hand, had represented geographically the farthest point of arrival for the 'Book of Islands'.39

It is no doubt symptomatic that it was in the transition from manuscript to print that the original conception of Pigafetta's book, its characteristic integration of narrative and maps, of literature and cartography, was first lost. The effects of printing, which led to the commercialization and literary decline of the 'Book of Islands' genre, were certainly significant. Perhaps most telling, however, was the substitution of the geographer's for the traveller's viewpoint. The literary life goes out of the 'Book of Islands' as soon as the first-hand narrative foundation is subtracted, as soon as the motion and change filtered through a traveller's subjectivity, which gives the narrative of travel its life, is lost. In any case, the heroic High Renaissance period of discovery and exploration, as far as Italy was concerned, came to an end with Pigafetta. His *First Voyage* represents the culminating achievement in the 'Book of Islands' tradition, no less than it epitomizes the Italian Americanist tradition of De Cuneo, Vespucci, and Verrazzano. Both Benedetto Bordone's 1528 *Libro de tutte l'isole* and Girolamo Benzoni's 1565 *Historia del Nuovo Mondo* stand as epigones with respect to the Vicentine Knight of Rhodes, within their respective generic traditions, and within the context of the general history of Italian Renaissance travel writing (although such a history is yet to be written).

Finally, however, the proper collocation of Pigafetta's *First Voyage* within the limited context of Italian literary history may well appear too narrow a preoccupation for one confronted with what must be considered a still vital classic of Western travel literature. Indeed, the heroic early modern function of travel finds one of its most mature expressions in Pigafetta's narrative. Through the dangers and vigils of the journey, the self of the traveller is reduced to its essentials, allowing one to see what those essentials are. Pigafetta's *First Voyage* is ultimately motivated and overshadowed by the presentiment of finality, of the terminability of human life. The monument that he erects to Magellan, to the achievement of the circumnavigation, but most of

all to himself, who survived and lived to tell of 'this long and dangerous navigation,' still endures as testimony to the power of that desire
to circumvent death which is at the root of all travel literature, which
seeks to fix and conserve through writing the instability and flux of
human movement through space and time.

Notes

* Unless otherwise indicated, parenthetic numbers refer to the numbering
  of the periods in the text, which follow the 1999 Canova Critical Edition.
1 'The Solitude of America,' *New York Times*, sec. 4, 6 February 1983.
2 Stephen Greenblatt, *Marvelous Possessions: The Wonder of the New World*
  (Chicago: University of Chicago Press, 1991), 80.
3 E.J. Leed, *The Mind of the Traveler: From Gilgamesh to Global Tourism* (New
  York: Basic Books, 1991), 28.
4 The extent to which Shakespeare's reading of Pigafetta's Patagonian
  encounters informs the Americanist thematics of *The Tempest* and the cre-
  ation of Caliban remains an open question. At least one recent commen-
  tator has observed that Shakespeare 'read Pigafetta more carefully than is
  usually noticed.' Bruce Chatwin, *In Patagonia* (New York: Summit Books,
  1977), 91.
5 'Fantasia y creatíon artistica en América Latina y el Caribe,' *Texto Critico*
  14 (1979): 6. On Shakespeare's *The Tempest* and the semantics of storms,
  which present points of differentiation between Old and New Worlds, see
  P. Hulme, *Colonial Encounters* (London: Methuen, 1986). For more on the
  contemporary Latin American reception of Pigafettas narrative, see
  H.E. Robles, 'The First Voyage around the World: From Pigafetta to
  García Márquez' *History of European Ideas* 6, no. 4 (1985): 385–404.
6 See T.J. Cachey Jr, 'Tasso's *Navigazione del mondo nuovo* and the Origins of
  Colombus Encomium (GL, XV, 31–31),' *Italica* 69, no. 3 (1992): 326–44
  and 'Dal Nuovo Mondo alle isole Fortunate,' *Le Isole Fortunate: Appunti di
  storia letteraria italiana* (Rome: L'Erma di Bretschneider, 1995), 203–62.
7 For the beginnings of research in this sense, see the discussion of the
  Renaissance poetics of the 'marvellous' and travel writing in Greenblatt,
  Marvelous Possessions, 77–82, 175–7nn69–80.

8 Penrose in her classic study *Travel and Discovery in the Renaissance* (Cambridge, MA: Harvard University Press, 1952) observed that 'as the first-hand narration of one of history's three greatest voyages, Pigafetta's book rivals Columbus's *Journal* and da Gama's *Roteiro*' (375).

9 This early translation and immediate reception beyond the Alps raised the famous red herring about the language in which Pigafetta composed the relation, now generally accepted to have been Italian. See the bio-bibliographical note.

10 The technology of writing as a symbol of European culture and as employed by Pigafetta constitutes an interesting theme in its own right, both implicitly and explicitly within the narrative (see, for example, 233, 377–8).

11 Pigafetta's language has been analysed from a linguistic perspective (see the studies by Sanvisenti, Busnelli, and Beccaria cited in the textual notes), but his importance (and that of contemporary Italian travel writing in general) in relation to literary historiography regarding the contemporary 'Questione della lingua' has not been particularly emphasized or developed.

12 See the bio-bibliographical note.

13 Raphael Nonsenso is said to have 'joined up with Amerigo Vespucci: You know those *Four Voyages* of his that everyone's reading about?' *Utopia*, trans. and intro. Paul Turner (Harmondsworth, UK: Penguin, 1965), 38–9.

14 See Canova's edition of Pigafetta, *Relazione del primo viggio attorno al mondo* (Padua: Atenore, 1999), in particular the section from the introduction titled "Esperienza e letteratura nella relazione" (64–102), for a discussion of Pigafetta's no less heavy dependence upon travel writers who had journeyed to the East and the Middle East, from Marco Polo to Lodovico Varthema.

15 The 'Book of Islands' genre and Pigafetta's *First Voyage* are early modern precursors of that discourse Edward Said has termed 'Orientalist': 'dealing with the Orient – dealing with it by making statements about it, authorizing views of it, describing it, by teaching it as a Western style for dominating, restructuring, and having authority over the Orient.' *Orientalism* (New York: Pantheon, 1978), 3.

16 Pigafetta was most likely a Knight in the Order of St John of Jerusalem before his departure on the voyage in 1519 departure. See the bio-bibliographical note.

17 *Novelle di Matteo Bandello*, ed. G.G. Ferrero (Turin: UTET, 1974), 287–8.

18 For Chiericati, see Leed, *The Mind of the Traveler.* His narrative describing a trip to Ireland in 1515 while he was Papal Nuncio at the Court of Henry VIII was published by J.P. Mahaffy, 'Two Early Tours in Ireland,' *Hermathena* 40 (1914): 1–16.

19 M. Masoero, 'Magellano, "bon pastore" e "bon cavaliero,"' in *La letteratura di viaggio dal Medioevo al Rinascimento: Generi e Problemi* (Alessandria, Italy: Edizioni dell'Orso, 1989), 51–62.

20 Leed, *The Mind of the Traveler,* 9.

21 *Letters from a New World: Amerigo Vespucci's Discovery of America*, ed. L. Formisano, trans. D. Jacobson (New York: Marsilio, 1992), 57–8.

22 Significantly, eighteenth-century Italian literary historiography already appears sensitive to this shift. Girolamo Tiraboschi, in that part of his *Storia della letteratura italiana* dedicated to the Renaissance period of discovery and exploration, excludes Pigafetta and the circumnavigation from his treatment since '[Pigafetta] was no more than a simple passenger, and the idea and the success of that great exploit are owed to Magellan and his companions among whom however we do find that there were two Genoese.' (Florence: Molini, Laudi, 1809), Tomo VII, pt. 1, 260.

23 C. Dionisotti thus describes the Italian literary tradition that would emerge from the Renaissance: 'It was, as the history of historiography teaches, a humanistic tradition, nourished by linguistic and literary successes, founded upon the persuasion that Italians indeed suffer the violence of historical events, but that they alone are capable by choice and by education, to oppose that ephemeral and blind violence with the perennial, lucid validity of discourse, of writing.' *Geografia e storia della letteratura italiana* (Turin: Einaudi, 1967), 27.

24 Vespucci, *Letters from a New World,* 57.

25 This passage has been termed 'perhaps the highest invitation to consider travel literature that which from the Odyssey forward it always has been: a literature of entertainment.' M. Guglielminetti, 'Il Messico a Venezia nel 1528: Benedetto Bordon e Hernán Cortés,' *L'impatto della scoperta dell'America nella cultura veneziana*, ed. A.C. Aricò (Rome: Bulzoni, c 1990), 108–9.

26 F.H.H. Guillemard, *The Life of Ferdinand Magellan* (London: George Philip & Son, 1890), 164-74.

27 *Marvelous Possessions*, 80.

28 'such a voyage as that I do not call a discovery, but merely a going to discovered lands. It is true that the navigation has been most profitable, which these days is what counts most, and especially in this kingdom, where inordinate greed reigns out of all order.' *Letters from a New World*, 17.

29 David Quint, 'The Boat of Romance and Renaissance Epic,' in *Romance: Generic Transformation from Chrétien de Troyes to Cervantes*, ed. K. and M. Brownlee (Hanover, NH: University Press of New England, 1985), 178–202.

30 For example, J. Crawfurd cites Pigafetta's description of the court of Brunei 'as giving the only authentic account we possess of a Malay court when first seen by Europeans, and before their policy, or impolicy, had affected Malayan society.' *A Descriptive Dictionary of the Indian Islands and Adjacent Countries* (1856; repr., London: Oxford University Press, 1971), 71.

31 For detailed commentary on these lists, on the manner of their compilation, and on the relevant scholarship, see A. Bausani, *L'Indonesia nella relazione di viaggio di A. Pigafetta* (Rome: Centro di cultura italiana Djakarta, 1972).

32 *Relazione del primo viaggio attorno al mondo*, ed. Andrea Canova (Padua: Antenore, 1999).

33 For discussion and bibliography regarding this text, for which unfortunately no modern critical edition exists, see the edition by L. De Sinner (Lipsiae; Berolini: Apud G. Reimer, 1824); R. Almagià, *Monumenta Cartografica Vaticana* I (1944), 105–17; A. Campana, 'Da codici del Buondelmonti,' *Silloge bizantina, in onore di Silvio Mercati* (Associazione nazionale per gli studi bizantini, 1957), 28–52; R. Weiss, 'Un umanistica antiquario: Cristoforo Buondelmonti,' *Lettere italiane* 16 (1964): 105–16; H. Turner, 'Christopher Buondelmonti and the *Isolario*,' *Terre Incognitae* 19 (1987): 11–28.

34 The maps that complement his narrative have always been attributed to Pigafetta without controversy. In fact, a first-hand witness to Pigafetta's reception at Rome upon his return, the historian Paolo Giovio, reports that 'In tanto subternavigati orbis miraculo fidelibus testimoniis comprobato, multa nostris admiranda, observandaque posteris *pictura et scripti* adnotata deposuit.' *Historiarum sui temporis* (Lutetia Parisiorum) 34 (1553): 72.

35 'The order imposed upon experience by the condition of mobility is an order of sequence, an order of "one-thing-after-another," a "progress." Motion resolves all orders of space – topografies, positions, scenes, containments, places – into an experiential order of continuously evolving appearances.' Leed, *The Mind of the Traveler,* 73.

36 Bartolomeo da li Sonetti was a Venetian shipmaster who printed an *isolario* around 1485 that included forty-nine maps of the Aegean and a series of sonnets derived in large measure from Buondelmonti's prose. Bordone, a Paduan illuminator, published in 1528 his *Libro de tutte l'isole del mondo.* See R.A. Skelton, *Theatrum Orbis Terrarum* (Amsterdam: 1966). This work was reprinted three times, for the last time just a few years before Tommaso Porcacchi brought out his *L'Isole più famose del mondo* (Venice: 1572).

37 M. Guglielminetti, 'Per un sottogenere della letteratura del viaggio: Gl'isolari fra Quattro e Cinquecento,' in *La letteratura di viaggio dal Medioevo al Rinascimento: generi e problemi* (Alessandria: Edizioni dell'Orso, 1989), 107–17.

38 Ibid., 116.

39 For a discussion of the relationship between cartography and literature during the Italian Renaissance, see T. Cachey, "Maps and Literature in Renaissance Italy," *History of Cartography,* vol. 3 (Chicago: University of Chicago Press, 2007), 450–60.

Bio-bibliographical Note

Little is known of Antonio Pigafetta's life before the circumnavigation (1519–22) beyond what he tells us himself in the dedicatory letter about his association with the papal ambassador and fellow Vicentine Francesco Chiericati, which led to his participation in Magellan's expedition. More survives regarding his activities between 1522 and 1525, namely, during the period in which he composed *The First Voyage Around the World* and sought patronage for its publication. The last archival trace to survive records the conferral of the *commenda*, or benefice, of Norcia, Todi, and Arquata upon Antonio Pigafetta by the Order of St John of Jerusalem (or Knights of Rhodes) on 3 October 1524. This honour is directly related to the dedication of his book to the Grand Master of the Knights of Rhodes, which concluded his two-year search for courtly patronage. Nothing more is heard of Pigafetta after this date, a situation which has encouraged biographers to posit a variety of hypotheses: these range from a heroic end aboard the galleys of the Knights of Rhodes in battle with the Turks to a return 'in patria' to the family's ancestral home in Vicenza.

Pigafetta belonged to a prominent noble Vicentine family that had arrived from Tuscany during the eleventh century and had quickly achieved prestige and wealth. Numerous members of the family attained distinction in political, economic, and academic spheres. Indeed, the historian Paolo Giovio, in his account of Pigafetta's meeting with Pope Clement VII, confuses Antonio with his relative, the Dominican friar Girolamo, who was noted at the time for his oratory and poetic production.[1] Giovio's error concerning Pigafetta's identity is typical of the historiographic confusion surrounding the origins of the explorer that has reigned until relatively recently. Pigafetta's birth has been variously assigned to anywhere between 1480 and the late 1490s; and there have been numerous proposals as to who his parents were, from among the various branches of the Pigafetta family.

An initial breakthrough was achieved by C. Manfroni and revealed in the preface to his 1928 edition of Pigafetta's narrative:[2] a crew list for the expedition found in the Archives of the Indies, and probably intended to indicate the heirs in case of death, included the names of the explorer's parents, 'Antonio Lombardo hijo de Juan e Anzola su mujer.' While archival research at the time did not succeed in identifying a corresponding couple, more recent work by G. Mantese has led to a resolution of the problem of Pigafetta's origins and also suggested his probable date of death. Through wills and other documents Mantese demonstrated the existence of Angela Zoga, wife of Giovanni Pigafetta, names corresponding to those on the crew list.[3] Later, on the basis of still other documents,[4] Mantese determined that Angela Zoga was Giovanni Pigafetta's second wife (hence the unusual expression 'hijo de Juan e Anzola su mujer'). A marriage contract written by the notary Gregorio da Malo informs us that, in March of 1492, Giovanni had married a noblewoman named Lucia, daughter of Marco Muzan, who thus would have been the mother of Antonio.[5] The birth of Antonio Pigafetta must therefore have been after 1492, and he would have been not older than twenty-seven when he embarked with Magellan. This corrects the tradition, dating back to the eighteenth century historiographers, that placed his birth during the 1480s. Further, in a will that Giovanni Pigafetta drew up in 1532, two other children are mentioned, Valentino and Serafina, while Antonio Pigafetta is not. From this, Mantese inferred that Antonio Pigafetta was already dead in 1532. If Pigafetta was already dead in 1532, then he would not have reached forty years of age, and it would thus have been impossible for him to have fought against the Turks with the Knights of Rhodes in the war of 1536, as some biographers have speculated.[6] That Pigafetta may have followed the Order to Malta when it transferred to the island in 1530 is perhaps suggested by one of the expressions he uses in his envoi: 'Then I came to Italy, where I *devoted myself forever,* and these my poor labours, to the famous and most illustrious Lord Philippe Villiers de l'Isle-Adam, the most worthy Grand Master of Rhodes' (1356; my emphasis). But the truth is that absolutely nothing is known about the last years of Pigafetta's life after 1525.[7]

The archival silence concerning Pigafetta's life before the circumnavigation and following the presentation of his *First Voyage* to the Grand Master is in some measure redressed by the engaging and relatively well-documented history of his peregrinations after his return from the voyage. Having disembarked with the eighteen survivors of the expedition on 8 September 1522, Pigafetta travelled to the imperial court at Valladolid, and presented to Charles V, as he writes in his envoi, things to be prized above gold and silver, among which 'a book, written by my hand, concerning all the matters that had occurred from day to day during our voyage' (1353). Pigafetta had come to court apparently of his own initiative and independently of the commander of the *Victoria*, Juan Sebastián de Elcano, who was summoned by the Emperor on 13 September, and appeared in October, together with the pilot Francisco Albo and the barber Hernando de Bustamante, before a court of enquiry into the voyage. Pigafetta seems to allude to a poor reception at the imperial court when he writes 'I left there as best I could and went to Portugal' (1354). Perhaps anti-Magellan sentiments had something to do with Pigafetta's lack of success at court. That Pigafetta's celebration of the heroic Portuguese commander as it has come down to us in his *First Voyage* might not have met with favour there is suggested by the more or less official version of the circumnavigation given by Peter Martyr (decade 5, bk. 7).[8] There, the court historiographer is clearly caught between a desire to magnify the undertaking but at the same time to undermine the reputation of Magellan, who is described as a traitor to his king and accused, among other things, of abusing the Spaniards.[9]

Already on 21 October 1522 the Mantuan ambassador, Antonio Bagarotto, reported from Valladolid to Isabella d'Este that the survivors of the expedition had brought back 'a very beautiful book'; and on 12 November the ambassador sent to Mantua extracts or a summary of that book, which may well have been Pigafetta's.[10] These letters represent first reports back to the court of Mantua which eventually led to Pigafetta's initial commitment to write the book for

Federico II Gonzaga, Marquis of Mantua. Francesco Chiericati, Pigafetta's original patron at the imperial court, wrote from Nuremberg to Isabella d'Este, Federico's famous mother, on 26 December 1522 concerning 'my Vicentine servant, whom I sent from Spain to India and who has returned very rich with the greatest and most marvellous things in the world, and a journal that he kept from the day he left Spain until the day he returned, which is a divine thing; and your illustrious signoria will have complete knowledge of it shortly.'[11]

According to Pigafetta's own account in his envoi, he proceeded to Lisbon, where he gave King João III an oral report, and then to France, where he gave the Queen Mother, Louise of Savoy, mother of Francis I, 'a gift of certain things from the other hemisphere' (1355). Most scholars pass over this stage quickly, as there does not appear to be any documentary support for these visits besides Pigafetta's own testimony. According to Ramusio, Louise of Savoy received a copy of Pigafetta's account and gave this text to J. Fabre (Jacques Lefèvre d'Etaples) so that it could be translated into French. This would have been the Paris imprint by Simon de Colines (the editio princeps of 1524–5, see below). Ramusio had the Colines text translated back into Italian for his own editions of the text in 1536 (Venice: Zoppini), and later as part of the *Navigazione e viaggi* (1550, vol. 1). While Ramusio's editions are derived from the Colines imprint, his account of the transmission of the text from Pigafetta to Louise of Savoy to Simon de Colines is without documentary support. In fact, Pigafetta himself makes no mention of giving a copy of his relation to Louise of Savoy, but simply 'a gift of certain things from the other hemisphere.'

Meanwhile, Francesco Chiericati wrote again from Nuremberg on 10 January 1523 to Isabella d'Este at Mantua announcing Pigafetta's arrival and expressing to her his hope that 'in a few days, your excellency will have great delight and recreation in listening to that servant of mine, who has recently returned from the circumnavigation of the world, recount all the great and marvellous things that he saw and recorded during that voyage.'[12] Upon his arrival in Mantua in January of 1523, Pigafetta would have begun the composition of the definitive version of his *First Voyage*, and it was at this time that he presumably received a commission for the work from Federico II

Gonzaga. Pigafetta was to continue work on the *First Voyage* at Mantua, Vicenza, and Rome (where he appears to have completed a version by April 1524). It was probably during the initial period at court in Mantua that he encountered the philosopher Pietro Pomponazzi, a Mantuan, who, lecturing on Aristotle at the University of Bologna soon after, on 23 March 1523, gave suggestive testimony regarding the implications of the voyage:

> I have received a letter sent to me by a friend of mine of the Veneto who accompanied the papal ambassador to the King of Spain and who, finding himself there, went along with an expedition sent by that king in the southern hemisphere; and he navigated there 25 degrees, after having passed the Torrid Zone. Now he writes to me that, leaving behind the Pillars of Hercules, they navigated in the southern hemisphere for three months and encountered more that three hundred islands separated one from the other, and that not only were they habitable but they were inhabited. What do you think of the reasoning of Aristotle and Averroes to demonstrate the opposite. Perhaps some of you will think that that merchant is telling me a sack of lies and that he is a big liar. No, dear sirs, it is not possible, he wasn't the only one on that voyage.[13]

Nothing else is known of the relations between Pomponazzi and Pigafetta except for this passage in which the philosopher refers to his 'amico veneto,' and which indicates Pigafetta's celebrity in Italy at this time. In fact, following a period of time spent with his family in Vicenza, Pigafetta was received by the Venetian doge Andrea Gritti in November of 1523. The Venetian diarist Marin Sanudo described the great interest elicited by Pigafetta's oral presentation before the entire Venetian College at the Ducal Palace: 'There appeared before the College a Vicentine named the Knight errant, friar of Rhodes, who had been exploring three years in India, and he recounted orally about those things, such that the College listened to him with great attention, and he told half the voyage: and after dinner he was again with the doge and he related those things at length, such that his Serenity and all those who heard him were stupefied by those things that are in India.'[14] This performance seemed to have had a resonance beyond the Hall of the Great Council since no sooner had Pigafetta returned from Venice to Vicenza than he was called in December to Rome by Pope Clement VII. On the way to Rome, as Pigafetta himself tells us in the envoi, he encountered the Grand Master of the Knights of Rhodes, Philippe Villiers de l'Isle Adam, to whom Pigafetta related his voyage and from whom Pigafetta received yet more encouragement and, apparently, promises of support.

Pigafetta worked on the book in Rome under the patronage of Pope Clement VII, a relationship that appears to have begun well enough. Pigafetta writes with some embarrassment on 2 February 1524 to the Marquis of Mantua explaining that a higher power and promise of publication had pre-empted the Marquis' original commission: 'I believe his Holiness desires it to be printed in his name: and to satisfy my promised debt to you, I will send the first to be printed to your illustrious signoria, or else I will write another one in my own hand.'[15] But the pope's promise to publish the book was not kept for reasons that are unknown. Apparently frustrated with the turn of events, Pigafetta sought to return to the service of the Marquis of Mantua in a letter of 16 April 1524 to the marquis.[16] He obtained a letter of recommendation from the Mantuan ambassador at the papal court at the time: Baldassare Castiglione. Castiglione wrote a revealing letter to the Marquis about Pigafetta one day before the explorer's own missive: 'That nobleman Pigafetta who went to the Antipodes recommends himself strongly to your excellency: and although he has had I don't know how little here from the pope together with many promises, if some benefice of St John's [The Order of the Knights of Rhodes] were to become available *accascando qualche beneficio de san Giohanni*], he nevertheless desires very much to serve your excellency: but I do not know if he would be contented with only a little.'[17] The letter is significant for the light it sheds on the patronage network within which Pigafetta was operating; it also provides a glimpse of the Vicentine's ambitious and jealous character, already suggested by his behaviour immediately following his return to Europe on the occasion of his presentation to Charles V.

Pigafetta was not going to sell himself short, and if that meant boldly pursuing his aim of publication and worthy compensation for his work, so be it. Castiglione's letter offers a glimpse of the state of play from Pigafetta's perspective during the spring and summer of 1524: on one side Clement VII and the Knights of Rhodes, on the other Mantua and the Venetian presses. Pigafetta's 1999 editor, Andrea Canova, has discovered in the Gonzaga register at the Vatican letters to Baldassare Castiglione sent by the lord of the castle of Mantua and secretary of Federico Gonzaga, Giovanni Giacomo Calandra, including one that attests to a visit by Pigafetta to Mantua during the summer of 1524. Calandra wrote to Castiglione on 9 July: 'I forgot to write to your Lordship to tell you that Pigafetta, who has been to the Antipodes, came by a few days ago with a book of his which he presented together with himself to the Marquis; and he expects some great compensation, and made it clear he won't be satisfied with a little, saying that he turned down deals with the Pope, the emperor, the Kings of Portugal, France and England: I don't now how he will get by. I think he is in a bad way.'[18] Eventually, Pigafetta received the support of the Marquis of Mantua in obtaining a licence to publish his work in Venice. Federico Gonzaga instructs his minister, Battista Malatesta, in a letter of 19 July 1524 to present a letter of Federico's to the doge Antonio Gritti in support of Pigafetta's request for a licence to print, and to support Pigafetta in any way possible. In addition, Malatesta put Pigafetta together with a printer, and made the arrangement that the work should be printed and that 'the Knight should now pay fifteen ducats to cover half of the expenses and that the profit will be divided.'[19] The fact that Pigafetta did not pay the sum and that the printing of the book was never accomplished has been thought to reflect Pigafetta's impoverished state upon his return to Europe, 'certainly not loaded with gold, pearls, and spices as many believed.'[20] On the other hand, Malatesta, in his letter to the Marquis of Mantua, after explaining the arrangements he had made, could not conceal a hint of exasperation when he wrote: 'however, as far as I can judge, he would like Your Excellency to give him that amount of money, and he has asked me faithfully to refer to you as much.'[21] Given what Castiglione and Calandra had already suggested about Pigafetta's pretensions ('I do not know if he would be contented with little'), one might just as easily suppose the Venetian printing never came off because Pigafetta was looking for an arrangement more favourable to his own interests. In any case, in the final account of his patrons and peregrinations in the *First Voyage*, and especially in the concluding envoi, the court of Mantua (and any reference to Venice) is conspicuously absent.

A better arrangement did in fact present itself only a few months later when on 3 October 1524, the Knights of Rhodes' vacant *commenda* of Norcia, Todi, and Arquata was conferred upon Pigafetta, and this act, as noted earlier, represents the last secure biographical datum regarding the Vicentine to survive. Significantly, the formal request for a benefice from the Order had been made on 25 July 1524, that is, more or less at the same time that Pigafetta was pursuing most intensely Mantuan-Venetian press patronage. In other words, there seem to have been parallel and competing paths in Pigafetta's pursuit of publication and adequate compensation. In the end, the patronage of the Knights of Rhodes must have represented the more attractive opportunity. The relationship between the date of the conferral of the benefice and the date of the completion of the manuscript and its presentation to the Grand Master remains an open question, as does the more general question of whether Pigafetta entered the Order of the Knights of Rhodes before or after the circumnavigation.

For the period between 25 January 1524 and 25 June 1525, the Grand Master was in Italy, where, according to *The First Voyage*, Pigafetta presented him with the manuscript. R.A. Skelton has observed that the presentation of the text might have been made to the Grand Master sometime between the date when Pigafetta applied for the benefice (25 July 1524) and when he received it (3 October 1524): 'if the presentation of his manuscript were designed to support his petition or to express his gratitude.'[22] But perhaps more telling is the other fact, also remarked on by Skelton, that Pigafetta's reference in the final paragraph to Louise of Savoy as 'Regent' can only refer to the period between February 1525 (Battle of Pavia) and January 1526 (Treaty of Madrid). Since the Grand Master was not in Italy after 25 June 1525, this passage and the presentation of the work would appear to date sometime between February and 25 June 1525. In other words, the benefice, requested and received between the summer and fall of 1524, would have represented the premise for Pigafetta's final preparation of the book for presentation to the Grand Master during the first months of 1525.

Pending future archival discoveries, the question of when Pigafetta first became a member of the Knights of Rhodes remains an open one. The tradition that knighthood had been conferred upon him in recognition of the achievement of the circumnavigation begins with Ramusio.[23] The view that he was already a member of the order before beginning his travels is based upon the argument that the time between his return (8 September 1522) and Sanudo's account of his presentation to the doge and reference to him as a 'friar of Rhodes' (7 November 1523) would have been insufficient to complete the enquiries into the nobility of his family, the novitiate, and other rituals involved in entering the order.[24] Da Mosto, on the other hand, pointed out that, in a time of military crisis for the Order, formalities were reduced to the minimum, and that it is more probable that Pigafetta was admitted by special procedure.[25] One should not neglect, however, the evidence presented by Pigafetta's narrative itself as possibly bearing on the question. The general ideological perspective of the document might be said to be entirely consistent with what one might expect from a member of the Order of St John of Jerusalem: from the portrayal of Magellan as a crusading hero (a member himself of the Military Order of St James [3, 589]) to more local observations like the famous passage 'When we cast them into the sea, the Christians went to the bottom face upward while the Indians always went down faces downward' (1336). The thesis that Pigafetta was a Knight of Rhodes before his departure is also supported by telling thematic features like the recurring topos of St Elmo's fire, as well as certain analogies and allusions that indicate, as Skelton has observed, that Pigafetta was familiar with both the eastern and western Mediterranean.[26] Finally, the work's generic affiliation with the *isolario* tradition, pointed out in this introduction, also suggests a fundamentally 'Rhodian' formation for our author, and leads us to believe that Pigafetta may well have been a member of the Order of St John of Jerusalem before departing with Magellan.

The text of Pigafetta's *First Voyage* survives in four manuscripts: one Italian (D = Milan, Bibl. Ambrosiana, L 103 Sup.), and three French (A = Paris, Bibliothèque Nationale, MS fr. 5650; B = MS fr. 24.224; and C = Yale University, Beinecke Rare Book and Manuscript Library, Phillipps MS 16405). All of the manuscripts include twenty-three coloured maps of the islands visited and date from the first half of the sixteenth century.

The publication of the Ambrosiana codex in 1800 by Carlo Amoretti (Milano: G. Galeazzi) made it possible to resolve the doubts about the language used by Pigafetta.[27] Since that time it is considered established that the Vicentine originally wrote his account in Italian. The autograph did not survive, and we possess only the Ambrosiana codex (D) in Italian, which originally belonged to the 'chevalier de Forrete': either Philibert de la Forest or Jean de Foret, both Knights of Malta and contemporaries of Philippe Villiers de l'Isle-Adam. The title at the beginning of the Ambrosiana codex, which is written by a later hand, reads *Notizie del Mondo Nuovo con le figure de' paesi scoperti, descritte da Antonio Pigafeta vicentino cavaglier di Rodi* (*News of the New World with Figures of the Discovered Countries, described by A.P., Vicentine Knight of Rhodes*). This title is clearly inexact referring as it does to only the American part of the voyage.

The Italian editor of a 1999 edition of the text, A. Canova, has noted that in two inventories of Ambrosiana manuscripts compiled in 1610 by Giorgio Longo and collaborators the codex is registered two times as 'Antonio Pigafetta Vicentino la navigatione et discovrimento dell'India Superiore' (The Navigation and Voyage of Upper India).[28] Thus the title given by these seventeenth century inventories corresponds to that of the three French manuscripts (*Navigation et descouvrement de a Indie superieuse faicte par moy Anthoyne Pigaphete vincentin chevalier de Rhodes* (A: The Navigation and Discovery of Upper India accomplished by me Antonio Pigafetta, Vicentine, Knight of Rhodes), *Navigation et discovrement de a Indie superieure faicte par moy Anthoine Pigaphete patricie vincentin chevalier de Rhodes* (B), *Navigation et descovrement de a Indie superieure et isles de Malucque ou naissent les cloux de Girofle. Faicte par Anthoine Pigaphete patricie vincentin chevalier de Rhodes* (C). Canova concludes that given the bad state of the Ambrosiana manuscript it is very likely that one or two of the outer pages were lost since the seventeenth century, and that *Navigatione e discovrimento dell'India Superiore* was the original title of the work presented by the Ambrosiana manuscript up until the middle of the nineteenth century. The Ambrosiana manuscript, which also contains the so-called *Regole sull'arte del navigare o trattato della sfera* (*Treatise on the Art of Navigation*),[29] is generally considered an apograph, that is, a direct copy of the original. Skelton's view, that the Ambrosiana text is 'the only remaining representative of the textual tradition deriving from Pigafetta's original draft,'[30] has now been corrected somewhat by Canova's edition, which is based on a more exacting collation of the surviving manuscripts.

The extremely rare first edition of the work mentioned earlier was printed in Paris by Simon de Colines, without date but probably in 1525. It is divided into 104 chapters and is entitled *Le voyage et navigation faict par les Espaignolz es isles de Mollucques, des Isles quilz ont trouve audict voyage, de roys dicelles, de leur gouverment et maniere de vivre, avec plusiers autres choses* (*The Voyage and Navigation of the Spaniards among the Moluccas, the Islands that they found during said voyage, the kings of these islands, their governments and manner of living, together with many other things*). According to the colophon, the work was translated from Italian into French. It is generally attributed, based on Ramusio's statement cited earlier, to the French editor Jacques Lefèvre d'Etaples, at the request of Louise of Savoy. A facsimile edition and translation of this edition by P.S. Paige was published in 1969 (*The Voyage of Magellan* [Englewood Cliffs, NJ: Prentice-Hall]).

The first Italian edition was prepared by Ramusio and published by Zoppini in Venice in 1536. It was essentially an Italian translation based on the Colines princeps, with the title *Il viaggio fatto da gli Spagniuoli atorno al mondo* (*The Voyage of the Spaniards Around the World*). The text was divided into 114 chapters and preceded by an anonymous *Avviso al lettore* as well as by the letter of Maximilian Transylvanus recounting the voyage (see below).

In 1550 Ramusio included Pigafetta's *First Voyage* in the first volume of the first edition of his *Navigazioni et viaggi* (Venezia: Eredi di Luc'Antonio Giunti) in a form that is very similar to that of the 1536 edition: *Viaggio attorno il mondo scritto per M. Antonio Pigafetta tradotto di lingua francese nella italiana* (*Voyage Around the World Written by Messer A. P. translated from French into Italian*). This edition includes a somewhat revised version of the Avviso of 1536, this time attributed to Ramusio, beneath the title *Discorso sopra il viaggio fatto dagli Spagnuoli intorno al mondo* (translated in Stanley, 181–2 and Nowell, 271–4) and is preceded by Maximilian Transylvanus's letter. The 1554 second edition of Ramusio's first volume appends a *Narrazione di un portoghese compagno di Odoardo Barbosa sopra la nave Vittoria* (see below). The third edition of Ramusio's *Navigazioni* (1563) introduced the division into chapters.

The text of Ramusio's first edition was translated in abbreviated form into English by Richard Eden in his *The Decades of the newe worlde or west India ... written by Peter Martyr* (London: G. Powell, 1555, repr. 1577). This is the text from which Shakespeare derived Caliban's American demon 'Setebos' (148 and note). A complete translation of the text was given for the first time in Samuel Purchas's *Hakluytus Posthumus or his Pilgrimes* (London, 1625, vol. I; 1905 ed., vol. II, 84–118).

The work was included in the celebrated eighteenth century *Histoire générale des voyages* of Antoine-Francois Prévost,[31] but did not otherwise appear in any new editions of Pigafetta before Carlo Amoretti's discovery and publication of the Ambrosiana manuscript in 1800 (Milano: G. Galeazzi). Amoretti published Italian, French (Paris: H.J. Jansen, 1801) and German (Gotha: Bey J. Perthes, 1801) editions of the text. The value of Amoretti's find was severely undermined however, by the fact that the text he published represented a rewriting or translation of Pigafetta's sixteenth century Italian. The editor also bowdlerized the text in an effort to 'exposit with the necessary decency the account of some strange customs written by him [Pigafetta] in frank terms which would offend the delicacy and modesty of the reader of good taste.' Unfortunately, the numerous translations in a variety of languages led to the dissemination of this corrupted text, including the English language editions prepared by

J. Pinkerton (*A General Collection of the Best and Most Interesting Voyages*, vol. XI [London: Longman, 1812], 288–420) and by Lord Stanley of Alderly and published in 1874 by the Hakluyt Society (*The First Voyage Round the World*).

On the occasion of the fourth centenary of the discovery of America, Andrea da Mosto prepared for the *Raccolta Colombiana* (vol. III, v, 1894) a diplomatic edition of the work which still remains important.[32] J.A. Robertson reproduced it in its entirety and added an English translation (*Magellan's Voyage Round the World*, Cleveland: A.C. Clark, 1906). This work included over 650 notes but unfortunately appeared in a limited edition of only 350 copies. C.E. Nowell reprinted Robertson's 1906 translation without Robertson's notes in *Magellan's Voyage Around the World* (Evanston, IL: Northwestern University Press, 1962).

On the occasion of the fourth centenary of the return of the *Victoria*, J. Denucé published an edition of the French ms. 5650 with variants from the Ambrosiana and the other French manuscripts.[33] Another French edition based upon ms. 5650, transcribed in modern French, was published by Léonce Peillard and published in Paris in 1956. The Yale-Beinecke manuscript was translated and edited by R.A. Skelton.

Several new editions of Pigafetta's narrative have recently appeared in Italy, all based upon the Ambrosiana manuscript. Two appeared during the late 1980s, including one by M. Masoero (Rovereto: Longo Editore, 1987) and another edited by L. Giovannini, which presented a more or less diplomatic transcription of the text: *La mia longa et pericolosa navigatione* (Milan: Edizioni Paoline, 1989). An abbreviated edition of the text, based upon the Ambrosiana manuscript and edited by M. Pozzi, has appeared in *Scopritori viaggiatori del Cinquecento e Seicento* (Milan-Naples: Riccardo Ricciardi, 1991), Tomo I, 509–71. More recently, Pozzi has edited a facsimile edition of the Ambrosiana codex (Vicenza: Neri Pozza, 1995). As mentioned, the most authoritative edition of the text, upon which the present English translation is based, is by A. Canova (Padua: Antenore 1999).

Of great importance for an adequate appreciation of Pigafetta's narrative are contemporary accounts by other participants in the expedition, as well as those by second-hand historiographic sources. Most of the first-hand sources were collected and published by M. Fernández De Navarrete in vol. IV of his *Colección de los viajes y descubrimientos que hicieron por mar los Españoles desde fines del siglo XV* (Madrid: Imprenta Real, 1825–37); several of these are translated into English in Lord Stanley of Alderly, *The First Voyage Round the World* (London: Hakluyt Society, 1874). An essential bibliographical essay treating these sources and the circumnavigation generally is M. Torodash's 'Magellan Historiography,' in *Hispanic American Historical Review* 51 (1971), 313–35.

Neither Magellan's own journals nor those of any of the other captains survived. The closest thing to an official report is the letter Juan Sebastián de Elcano (originally master of the *Concepción*, and commander of the *Victoria* after August 1521) wrote to Charles V (dated 6 September 1522) and the account of Elcano's oral testimony given 18 October 1522 at Valladolid. These documents are printed by M. Mitchell in *Elcano, The First Circumnavigator* (London: Herder 1958, 178–82). They are mainly concerned with the conduct of the fleet and the relations between its senior officers, about which Pigafetta says very little. Also significant is the fact that Gonzalo Fernández de Oviedo y Valdés refers to information given him verbally by Elcano more than once in his *Historia general y natural de las Indias* (prólogo de J. Natalicio Gonzalez; notas de José Amador de Los Rios, 14 vols., [Asuncion del Paraguay: Editorial Guarania, 1944], Tomo IV, Bk. XIX, Part II, chaps. 1–24).

The only surviving nautical documents written on the voyage or from memory are a handful of pilots' logs including most importantly the *Diario ó derrotero* of the pilot Francisco Albo, who began the voyage as boatswain in the *Trinidad* and ended it as pilot of the *Victoria*, the only ship to complete the first circumnavigation.[34] Albo is more precise in the reporting of latitudes and longitudes than Pigafetta but his account begins only two months into the voyage with the departure from Cape St Augustine in Brazil (29 November 1519).

A *Roteiro* by a 'nameless' Genoese pilot, to be identified perhaps as Leone Pancaldo of Savona or Juan Bautista de Punzorol (or de Poncerva), both of whom were taken prisoner in the *Trinidad* at

Ternate, is an account of the voyage from Spain to the Moluccas, edited by Berchet in the *Raccolta di documenti e studi colombiani*, p. III, vol. II (Rome: Ministero della Pubblica Istruzione, 1893), 272–87.[35] According to Torodash, 'nothing can be gained from a reading of this rather boring account,' but it formed the basis for the report made by Antonio de Brito, the Portuguese governor who captured the crew of the *Trinidad*, which had been forced to return to Ternate in November 1522. Brito addressed a letter to King João III of Portugal dated 6 May 1523 that was printed by Navarrete, 305–11.

Four other first-hand accounts survive, including one by seamen Ginés de Mafra, who returned with Pancaldo on the *Trinidad* to Spain, one of only five survivors of the fifty-three men left with Juan Carvalho at Tidore, published by Antonio Blázquez y Delgado Aguilera, 'Descubrimiento del Estrecho de Magallanes,' in *Tres Relaciones* (Madrid, 1920). The other three include the brief diary of an anonymous Portuguese companion of Duarte Barbosa (perhaps Vasco Gomes Gallego, who sailed as a common seaman on the *Trinidad*, or more likely Basco Gallego who sailed as pilot of the *Victoria*), first published in Ramusio's second edition of volume I of his *Navigazioni* (1554) at fols. 408v.-409r; Stanley provides a translation, 30–2; the narrative of a seaman identified as Martín López de Ayamonte who deserted at Timor and was later taken by the Portuguese, published by Antonio Baião under the title 'A Viágem de F.M. por una Testemunha Presencial,' in *Arquivo Histórico de Portugal* (Lisbon, 1933; vol. I, pts. 5 and 6, 276–81); and a *derrotero* by another unnamed seaman discovered in a manuscript in the University of Leiden library and published in 1937 by M. de Jong, *Um Roteiro inédito* (Coimbra: Faculdade de letras, 1937).

Among the second-hand sources, the earliest printed narrative was by Maximilian Transylvanus, Peter Martyr's student and secretary to Charles V (the text is dated 22 October 1522): *De Moluccis Insulis*, ed. Johann Schöner, Charles Coote, and Henry Stevens (London: H. Stevens, 1888), 101–46; and Nowell, 269–309.[36] It was printed in Rome in 1523 and at Cologne in January 1524, and in later travel collections beginning with Ramusio's (1536, and in vol. I of the *Navigazioni e viaggi*, 1550). Like Peter Martyr and others, Maximilian obtained his information from Elcano and Francisco Albo and Hernando Bustamante at court in Valladolid. He was married to the niece of Cristóbal de Haro, the principal backer of Magellan's adventure, and thus may have had stronger than scholarly curiosity about the voyage. Skelton notes that Maximilian 'made a serious attempt to display the circumnavigation against the background of politics and diplomacy in the Far East.'[37] As noted earlier, Peter Martyr, 'the first historian of America,' includes an account of Magellan's circumnavigation in his *De Orbe Novo* (decade 5, book 7). Antonio de Herrera y Tordesillas gives an account of the circumnavigation in his *Historia general de los hechos de los Castellanos en las islas y tierre firme del Mar Océano* (prólogo de J. Natalicio Gonzalez [Asuncion del Paraguay: Editorial Guarania, 1944], tomo III, Decada Segunda, libro quarto and tomo IV, Decada Tercera, Libro septimo). Herrera was the official historiographer of the Indies from 1596 and had access to sources many of which have since been lost.

The Portuguese historians Gaspar Correa, *Lendas da India*, composed before 1563 (Lisbon: Typ. da Academia Real das Sciencas, 1858–66), and João de Barros, *Asia* (Lisbon, 1552–1615), represent other important sources. Torodash observes with regard to Barros that this Portuguese royal chronicler not only used a great deal of first-hand material, but also had access to the correspondence between Magellan and Francisco Serrão and may even have used the lost account of the voyage written by Magellan himself.[38] Both Barros and Correa utilized Antonio de Brito's letter as well as information and documents captured from the Spanish at Ternate. The sections on Magellan from Correa's *Lendas da India* have been translated, and are available in Stanley (244–56) and in Nowell (312–28).

Notes

1 P. Giovio, *Historiarum sui temporis*, ed. Dante Visconti (Rome: Istituto poligrafico della Stato, Libreria della Stato, 1957) 172. The family produced two later geographical writers of note: Marcantonio Pigafetta, author of *Itinerario da Vienna a Constantinopoli* (London: 1585), and

Filippo Pigafetta (1533–1604), who published an Italian version of Ortelius's *Theatrum* (1608) and the *Relatione del reame del Congo* (1591), which
was translated into English (1597), Latin, French, Dutch, and German.

2 The original document is in Seville in the Archivio General de las Indias,
Contración 5090, c. 52 and was published by P. Pastella and C. Bayle, *El
descubrimento del Estrecho de Magalanes* (Madrid, 1920), 223. Manfroni used
this document in 'I genitori di Antonio Pigafetta,' *Archivio Veneto-
Tridentino* 2 [1922], 189–92 and in the introduction to his edition,
A. Pigafetta, *Il primo viaggio intorno al mondo* (Milan, 1956), 10–11.

3 'I genitori di Antonio Pigafetta,' *Archivio Veneto* 67 (1960): 26–37.

4 G. Mantese, *Memorie Storiche della Chiesa vicentina*, vol. 3, pt. 2 (Vicenza: N.
Pozza, 1964), 847–54.

5 Antonio Pigafetta's father, Giovanni, was born between 1440 and 1450. It
is possible to reconstruct his public career from archival documents,
where he first appears 21 December 1475: Giovanni was registered as a
notary after 1493 although he appears never to have practised. In 1500
he was member of the city's Major Council; in 1520 he was vicar of Bren-
dola; and in 1528 he was 'minister' of the Third Order Franciscan confra-
ternity (Canova, *Relazione*, 1999, 22).

6 Mantese discovered yet another interesting document that sheds light on
both the paternity and the death of Antonio Pigafetta. In a will dated
25 June 1524, Giovanni, apparently in an attempt to lure his globe-
trotting son back home, left to Antonio, together with his other son,
Valentino, the income of his estate, with the condition 'se vorrà abitare
nella sua patria' (if he will live in his homeland). But Antonio appears
never to have returned home to settle in Vicenza. Other studies of
Mantese on Pigafetta include 'Vicenza ai tempi della guerra di Cambrai,'
in *Archivio Veneto* 109, no. 146 (1978): 199 and 'Il Secolo XV: inizio della
dominazione veneziana e guerra di Cambrai,' in *Malo e il suo Monte*
(Malo: Amministrazione Comunale, 1979), 89–90, 481–2.

7 Canova reports that according to a family tradition referred to him by
Signora Rita Pigafetta, Antonio died in Greece fighting against the Mus-
lims. Georg Schurhammer proposed that Pigafetta entered into the service
of the Turkish court of Ibrahim Pascià after 1525, passing himself off as a
Portuguese ('Una ipotesi sulla fine di Antonio Pigafetta,' *Bollettino della reale
Società geografica italiana*, 6, no. 10 [1933]: 488–97, later in *Orientalia*

[Lisbon: *Centro de Estudos Históricos Ultramarinos*, 1965], 455–61). This theory was dismissed by S.E. Morison, *European Discovery of America*, vol. 2, *The Southern Voyages 1492–1616* (New York: Oxford University Press, 1974; hereafter cited as Morison, *The Southern Voyages*).

8 According to Ramusio, Martyr had written an earlier account of the voyage and sent it to Pope Adrian VI in Rome. There it would have been lost during the sack of 1527. *Discourse*, trans. Stanley, in H.E.J. Stanley, *The First Voyage Round the World by Magellan*. London: the Hakluyt Society, 1874, 181.

9 Antonello Gerbi wondered if Pigafetta might have been aware of the animosity that the chronicler of Spain bore Magellan, since he apparently did not provide Martyr with any information (their accounts are at odds on several points); Martyr in fact states that the eighteen survivors were illiterate in *Nature in the New World* (101). Pigafetta's desire to protect his literary capital is evident in his coming to court independently; that he would have guarded it from the competing pen of Martyr is highly plausible.

10 The relevant letters were published by G. Berchet, *Raccolta Colombiana* 1, *Fonti italiane per la storia della scoperta del nuovo mondo* (Rome: Ministero della Pubblica istruzione 1892), pt. 3 172–84.

11 Ibid., 175. The marchioness responded 2 January 1523: 'concerning the itinerary that you promised to send us, we say to you that we will be very pleased to receive it, and we ask you to send it as soon as possible, and we await it with the greatest desire' (cited in Canova, *Relazione*, originally published in Antonio Ciscato, *Antonio Pigafetta viaggiatore vicentino del secolo XVI* (Vicenza: Fratelli Giuliam, 1898), 86.

12 Berchet, *Fonti italiane*, 176. After receiving the itinerary, Isabella d'Este invited Pigafetta to be received by her in a letter of 3 February 1523: 'if that servant of yours who returned from those parts is well informed, and whom we envy greatly, will present himself here, we will be very pleased to speak with him, understanding that it is more delightful to hear about these incredible and novel matters from a living voice than through writings.' Cited by Canova, *Relazione*, 27, from Ciscato, *Pigafetta*, 89–90.

13 Bruno Nardi first noted the passage and we cite from his *Studi su Pietro Pomponazzi* (Florence: F. Le Monnier 1965), 42–3.

14 Marin Sanudo, *I Diarii (1496–1533): pagine scelte*, Paolo Margarol (Vicenza: N. Pozza, 1997). 35, col. 173.

15 An offer graciously accepted by Gonzaga in a letter of February 26, 1524. Berchet, 178–180.

16 Ibid., 179.

17 Ibid., 182.

18 Cited in Canova, 32, from Ms. Vat. Lat. 8211, f. 139v.

19 Ibid., 183; Pigafetta's formal request to the doge is dated 5 August. Ibid., n. 3; Marin Sanudo records the granting of the privilege in *Diarii* 36, col. 293b.

20 Masoero, 22.

21 Berchet, 183.

22 R.A. Skelton. *Magellan's Voyage: A Narrative Account of the First Circumnavigation by Antonio Pigafetta* (New Haven: Yale University Press, 1969), 16.

23 '[Pigafetta], having gone on the voyage and returned in the ship, *Victoria*, was made a Knight of Rhodes.' *Discourse*, 182.

24 Manfroni, 11–13.

25 Da Mosto, 29.

26 Skelton, 6–7.

27 For a detailed discussion of this problem and the relations between manuscripts, as well as bibliography, see Skelton, 16–27, but also Canova, 127–58, whose philological work and collocation of the testimonies has surpassed Skelton's.

28 Regarding the historical inventories (Z 62 inf.; Z 35 inf.) of the Ambrosiana, see C. Pasini, 'Antichi cataloghi manoscritti dei codici della Biblioteca Ambrosiana,' *Aevum*, 69 (1995): 667–8.

29 This work has never been much appreciated. Torodash says, 'To the historian it is, for the most part, an incomprehensible piece of curiosa' (326). Stanley provides an English translation of Amoretti's abridged version in pages 164–74.

30 Skelton, 17.

31 Cited by Tiraboschi (260) as occurring in vol. 37 of the eighty-volume Paris edition (Didot, 1748–89).

32 Camillo Manfroni published in 1928 an edition based on Da Mosto in modernized Italian which in not without omissions and errors. *Relazione*

del primo viaggio (Milan: Alpes; reprinted in 1983 by the Casso di Risparmio di Verona).

33 *Relation du premier voyage autor du monde* (Anvers-Paris: G. Jaussens-E. Leroux, 1923).

34 Navarrete, 209–47; English translation in Stanley, 211–36.

35 English translation in Stanley, 1—9.

36 English translations in Stanley, 179–210.

37 Skelton, 5.

38 Torodash, 138.

Note on the Text and Translation

This edition is based on the recent authoritative Italian edition of the Ambrosiana manuscript prepared by Andrea Canova (Padua: Antenore: 1999). The paragraphing and the spacing between the paragraphs follow those of the Ambrosiana manuscript. The numbering of the paragraphs was an innovation introduced by Mariarosa Masoero in her edition of the text (Rovereto: Longo, 1987), which was followed by Mario Pozzi in his facsimile edition of the Ambrosiana manuscript (Vicenza: Neri Pozza, 1995). This presentation and paragraph numbering of the text has been adopted here. In addition, we have utilized the numbering of the periods introduced by Canova, and it is to these that the references in the notes refer. The twenty-three maps are included in the edition at the appropriate place, that is, at the point where they appear in the Ambrosiana manuscript. All bracketed material, in the text and accompanying the maps, are interpolations of the editor.

The classic Robertson translation (Cleveland: Arthur H. Clark, 1906) has been thoroughly revised for this edition. Besides the general updating which has been effected by revising the translation against the most currently authoritative text of the original, numerous and in some cases crucial errors of the Robertson translation have been corrected. For example, quite inexplicably, Robertson has translated Pigafetta's nationality as 'Venetian' instead of 'of Vicenza' at the works very outset (1). Another example is the expression in the work's final paragraph where according to Robertson's rendering Pigafetta reports his return to Italy 'where I established my permanent abode' (1356). This was an unfortunate and misleading interpolation based upon the translator's misunderstanding of the original: 'Poi me ne venni ne la

Italia, ove donnai per sempre me medesimo e queste mie poche fatiche a lo inclito e illustrissimo signor Filipo de Villers Lisleadam, gran maestro de Rodi dignissimo' (Then I came to Italy, where I devoted myself forever, and these my poor labours to the famous and most illustrious Lord Philipp de Villiers l'Isle-Adam, the most worthy Grand Master of Rhodes). The translation has been revised for both style, content, and occasionally for interpretation, as when in Pigafetta's eulogy to Magellan, the word *fortuna*, meaning 'tempest' or 'fortune,' is taken in its more literal sense by the present editor. Contrary to Robertson's practice, place names, including the many toponyms for the Philippines and Moluccas as well as proper names, when clearly identifiable, have been rendered with their modern equivalents. The Robertson translation's principal virtue, however, has been maintained, that is, its accurate portrayal of Pigafetta's prose style, achieved primarily through a highly literal rendering.

Finally, I would like to take this opportunity to thank the readers of the University of Toronto Press for their valuable suggestions, Regan O'Kon and Demetrio Yocum for their reliable editorial assistance, and Shannon Carter and Robin Hoeppner for their technical support and help during the preparation of the manuscript.

Chronology of the Voyage

28 March 1518: Charles V issues a *capitulación* stipulating a fleet of five ships and some 250 officers and men for the expedition.

5 May 1519: A royal decree orders that 235 men should depart [Pigafetta says that 237 men were on board (21)]. The lists published by Navarette come to 239 men: 62 on the *Trinidad*, 57 on the *San Antonio*, 45 on the *Victoria*, 44 on the *Concepción* and 31 on the *Santiago*.

8 May 1519: A royal *cédula* is issued including seventy-four paragraphs of minute instructions for the voyage.

May 1519: Antonio Pigafetta arrives in Seville in time to join the expedition and participate in final preparations.

10 August 1519: The fleet departs Seville, anchoring at Sanlúcar de Barrameda, the outport of Seville, for more than a month, in order to add to the provisions.

24 August 1519: Magellan makes his last will and testament.

20 September 1519: The fleet weighs anchor from Sanlúcar and shapes its course south-west. Three years pass before the *Victoria* returns.

26 September 1519: The fleet reaches Tenerife in the Canaries (28).

3 October 1519: The fleet departs Tenerife and follows a south-west course down to latitude 27° N, then changing to south by west.

18 October 1519: The fleet experiences a series of storms off Sierra Leone (32).

29 November 1519: The fleet reaches Cabo Santo Agostinho at latitude 8° 21′ S, now Cabo Branco, to the north of Recife (46).

13 December 1519: The fleet reaches Rio de Janeiro at latitude 22° 54′ S.

20 December 1519: Trial, conviction, and execution of Antonio Salamone, master of the *Victoria*, who had been caught in the act of sodomy with an apprentice seaman off the coast of Guinea.

26 December 1519: The fleet departs Rio de Janeiro.

11–12 January 1520: The fleet reaches the Rio de la Plata (98), which Magellan calls Rio de Solis after the explorer killed by natives there in 1516.

2 February 1520: The fleet departs its anchorage near Montevideo.

13 February 1520: The fleet experiences storms off Bahia Blanca.

27 February 1520: The fleet anchors off a broad bay; they call it Bahia de los Patos for the immense number of penguins.

31 March 1520: The fleet enters Puerto San Julián (in 49° 30′ S), where it remains for five months, until 24 August. Here the encounters with the Patagonian giants and the mutiny take place (107–88).

1 April 1520: During the night between 1–2 April, Juan de Cartagena attempts to kill the master of the *San Antonio*, Juan de Elorriaga, and put in chains Alvaro de Mesquita. Gaspar de Quesada and Juan Sebastián del Cano take possession of the *Concepción* and Luis de Mendoza of the *Victoria*. Magellan suppresses the mutiny. A court martial is held and forty men are found guilty and condemned to death, including Gaspar de Quesada.

3 May 1520: The *Santiago* is lost while searching for the strait (180).

24 August 1520: The voyage is resumed.

14 September 1520: The four remaining ships of the fleet reach Rio Santa Cruz at latitude 50° S, where they remain until 18 October.

21 October 1520: The fleet reaches Cabo Vírgenes on the feast of St Ursula and the Eleven Thousand Virgins at latitude 52° 20´ S, longitude 68° 21´ W (192).

1 November 1520: Magellan discovers and names the strait Todos los Santos in honour of All Saints' Day.

November 1520: Estevão Gomez succeeds in the one successful mutiny of the voyage and together with the pilot Hierónimo Guerra takes command of the *S. Antonio* and returns to Spain, arriving 6 May 1521 (205–8).

28 November 1520: The fleet, consisting of *Trinidad, Concepción,* and *Victoria* pass Cabo Pilar (which Magellan names Deseado) on Desolation Island, and enters the Pacific Ocean: 'Wednesday, 28 November 1520, we debouched from that Strait, engulfing ourselves in the Pacific Sea' (238).

1 December 1520: After steering north along the coast of present-day Chile, the fleet sights Cabo Tres Montes in latitude 47° S.

24 January 1521: The fleet sights the uninhabited Islas Infortunatas identified by most authorities as Puka Puka in the Tuamoto archipelago in 14° 50´ S (248).

4 February 1521: The fleet sights the Isla de los Tiberones, probably Caroline in 10° 00´ S.

13 February 1521: The fleet reaches the equator.

6 March 1521: The fleet sights the Islas de Ladrones or Las Islas de Velas Latinas, identified as Guam and Rota of the Marianas (264).

9 March 1521: The fleet departs from the Marianas on a course west by south.

16 March 1521: The fleet sights the mountains of Samar in the Philippines and anchors at the island of Suluan at latitude 11° N: 'At dawn on Saturday, 16 March 1521, we came upon a high land at a distance of three hundred leagues from the islands of thieves' (293).

18 March 1521: Europeans make their first contact with Filipinos on Homonhon Island.

25 March 1521: Pigafetta falls overboard and is nearly drowned: 'I was aided not, I believe, indeed, through my merits, but through the mercy of that font of charity [the Virgin]' (336).

28 March 1521: The fleet anchors off Limasawa (Pigafetta's Mazaua) at the southern entrance to Suriago Strait; Magellan and his men are well received there by the natives and good relations are established with Rajah Colambu (352–437).

31 March 1521: Magellan has Easter mass celebrated on Limasawa Island (400–8).

6 April 1521: The fleet departs Limasawa.

7 April 1521: The fleet enters the port of Cebu, where, following negotiations, merchandise is exchanged for provisions, and good relations are established (456–62).

14 April 1521: The Sultan Humabon is baptized (and renamed Don Carlos) by the flagship's chaplain with all pomp and circumstance. Rajah Colambu is also baptized and named Don Juan after the Infante (558–564). Magellan cures a sick elder, which leads to the burning of native idols (594–609).

27 April 1521: Magellan and sixty of his men in three longboats attack Rajah Lapu Lapu and his forces on Mactan. They are driven back to the ships and Magellan is killed (696).

1 May 1521: Massacre of Europeans in the island of Cebu, including Duarte Barbosa and twenty-five shipmates (704–14). At this time, the *Concepción* is abandoned (721). Only about 110 men still survive. João Carvalho was elected captain-general.

21 June 1521: *Victoria* and *Trinidad* depart Palawan. They arrived at Brunei on the north-eastern coast of Borneo on 9 July (784).

29 July 1521: The Europeans attack a group of junks off Brunei, capturing four and killing several others (838–41).

15 August 1521: *Victoria* and *Trinidad* call at Cimbonbon (Banguey) on the south side of Balabac Strait, where they remain forty-two days repairing the ships and gathering provisions (882).

September 1521: Carvalho is degraded to his former rank of flag pilot; Gómez de Espinosa is elected captain-general and captain of the *Trinidad*; Juan Sebastián de Elcano is elected captain of *Victoria*.

27 September 1521: The voyage is resumed and a junk carrying the governor of Palawan is sacked and the governor held for ransom (896–901).

26 October 1521: The two ships experience storms in the Celebes Sea (928).

6 November 1521: *Victoria* and *Trinidad* arrive at the Moluccas: 'Therefore we thanked God and as an expression of our joy discharged all our artillery' (945).

8 November 1521: *Trinidad* and *Victoria* enter the harbour of Tidore, most important of the five principal Moluccas, which include Ternate, Motir, Makian, and Batjan (948): 'so that they spent from Seville to Maluco two years, two months and twenty-eight days, for they sailed on the tenth of August of 1519' (Genoese pilot).

9 November 1521: The Europeans are received at Tidore by the Sultan Manzor, who declares that he and all his people wish to become vassals of the emperor Charles V.

18 December 1521: The *Victoria* and the *Trinidad* lift anchor to depart but the *Trinidad* springs a leak.

21 December 1521: *Victoria*, under the command of Elcano, sets sail for a nine-month-long return voyage via the Cape of Good Hope, with forty-seven of the original crew and thirteen natives on board (eighteen Christian and three Indonesians survive). Gómez de Espinosa stays behind with fifty-three men to repair the *Trinidad* before attempting to return across the Pacific to New Spain, where the cargo is to be carried across the Isthmus of Panama and shipped to Spain (1190).

6 April 1522: *Trinidad* sets sail from Tidore and struggles as far as latitude 43° N, before it is decided to return to Tidore. The ship and crew are eventually captured by the Portuguese captain António de Brito. Only four of the *Trinidad's* crew eventually return to the Iberian Peninsula. Espinosa spends four and a half years in captivity in the east before returning to Spain.

10 January 1522: *Victoria* reaches Alor (Pigafetta's Malua) in 8° 20´ S latitude (1222).

25 January 1522: *Victoria* departs Alor and arrives the next day at the island of Timor, along which the ship coasts for three weeks while trading for provisions (1238).

10–11 February 1522: *Victoria* sails from Timor into the Indian Ocean, called Laut Chidol (1323).

6 May 1522: *Victoria* doubles the Cape of Good Hope, according to Pigafetta (1329). In fact, according to Albo, the sailors are convinced they doubled the Cape 8 May, but then realize that they are in error. The fleet double the Cape 16 May and entered the Atlantic 22 May.

8 June 1522: *Victoria* crosses the equator for the fourth time since leaving Spain.

9 July 1522: *Victoria* anchores in the port of Ribeira Grande on the Cape Verde island of Santiago. Between Timor and Cape Verde fifteen Europeans and ten Indonesians have died aboard the *Victoria*.

15 July 1522: *Victoria* departs hastily from the Cape Verde islands. Thirteen members of the crew are detained by the Portuguese authorities.

28 July 1522: Tenerife of the Canary Islands is sighted.

7 August 1522: The volcanic island of Pico in the Azores was sighted.

21 August 1522: *Victoria* heads for Cape St Vincent and arrives there 4 September.

6 September 1522: *Victoria* enters the harbour of Sanlúcar de Barrameda, and anchors off a quay at Seville on 8 September. Only eighteen Christians and three Indonesians survive.

THE FIRST VOYAGE AROUND THE WORLD

The First Voyage around the World
(1519–1522)

[1] Antonio Pigafetta, patrician of Vicenza and Knight of Rhodes, to the most illustrious and excellent Lord, Philipe Villiers de l'Isle-Adam, renowned Grand Master of Rhodes, his most honoured lord[1] [1].

[2] Inasmuch as, most illustrious and excellent Lord, there are many curious persons who not only take pleasure in knowing and hearing the great and wonderful things that God has permitted me to see and suffer during my long and dangerous voyage, herein described, but who also wish to know the means and manners and paths that I have taken in making that voyage; and who do not lend full credence to the end unless they have a perfect assurance of the beginning: therefore, your most illustrious Lordship must know that, finding myself, in the year of the nativity of Our Saviour 1519 in Spain, in the court of the most serene King of the Romans, [2] with the reverend Monsignor, Francesco Chiericati,[3] then apostolic protonotary and ambassador of Pope Leo X of holy memory (and who has since ascended to the bishopric of Aprutino and the lordship of Teramo),[4] and having obtained much information from many books that I had read, as well as from various persons, who discussed the great and marvellous things of the Ocean Sea with his Lordship, I determined, with the good grace of His Caesarean Majesty, and of his Lordship abovesaid, to experience myself and to see those things that might satisfy me somewhat, and that might grant me some renown with posterity [2].

[3] Having heard that a fleet of five vessels had been fitted out in the city of Seville for the purpose of going to discover the spicery in the islands of Molucca,[5] under command of Captain-General Ferdinand

Magellan, a Portuguese gentleman, *comendador* of the Order of Santiago de la Spada,[6] [who] had many times travelled the Ocean Sea in various capacities, acquiring great praise, I set out from the city of Barcelona, where His Majesty was then residing, bearing many letters of recommendation, and by ship I went as far as Malaga, and from there, travelling by land, I reached Seville,[7] and having been there about three full months, waiting for the said fleet to be set in order for the departure, finally, as your most excellent Lordship will learn below, we commenced our voyage under most happy auspices [3].

[4] And inasmuch as when I was in Italy and going to see His Holiness Pope Clement,[8] you by your grace showed yourself very kind and good to me at Monterosi,[9] and told me that you would be pleased if I would copy down for you all those things that I had seen and suffered during the voyage; and although I have had little opportunity, yet I have tried to satisfy your desire according to my poor ability [4]. Therefore, I offer you, in this little book of mine, all my vigils, hardships, and wanderings, begging you, when you will take some rest from your continual Rhodian cares, to deign to skim them, by which I shall receive no slight recompense from your most illustrious Lordship, to whose good grace I consign and commend myself [5].

[5] The captain-general having resolved to make so long a voyage through the Ocean Sea, where furious winds and great storms are always reigning, but not desiring to make known to any of his men the voyage that he was about to make, fearing they might be cast down at the thought of doing so great and extraordinary a deed, as he did accomplish with the aid of God (the captains who accompanied him, hated him exceedingly, I know not why, unless because he was a Portuguese, and they Spaniards) [6].[10] Desiring therefore to accomplish that which he promised under oath to the emperor, Don Carlo, king of Spain, and so that the ships might not become separated from one another during the storms and night, he prescribed the following orders and gave them to all the pilots and masters of his ships:[11] these were [to the effect] that he should always precede the other ships at night and they were to follow his ship which would have a large torch of wood, which they call *farol*,[12] which he always carried hanging from the poop of his ship [7]. This was a signal that

they should continue to follow him [8]. If he showed another light with a lantern or by means of a piece of rush wicking called *strengue*,[13] made of esparto that is well beaten in the water and then dried in the sun or in the smoke (a most excellent material for such use), they were to answer him so that he might know by that signal whether all of the ships were coming together [9]. If he showed two lights without the farol, they were to veer or take another tack [10]. When the wind was not favourable or suitable for us to continue on our course, or when he wished to sail slowly, he showed three lights, so that they were to take away the *bonneta* (bonnet sail), which is a part of the sail that is fastened below the mainsail; when the weather is good, in order to make better time, it is taken away so that it may be easier to furl the mainsail when it is struck hastily during a sudden squall [11]. If he showed four lights, they were to strike all the sails, after which he showed a signal by one light [12]. When he was standing still, if he showed many lights, or fired a mortar, it was a signal of land or of shoals [13]. Then he showed four lights when he wished to have the sails set full, so that they might always sail in his wake by the torch on the poop [14]. When he desired to set the bonnet sail, he showed three lights [15]. When he desired to alter his course, he showed two [16]. Then if he wished to ascertain whether all the ships were following and whether they were coming together, he showed one light, so that each one of the ships might do the same and reply to him [17].

[6] Three watches were set nightly: the first at the beginning of the night, the second (which they call *modora*)[14] in the middle, and the third at the end [of the night] [18]. All of the men in the ships were divided into three *colonelli*:[15] the first was that of the captain or boatswain, those two alternating nightly; the second, of either the pilot or boatswain's mate; and the third, of the master [19]. Thus did the captain-general order that all the ships observe the above signals and watches, so that their voyage might be more secure [20].[16]

[7] On Monday morning, 10 August, St Lawrence's day, in the abovesaid year, the fleet, having been supplied with all the things necessary for the sea and with men of every sort[17] (our number was 237),[18] the five ships made ready in the morning to leave the Mole of Seville,[19] and discharging many pieces of artillery, the ships set their

foresails to the wind, and descended the river Betis, at present called
Guadalquivir,[20] passing by a village called San Juan de Aznalfarache,
once a large Moorish settlement, in the midst of which was once a
bridge that crossed the said river, and led to Seville, where two columns
of that bridge have remained even to this day at the bottom of the
water; and when ships sail by there, they need men who know well the
location of the columns, so as to avoid them [21]. And it is necessary to
pass them when the river is at high tide, as with many other places
along the river that have insufficient depth for ships that are laden and
too large to pass [22]. Then the ships reached another village called
Coria,[21] and passed by many other villages along the river, until they
came to a castle of the duke of Medina-Sidonia, called Sanlúcar, which
is a port by which to enter the Ocean Sea, in an east and west direction
with the Cape of San Vincente, which lies in thirty-seven degrees of latitude, and ten leagues from the said port [23].[22] From Seville to this
point [Sanlúcar], it is seventeen or twenty leagues by river [24].

[8] Some days after, the captain-general, with his other captains,
descended the river in the small boats belonging to their ship, and we
remained there for a considerable number of days in order to finish
[providing] the fleet with some things that it needed [25]. Every day
we went ashore to hear mass in a village called Our Lady of
Barrameda, near Sanlúcar [26]. Before the departure, the captain-
general wished all the men to go to confession, and he would not
allow any woman to sail in the fleet for the sake of better order [27].

[9] We left that village called Sanlúcar on Tuesday, 20 September, of
the same year, and took a southwest course, and on the twenty-sixth of
the same month we reached an island of the Grand Canary islands,[23]
called Tenerife, which lies in a latitude of twenty-eight degrees, [land-
ing there] in order to get meat, water, and wood [28]. We stayed there
for three and one-half days in order to furnish the fleet with those supplies, and then we went to a port of the same island called Monte
Rosso[24] to get pitch, staying [there] two days [29].

[10] Your most illustrious Lordship must know that among these
Grand Canary islands, there is one where not a single drop of fresh water
is to be found; but that at midday a cloud descends from the sky and
encircles a large tree which grows in that island, the leaves and branches

of which distil a great quantity of water; and at the foot of the tree runs a trench that resembles a fountain, where all the water falls, and from which the people living there, and the animals, both domestic and wild, amply satisfy themselves every day with this water and no other [30].[25]

[11] At midnight on Monday, 3 October, the sails were trimmed toward the south, and we took to the open Ocean Sea, passing between Cape Verde and its islands in fourteen and one-half degrees [31]. Thus for many days did we sail along the coast of Ghinea, or Ethiopia; here there is a mountain called Sierra Leone, which lies in eight degrees of latitude, with contrary winds, calms, and rains without wind, until we reached the equinoctial line, where we had sixty days of continual rain, contrary to the opinion of the ancients [32].[26] Before we reached the line, at fourteen degrees, many furious squalls of wind and currents of water struck us head on [33]. Since we were unable to advance, and so as to avoid being wrecked, all the sails were struck; and in this manner did we wander here and there on the sea, waiting for the squall to cease, for it was very violent [34]. When it rained there was no wind; when the sun shone, it was calm [35].[27]

[12] Some large fish with fearsome teeth called *tiburoni*[28] came to the side of the ships, and whenever they find men in the sea they devour them [36]. We caught many of them with iron hooks, although they are not good to eat unless they are small, and even then they are not very good [37].

[13] During those storms the Holy Body, that is to say St Elmo,[29] appeared to us many times in the form of light [38]. Once he appeared during an exceedingly dark night, with the brightness of a blazing torch, on the maintop, where he stayed for about two hours or more, to our consolation, for we were weeping [39]. When that blessed light was about to leave us, so dazzling was the brightness that it cast into our eyes, that we all remained for more than an eighth of an hour blinded and calling for mercy, for truly we thought that we were dead men [40]. The sea suddenly grew calm [41].[30]

[14] I saw many kinds of birds, among them one that had no anus [42]. Another, [which] when the female wishes to lay its eggs, it does so on the back of the male and there they are hatched; the latter bird has no feet, and always lives in the sea;[31] also, [there is] another kind

that lives on the ordure of the other birds, and in no other manner; for I often saw this bird, which is called *cagassela*, fly behind the other birds, until they are constrained to drop their ordure [43]. Immediately, the *cagassela* seizes it and lets the bird go [44].[32] I also saw many flying fish, and many others collected together, so that they resembled an island [45].[33]

[15] After we had passed the equinoctial line going south, we lost the North Star, and hence we sailed south-south-west until [we reached] a land called 'the land of Verzin,'[34] which lies in twenty-three and one-half degrees of the Antarctic Pole [south latitude],[35] and it is the land extending from the Cape of Santo Agostinho, which lies in eight degrees of the same pole,[36] where we got a plentiful refreshment of fowls, potatoes, many sweet pine cones (in truth the most delicious fruit that can be found),[37] the flesh of the *anta*,[38] which resembles beef, sugar cane, and innumerable other things, which I shall not mention in order not to be prolix [46].[39] For one fish hook or one knife, those people gave five or six chickens; for one comb, a pair of geese; for one mirror or one pair of scissors, as many fish as would be sufficient for ten men; for a bell or a lace, one basketful of potatoes (these potatoes resemble chestnuts in taste, and are as long as turnips); for a king of diamonds, which is a playing card,[40] they gave me six fowls and thought that they had even cheated me [47].[41] We entered that port on St Lucy's day,[42] and on that day had the sun on the zenith and we were subjected to greater heat on that day and on the other days when we had the sun on the zenith than when we were beneath the equator [48].

[16] That land of Verzin is very bounteous and is larger than Spain, France, and Italy put together [49].[43] It belongs to the king of Portugal [50].[44] The people of that land are not Christians, and do not worship anything; they live according to the dictates of nature, and reach an age of 125 and 140 years [51].[45] Both the men and the women go naked [52]. They live in certain long houses which they call *boii*,[46] and sleep in cotton hammocks called *amache*,[47] which are fastened in those houses by each end to large beams; a fire is built on the ground between the beams [53]. In each one of those boii, there are one hundred men with their wives and children, and they make a

great racket [54]. They have boats called *canoe*[48] made of a single but flattened[49] tree, hollowed out by the use of stone[50] (those people employ stones as we do iron, as they have no iron); thirty or forty men occupy one of those boats [55]. They paddle with blades like a baker's peel,[51] and thus, black, naked, and shaven, they resemble, when paddling, the inhabitants of the Stygian marsh [56].[52]

[17] The men and women are proportioned like us [57]. They eat the human flesh of their enemies, not because it is good, but because it is a certain established custom [58]. That custom, which is mutual, was begun by an old woman, who had but one son who was killed by his enemies [59]. In return some days later, that old woman's friends captured one of the company who had killed her son, and brought him to the place of her abode [60]. When she saw him, remembering her son, she ran upon him like an infuriated bitch, and bit him on the shoulder [61]. Shortly afterward he escaped to his own people, whom he told that they had tried to eat him, showing them [in proof] the marks on his shoulder [62]. Whomever the latter captured afterward at any time from the former they ate, and the former did the same to the latter, so that such a custom has sprung up in this way [63].[53] They do not eat the bodies all at once, but everyone cuts off a piece, and carries it to his house, where he smokes it [64]. Then every eight days, he cuts off a small bit, which he eats thus smoked with his other food to remind him of his enemies [65].[54] The above was told me by the pilot, João Carvalho, who came with us, and who had lived in that land for four years [66].[55]

[18] Those people paint the whole body and the face in a wonderful manner with fire in various fashions, as do the women also; the men are smooth shaven and have no beard, for they pull it out; they clothe themselves in a dress made of parrot feathers, with large round arrangements at their buttocks made from the largest feathers, and it is a ridiculous sight [67]. Almost all the men, except the women and children, have three holes pierced in the lower lip, where they carry round stones, one finger or thereabouts in length and hanging down outside [68]. Those people are not entirely black, but olive skinned; they keep the privies uncovered, and the body is without hair, while both men and women always go naked [69]. Their king is called *cacich*

[70].[56] They have an infinite number of parrots, and gave us eight or ten for one mirror; and little monkeys[57] that look like lions, only [they are] yellow, and very beautiful [71]. They make round white bread from the marrowy substance of trees, which is not very good, and is found between the wood and the bark and resembles ricotta [72].[58] They have swine that have their navels on their backs,[59] and large birds with beaks like spoons and no tongues [73].[60]

[19] For one hatchet or a large knife, they gave us one or two of their young daughters as slaves, but they would not give us their wives in exchange for anything at all [74].[61] The women will not shame their husbands under any considerations whatever, according to what was told to us [75]. They refuse to consent to their husbands by day, but only by night [76]. The women cultivate the fields, and carry all their food from the mountains in panniers or baskets on the head or fastened to the head, but they are always accompanied by their husbands, who are armed only with a bow of Brazil wood or of black palm wood, and a bundle of cane arrows, doing this because they are jealous [of their wives] [77].[62] The women carry their children hanging [in] a cotton net from their necks [78].

[20] I omit other particulars, in order not to go on too long [79]. Mass was said twice on shore, during which those people remained on their knees with so great contrition and with clasped hands raised aloft, that it was an exceeding great pleasure to behold them [80].[63] They built us a house as they thought that we were going to stay with them for some time, and at our departure they cut a great quantity of Brazil wood to give us [81]. It had been about two months since it had rained in that land, and when we reached that port, it happened to rain, whereupon they said that we came from the sky and that we had brought the rain with us [82]. Those people could be converted easily to the faith of Jesus Christ [83].[64]

[21] At first those people thought that the small boats were the children of the ships, and that the latter gave birth to them when they were lowered into the sea from the ships, and when they were lying so alongside the ships (as is the custom), they believed that the ships were nursing them [84].[65] One day a beautiful young woman came to the flagship, where I was, for no other purpose than to find some

action [85].[66] While waiting there, she cast her eyes upon the master's room, and saw a nail longer than one's finger, and picking it up very delightedly and neatly, she trust it through the lips of her vagina, and bending down low immediately departed, as the captain-general and I witnessed [86].[67]

[22] Some words of those people of Verzin [87]:[68]

1] For millet *maiz*
2] For flour *hui*
3] For fishhook *pinda*
4] For knife *tasce*
5] For comb *chigap*
6] For scissors *pirame*
7] For bell *itanmaraca*
8] For good, better *tum maragathum*

[23] We remained in that land for thirteen days [88].[69] Then proceeding on our way, we went as far as thirty-four and one-third degrees toward the Antarctic Pole, where we found people at a freshwater river,[70] called Cannibals, who eat human flesh [89].[71] One of them, almost a giant in stature, came to the flagship in order to assure [the safety of] his companions [90]. He had a voice like a bull [92]. While he was on board the ship, the others carried away their possessions from the place where they were living into the interior, for fear of us. Seeing that, we landed one hundred men in order to find an interpreter and converse with them, or to capture one of them by force [93]. They fled, and in fleeing they took such long strides that we, although running, could not catch up with them [94]. There are seven islands in that river, in the largest of which precious gems are found [95]. That place is called Cape Santa Maria; it was formerly thought that one passed from there to the sea of Sur, that is to say the South Sea,[72] but it was never further explored [96]. Now the name is not [given to] a cape, but [to] a river, with a mouth seventeen leagues in width [97].[73] A Spanish captain called Juan de Solis was eaten by these Cannibals for trusting them too far, together with sixty men who were going to discover lands like us [98].[74]

[24] Then proceeding on the same course toward the Antarctic Pole, coasting along the land, we encountered two islands full of geese and seawolves [99].[75] Truly, the great number of those geese cannot be told; in one hour we loaded the five ships [with them] [100]. Those geese are black and have all their feathers alike both on body and wings, and they do not fly and live on fish [101]. They were so fat that it was necessary to skin them rather than to pluck them [102]. Their beak is like that of a crow [103]. The seawolves are of various colours, and as large as a calf, with a head like that of a calf, ears small and round, and large teeth; they have no legs but only feet with small nails attached to the body, which resemble our hands, and between their fingers the same kind of skin as the geese [104]. They would be very fierce if they could run; they swim, and live on fish [105]. The ships suffered there a very great storm, during which the three holy bodies appeared to us many times, that is to say, St Elmo, St Nicholas, and St Clare; whereupon the storm immediately ceased [106].[76]

[25] Leaving there, we finally reached forty-nine and one-half degrees toward the Antarctic Pole [107].[77] Since it was winter, the ships entered a safe port to winter [108].[78] We passed two months there without seeing any people [109]. One day we suddenly saw a naked man of giant stature on the shore of the port, dancing, sing-ing, and throwing dust on his head [110]. The captain-general sent one of our men to the giant so that he might perform the same actions as a sign of peace, and having done that, the man led the giant to a small island where the captain-general was waiting [111]. When the giant was in the captain-general's and our presence he marvelled greatly, and made signs with one finger pointed upward, indicating that he believed that we had come from the sky [112]. He was so tall that we reached only to his waist, and he was well propor-tioned;[79] his face was large and painted red all over, while about his eyes he was painted yellow; and he had two hearts painted on the middle of his cheeks; his scanty hair was painted white; he was dressed in the skins of animals skilfully sewn together, and that ani-mal has a head and ears as large as those of a mule, a neck and body like those of a camel, the legs of a deer, and the tail of a horse, like which it neighs [113]. That land has very many of those animals

[114].[80] His feet were shod with the same kind of skins and covered his feet in the manner of shoes, and in his hand he carried a short, heavy bow, with a cord somewhat thicker than those of the lute, and made from the intestines of the same animal, and a bundle of rather short cane arrows feathered like ours, and with points of white and black flint stones in the manner of Turkish arrows, instead of iron, fashioned by means of another stone [115].

[26] The captain-general had the giant given something to eat and drink, and among other things that were shown to him was a large steel mirror [116]. When he saw his reflection, he was greatly terrified and jumped back, throwing three or four of our men to the ground [117]. After that the captain-general gave him some bells, a mirror, a comb, and some beads and sent him ashore with four armed men [118]. When one of his companions, who would never come to the ships, saw him coming with our men, he ran to the place where the others were [119]. They came one after the other, completely naked [120]. When our men reached them, they began to dance and to sing, lifting one finger to the sky, and showing our men some white powder made from the roots of an herb, which they kept in earthen pots, and which they offered our men to eat because they had nothing else [121].[81] Our men made signs inviting them to the ships, and suggesting that they would help them carry their possessions; thereupon, those men quickly took only their bows, while their women laden like asses carried everything [122].

[27] The latter are not so tall as the men but are very much fatter [123]. When we saw them we were greatly surprised: their breasts are one-half cubit long,[82] and they are painted and clothed like their husbands, except that in front of their private parts they have a small skin that covers them [124]. They led four of those young animals [the guanaco], fastened with thongs like a halter [125]. When those people wish to take some of those animals, they tie one of these young ones to a thornbush; thereupon, the large ones come to play with the little ones, and those people kill them with their arrows from their place of hiding [126]. Our men led eighteen of those people, both men and women, to the ships, and they were returned to both sides of the port so that they might catch some of those animals [127].

[28] Six days later, a giant painted and clothed in the same manner was sighted by some [of our men] who were cutting wood [128]. He had in his hand a bow and arrow; when he approached our men, he first touched his head, face, and body, and then did the same to our men, afterward lifting his hands toward the sky [129]. When the captain-general was informed of it, he ordered him to be taken in the small boat, and brought to that island in the port where our men had built a house for the smiths and for the storage of some things from the ships [130]. That man was even taller and better built than the others and as tractable and amiable [131]. Jumping up and down, he danced, and when he danced, at every leap, his feet sank a palm's depth into the earth [132]. He remained with us for many days, so long that we baptized him, calling him John [133]. He pronounced the name Jesus, the Pater Noster, Ave Maria, and his own name as distinctly as we, but with an exceedingly loud voice [134]. Then the captain-general gave him a shirt, a woollen jerkin, cloth breeches, a cap, a mirror, a comb, bells, and other things, and sent him away to his companions; he left us very joyous and happy [135]. The following day he brought one of those large animals to the captain-general, in return for which many things were given to him, so that he might bring some more to us; but we did not see him again [136]. We thought that his companions had killed him because he had conversed with us [137].

[29] After fifteen days we saw four of those giants without their weapons for they had hidden them in certain bushes as the two whom we captured showed us [138]. Each one was painted differently [139]. The captain-general detained two of them, the youngest and best proportioned, by means of a very cunning trick, in order to take them to Spain; had he used any other means [than those he employed], they could easily have killed some of us [140]. The trick that he employed to capture them was as follows: he gave them many knives, scissors, mirrors, bells, and glass beads [141]. And those two having their hands filled with those things, the captain-general had two pairs of iron manacles brought, such as are fastened on the feet, and made motions as if to make a gift of them, whereat they were very pleased, since those manacles were of iron, but they did not

know how to carry them, and they were grieved at leaving them behind [142]. They had no place to put those gifts; for they had to hold the skin wrapped about them with their hands [143]. The other two giants wished to help them, but the captain refused [144]. Seeing that they were loath to leave those manacles behind, the captain made them a sign that he would put them on their feet, and that they could carry them away [145]. They nodded assent with the head [146]. Immediately, the captain had the manacles put on both of them at the same time, and when our men were driving home the cross bolt, the giants began to suspect something, but since the captain reassured them, they nevertheless remained still [147]. When they then saw that they were deceived, they raged like bulls, calling loudly for Setebos[83] to aid them [148]. As soon as we were able to bind the hands of the other two, we sent them ashore with nine of our men, in order that the giants might guide them to the place where the wife of one of the two whom we had captured was; for the latter expressed his great grief at leaving her by signs so that we understood [that he meant] her [149]. While they were on their way, one of the giants freed his hands, and took to his heels with such swiftness that our men lost sight of him [150]. He went to the place where his associates were, but he did not find [there] one of his companions who had remained behind with the women, for he had gone hunting [151]. He immediately went in search of the latter, and told him all that had happened. The other giant endeavoured so hard to free himself from his bonds, that our men struck him, wounding him slightly on the head, whereat he, raging, led them to where the women were [153]. João Carvalho, the pilot and commander of those men, refused to bring back the woman that night, but determined to sleep there, for night was approaching [154]. The other two giants came, and seeing their companion wounded, hesitated, but said nothing then, but with the dawn, they spoke to the women; [whereupon] they immediately ran away (and the smaller ones ran faster than the larger), leaving all their possessions behind them [155]. Two of them turned aside to shoot their arrows at our men; the other was leading away those small animals of theirs they use to hunt, and thus fighting, one of them pierced the thigh of one of our men with an arrow, and he died immediately [156].[84] When the giants saw that, they ran away quickly [157]. Our men had muskets and crossbows, but they could never wound any of the giants [158]. When the latter fought, they never stood still, but leaped here and there [159]. Our men buried their dead companion, and burned all the possessions left behind by the giants [160]. Truly, those giants run faster than horses and are exceedingly possessive of their wives [161].[85]

[30] When those people feel sick to their stomachs, instead of purging themselves, they thrust an arrow down their throat for two span or more and vomit [a substance of a] green colour mixed with blood, for they eat a certain kind of thistle [162].[86] When they have a headache, they cut themselves across the forehead; and they do the same on the arms or on the legs and in any part of the body, letting much blood [163]. One of those whom we had captured, and whom we kept in our ship, said that the blood refused to remain there [in the place of the pain], and consequently causes them suffering [164]. They wear their hair cut with the tonsure, like friars, but longer; and they have a cotton cord wrapped about the head, in which they stick their arrows when they go hunting [165]. They bind their privies close to their bodies because of the very great cold [166]. When one of those people die, ten or twelve demons all painted appear and dance very joyfully about the corpse [167]. One of those demons is seen to be much taller than the others, and he cries out and rejoices more [168]. They paint themselves in the same manner as the demon appears painted to them [169]. They call the larger demon Setebos and the others Cheleulle [170]. That giant also told us by signs that he had seen the demons with two horns on their heads and long hair hanging down to the feet belching forth fire from mouth and buttocks [171]. The captain-general named those people Patagoni [172].[87] They all clothe themselves in the skins of that animal mentioned earlier; and they have no houses except those made from the skin of the same animal, and they wander here and there with those houses just as the gypsies do; they live on raw flesh and on a sweet root that they call chapae [173]. Each of the two whom we captured ate a basketful of biscuit, and drank half a pail of water at a gulp [174]. They also ate rats without skinning them [175].

[31] We remained in that port, which we called 'Port St Julian,' about five months where many things happened [176].[88] In order that your most illustrious Lordship[89] may know some of them, it happened that as soon as we had entered the port, the captains of the other four ships plotted treason in order that they might kill the captain-general; and these men were the overseer of the fleet, one Juan de Cartagena, the treasurer, Luis de Mendoza, the accountant, Antonio Coca, and Gaspar de Quesada; and when the treason was discovered, the overseer of the men was quartered, and the treasurer was killed by dagger blows [177]. Some days after that, Gaspar de Quesada was banished with a priest[90] in that land of Patagonia for planning another plot [178]. The captain-general did not wish to have him killed, because the emperor, Don Carlo, had appointed him captain [179].[91]

[32] A ship called *Santiago* was lost in an expedition made to explore the coast [180]. All the men were saved as by a miracle, not even getting wet [181]. Two of them barely made it to the ships and told us about it; consequently, the captain-general sent some men with bags full of biscuits [182]. It was necessary for us to bring them food for two months, while each day supplies from the ship [that was wrecked] were recovered [183]. The journey there was twenty-four leagues long (or one hundred miles), and the path was very rough and full of thorns. The men were four days on the road, sleeping at night in the bushes; they found no drinking water, but only ice, which caused them the greatest hardship [185].[92] There were very many long shellfish that are called *missiglioni*[93] in that port (they had pearls in them), but they were too small to be eaten [186]. Incense, ostriches, foxes, sparrows, and rabbits much smaller than ours were also found [187]. We erected a cross on the top of the highest summit there, as a sign in that land that it belonged to the king of Spain; and we called that summit 'Monte de Cristo' [188].

[33] Departing from there, we found, in fifty-one degrees less one-third degree, toward the Antarctic Pole, a river of fresh water[94] in which the ships were almost lost because of the furious winds; but God and the holy bodies aided them [189]. We stayed about two months in that river[95] in order to supply the ships with water, wood, and fish, [the latter being] one cubit in length and more, and covered with

scales:[96] they were very good although there were too few of them
[190]. Before leaving that river, the captain-general and all of us confessed and received communion as true Christians [191].

[34] Upon reaching fifty-two degrees toward the Antarctic Pole, we
discovered most miraculously a strait on the day of the [Feast of the]
Eleven Thousand Virgins, whose cape we named the Cape of the Eleven
Thousand Virgins [192].[97] That strait is 110 leagues or 440 miles long,
and it is one-half league broad, more or less, and it leads to another sea
called the Pacific Sea, and is surrounded by very lofty mountains laden
with snow [193]. There it was impossible to find bottom [for anchor-
ing], and [it was necessary to fasten] the moorings[98] on land twenty-five
or thirty fathoms away, and if it had not been for the captain-general, we
would not have found that strait, for we all thought and said that it was
closed on all sides [194].[99] But the captain-general, who knew that he
had to make his journey by means of a well-hidden strait, which he had
seen depicted on a map in the treasury of the king of Portugal, which
was made by that excellent man, Martin of Bohemia,[100] sent two ships,
the *San Antonio* and the *Concepción* (for thus they were called), to discover what was at the end of the bay [195].

[35] We with the other two ships, the flagship, called *Trinidad*, and
the other the *Victoria*, stayed inside the bay to wait for them [196]. A
great storm struck us that night, which lasted until the middle of the
next day, and forced us to lift anchor and be driven here and there
about the bay [197].[101] The other two ships suffered a headwind and
could not double a cape formed by the bay almost at its end, as they
were trying to return to join us; so that they thought that they would
have to run aground [198]. But on approaching the end of the bay,
and thinking that they were lost, they saw a small opening that did
not appear to be an opening, but a cove,[102] and like desperate men
they hauled into it, and thus they discovered the strait by chance, and
seeing that it was not a cove, but a strait with land, they proceeded
farther and found a bay [199].[103] And then farther on they found
another strait and another bay larger than the first two [200].[104] Very
joyful, they immediately turned back to report to the captain-general
[201]. We thought that they had been wrecked, first, by reason of the
violent storm, and second, because two days had passed and they had

not appeared, and also because of certain smoke signals made by two of their men who had been sent ashore to notify us [202]. And so, while in suspense, we saw the two ships, with sails full and banners flying to the wind, coming toward us [203]. Upon approaching us, they suddenly discharged a number of mortars [...] and cheers; then, all together, thanking God and the Virgin Mary, we went to explore farther on [204].

[36] After entering that strait, we found two openings, one to the southeast and the other to the southwest [205].[105] The captain-general sent the ship *San Antonio* together with the *Concepción* to ascertain whether that opening which was toward the southeast had an exit into the Pacific Sea [206]. The ship *San Antonio* would not wait for the *Concepción* because it intended to flee and return to Spain, which it did [207]. The pilot of that ship was one Estevão Gomez,[106] and he hated the captain-general exceedingly, because before that fleet was fitted out, he had gone to the emperor to request some caravels to go and explore, but His Majesty did not give them to him because of the coming of the captain-general [208]. On that account he conspired with certain Spaniards, and the next night they captured the captain of their ship, a cousin-german of the captain-general, one Alvaro de Mezquita, whom they wounded and put in irons, and in this condition took to Spain [209]. The other giant whom we had captured was in that ship, but he died when they came into the warmer climate [210]. The *Concepción*, as it was unable to keep up with that ship, waited for it, sailing about here and there [211]. The *San Antonio* turned back during the night and fled through the same strait [212].

[37] We had gone to explore the other opening toward the southwest, finding, however, that the same strait continued [213]. We came upon a river that we called the 'river of Sardines,' because there were many sardines near it,[107] and so we stayed there for four days in order to await the two ships [214]. During that period we sent a well-equipped boat to discover the cape of the other sea [215]. The men returned within three days, and reported that they had seen the cape and the open sea [216]. The captain-general wept for joy, and called that cape, 'Cape Deseado,' for we had desired it for a long time [217].[108] We turned back to look for the two ships, but we found only the *Concepción*, and upon asking them

where the other one was, João Serrão,[109] who was captain and pilot of the *Concepción* (and also of that ship that had been wrecked), replied that he did not know, and that he had never seen it after it had entered the opening [218]. We sought it in all parts of the strait, as far as that opening through which it had fled [219]. The captain-general sent the ship *Victoria* back to the entrance of the strait to ascertain whether the ship was there, and orders were given them, if they did not find it, to plant a banner on the summit of some small hill with a letter in an earthen pot buried in the earth near the banner, so that if the banner were seen the letter might be found, and the ship might learn the course that we were sailing, for this was the arrangement made between us in case we became separated [220]. Two banners were planted with their letters: one on a little eminence in the first bay, and the other in an islet in the third bay where there were many seawolves and large birds [221].[110]

The captain-general waited for the ship with his other ship near the river of Isleo,[111] and he had a cross set up in an islet near that river, which flowed between high mountains covered with snow and emptied into the sea near the river of Sardines [222]. Had we not discovered that strait, the captain-general had determined to go as far as seventy-five degrees toward the Antarctic Pole, where in that latitude, during the summer season, there is no night, or if there is any night it is but short, and so in the winter with the day [223].

[38] In order that your most illustrious Lordship may believe it,[112] when we were in that strait, the nights were only three hours long, and it was then the month of October [224]. The land on the left-hand side of that strait turned toward the southeast and it was low [225].[113] We called that strait the 'strait of Patagonia,'[114] where one finds the safest of ports every half league in it, excellent waters, the finest of wood (but not of cedar), fish, sardines, and *missiglioni*, while small-age,[115] a sweet herb (although there is also some that is bitter), grows around the springs, of which we ate for many days as we had nothing else [226]. I believe that there is not a more beautiful or better strait in the world than that one [227]. In that Ocean Sea one sees a very amusing fish hunt: the fish [that hunt] are of three sorts, and are one cubit and more in length, and are called *dorado, albicore,* and *bonito,*[116] which follow the flying fish called *colondrini,*[117] which are one span and more in length and very good to eat [228]. When the above three kinds [of

fish] find any of those flying fish, the latter immediately leap from the water and fly, as long as their wings are wet, more than a crossbow's flight [229]. While they are flying, the others run along behind them under the water following the shadow of the flying fish; the latter have no sooner fallen into the water than the others immediately seize and eat them: it is a truly beautiful thing to see [230].[118]

[39] Words of the Patagonian giants:[119]

1] For head *her*
2] For eye *other*
3] For nose *or*
4] For eyebrows *occhechel*
5] For eyelids *sechechiel*
6] For nostrils *oresche*[120]
7] For mouth *xiam*
8] For lips *schiahame*
9] For teeth *phor*
10] For tongue *schial*
11] For chin *sechen*
12] For hair *archir*
13] For face *cogechel*
14] For throat *ohumez*
15] For occiput *schialeschin*
16] For shoulders *pelles*
17] For elbow *cotel*
18] For hand *chene*
19] For palm of hand *canneghin*
20] For finger *cori*
21] For ears *sane*
22] For armpit *salischin*
23] For breasts *othen*
24] For chest *ochij*
25] For body *gechel*
26] For penis *sachet*
27] For testicles *sacaneos*
28] For vagina *isse*
29] For communication with women *io hoi*
30] For thighs *chiaue*
31] For knee *tepin*
32] For rump *schiaguen*
33] For buttocks *hoij*
34] For arm *mar*
35] For pulse *holion*
36] For legs *coss*
37] For foot *thee*
38] For heel *tere*
39] For ankle *perchi*
40] For sole of foot *caotscheni*
41] For fingernails *colim*
42] For heart *thol*
43] For to scratch *gechare*
44] For cross-eyed man *calischen*
45] For young man *calemi*
46] For water *holi*
47] For fire *ghialeme*
48] For smoke *giaiche*
49] For no *ehen*
50] For yes *rey*
51] For gold *pelpeli*
52] For lapis lazuli *secheg*
53] For sun *calexchen*
54] For stars *settere*
55] For sea *aro*

56] For wind *oni*

57] For storm *ohone*

58] For fish *hoi*

59] For to eat *mechiere*

60] For bowl *elo*

61] For pot *aschanie*

62] For to ask *ghelhe*

63] For come here *hon si*

64] For to look *choime*

65] For to walk *rey*

66] For to fight *oamaghce*

67] For arrows *sethe*

68] For dog *holl*

69] For wolf *ani*

70] For to go a long distance *schien*

71] For guide *anti*

72] For snow *then*

73] For to cover *hiam*

74] For ostrich, a bird *hoihoi*

75] For its eggs *iam*

76] For the powder of the herb they eat *chapae*

77] For to smell *os*

78] For parrot *cheche*

79] For birdcage *cleo*

80] For missiglioni *siameni*

81] For red cloth *terechai*

82] For cap *aichel*

83] For black *ainel*

84] For red *taiche*

85] For yellow *peperi*

86] For to cook *yrocoles*

87] For belt *cathechin*

88] For goose *cache*

89] For their big devil *Setebos*

90] For their small devils *Cheleule*

All the above words are pronounced in the throat, for such is their method of pronunciation [232].

[40] That giant whom we had in our ship told me those words; for when he, upon asking me for *capac*, that is to say, bread, as they call that root which they use as bread, and *oli*, that is to say, water, saw me write those words, and afterward when I, with pen in hand, asked him for other words, he understood me [233]. Once I made the sign of the cross, and, showing it to him, kissed it, he immediately cried out 'Setebos', and made me a sign that if I made the sign of the cross again, Setebos would enter into my body and cause me to die [234]. When that giant was sick, he asked for the cross, and embraced it and kissed it many times [235]. He decided to become a Christian before his death; we called him Paul [236]. When those people wish to make a fire, they rub a sharpened piece of wood against another piece until the fire catches in the pith of a certain tree, which is placed between those two sticks [237].

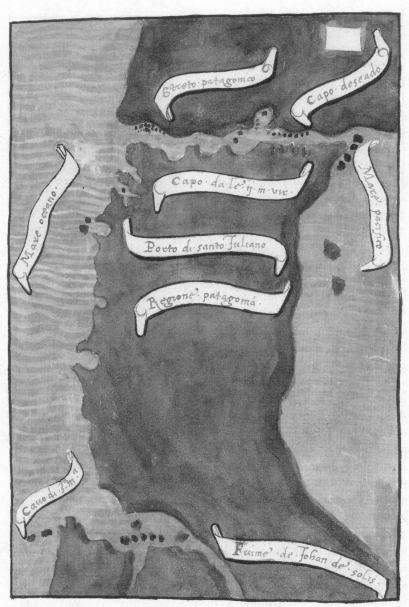

[Chart of the Patagonian Strait (I)]

[Chart of the Unfortunate Islands (II)][121]

[41] Wednesday, 28 November 1520,[122] we debouched from that strait, engulfing ourselves in the Pacific Sea [238]. We were three months and twenty days without taking on any food or water [239]. We ate biscuit, which was no longer biscuit, but [had been reduced to] fistfuls of powder swarming with worms, for they had eaten the better part (it stank strongly of rat urine); and we drank yellow water that had been putrid for many days, and we also ate some ox hides that covered the top of the main yard to prevent the yard from chafing the shrouds, and which had become exceedingly hard because of the sun, rain, and wind [240]. We left them in the sea for four or five days, and then placed them for a few moments on top of the embers, and thus we ate them; and often we ate sawdust from boards [241]. Rats were sold for one-half ducat apiece, if only one could get them [242]. But worse than all the other misfortunes was the following: the gums of both the lower and upper teeth of some of our men swelled, so that they could not eat under any circumstances and therefore died [243]. Nineteen men died from that sickness, as well as the giant together with an Indian from the country of Verzin;[123] twenty-five or thirty men fell sick [during that time], in the arms, legs, or in some other place, so that only a few remained well [244]. By the grace of God, I suffered no infirmity [245].

[42] We sailed about four thousand leagues during those three months and twenty days through an open stretch in that Pacific Sea [246]. In truth it is very pacific, for during that time we did not suffer any storm, and we saw no land except two desert islets, where we found nothing but birds and trees [247]. We called them the Unfortunate Islands;[124] they are two hundred leagues apart [248]. We found no anchorage, [but] saw many sharks near them [249]. The first islet lies in fifteen degrees and the other in nine [250]. Daily we made runs of fifty, sixty, or seventy leagues with the wind at the windward side or at the stern,[125] and had not God and His blessed mother given us such good weather we would all have died of hunger in that exceedingly vast sea [251]. In truth I believe no such voyage will ever be repeated [252].[126]

[43] When we left that strait, if we had sailed continuously westward we would have circumnavigated the world without finding other land than the Cape of the Eleven Thousand Virgins, which is a cape of that strait on the Ocean Sea, straight east-west from Cape Deseado on the Pacific Sea, and both of those capes lie in a latitude of exactly fifty-two degrees toward the Antarctic Pole [253].

[44] The Antarctic Pole is not so starry as the Arctic [254]. Many small stars clustered together are seen, which have the appearance of two clouds with little distance between them, and they are somewhat dim;[127] in the midst of them are two large and not very luminous stars, which move only slightly: those two stars are the Antarctic Pole [255]. Our loadstone, although it moved here and there, always pointed toward its own Arctic Pole, although it did not have so much strength as on its own side, and on that account when we were in that open expanse, the captain-general asked all the pilots: 'Are you still sailing forward in the course that we laid down on the maps [256]?' All replied: 'By your course exactly as laid down [257].' He answered them that they were pointing wrongly, which was a fact, and that it would be fitting to adjust the compass, for it was not receiving so much force from its side [258].[128] When we were in the midst of that open expanse, we saw a cross with five extremely bright stars straight toward the west, those stars being exactly placed in relation to one another [259].[129]

[Chart of the three 'Islands of Thieves' (III)][130]

[45] During those days we sailed between west and north-west and north-west by west, and north-west, until we reached the equinoctial line at the distance of 122 degrees from the line of demarcation [260].[131] The line of demarcation is thirty degrees from the meridian, and the meridian is three degrees eastward from Cape Verde [261]. We passed a short distance from two exceedingly rich islands while on that course, one in twenty degrees of the latitude of the Antarctic Pole, by name Cipangu, and the other in fifteen degrees, by name Sumbdit Pradit [262].[132] After we had passed the equinoctial line we sailed west-north-west, and west by north, and then for two hundred leagues toward the west, changing our course to west by south until we reached thirteen degrees toward the Arctic Pole in order that we might approach nearer to the land of Cape Catigara, and that cape (begging the pardon of cosmographers, for they have not seen it) is not found where they thought it to be, but to the north in twelve degrees or thereabouts [263].[133]

[46] About seventy leagues on the above course, and lying in twelve degrees of latitude and 146 in longitude, we discovered on Wednesday, 6 March a small island to the northwest, and two others toward the southwest [264]. One of them was higher and larger than the other two [265].[134] The captain-general wished to stop at the large island and get some fresh food, but he was unable to do so because the inhabitants of that island entered the ships and stole whatever they could lay their hands on, in such a manner that we could not defend ourselves from them [266]. The men wanted to strike the sails so that we could go ashore [267]. The natives very deftly stole from us the small boat that was fastened to the poop of the flagship;[135] thereupon, the captain-general in wrath went ashore with forty armed men, and they burned some forty or fifty houses together with many boats, killed seven men, and recovered the small boat; we departed immediately pursuing the same course [268]. Before we landed, some of our sick men begged us if we should kill any man or woman to bring the entrails to them, since by eating them they would recover immediately [269].[136]

[47] When we wounded any of those people with our crossbow shafts, which passed completely through their loins from one side to the other, they, looking at it, pulled on the shaft now on this and now on that side, and then drew it out, with great astonishment, and so died; others who were wounded in the breast did the same, which moved us to great compassion [270]. Those people seeing us departing followed us with more than one hundred boats for more than one league [271]. They approached the ships showing us fish, feigning that they would give them to us, but then threw stones at us and fled [272]. And although the ships were under full sail, they passed between them and the small boats [fastened astern] very adroitly in those small boats of theirs [273]. We saw some women in their boats who were crying out and tearing their hair, for love, I believe, of their dead [274].

[48] Each one of those people lives according to his will, for they have no lords [275]. They go naked, and some are bearded and have tangled black hair that reaches to the waist; they wear small palm-leaf hats, as do the Albanians, and they are as tall as we, and well built [276]. They worship nothing [277]. They are olive-skinned, but are born white; their teeth are red and black, for they think that is most beautiful [278]. The women go naked except that they cover their privies with a narrow strip of bark as thin as paper, which grows between the tree and the bark of the palm [279]. They are beautiful, delicately formed, and whiter than the men; they wear their hair, which is exceedingly black, loose and hanging down to the ground [280]. The women do not work in the fields but stay in the house, weaving mats, baskets, and other things needed in their houses from palm leaves [281]. They eat coconuts, potatoes, birds, figs a span in length [bananas], sugar cane, and flying fish, besides other things [282]. They anoint the body and the hair with coconut and beneseed [benzoin] oil [283].

[49] Their houses are all built of wood covered with planks and thatched with leaves of the fig tree [banana tree] two fathoms long, and they have wooden-beam floors and windows; the rooms and the beds are all furnished with the most beautiful palm-leaf mats [284]. They sleep on palm straw that is very soft and fine [285]. They use no weapons, except a kind of a spear pointed with a fishbone at the end [286]. Those people are poor, but ingenious and very thievish, on account of which we called those three islands 'the Islands of Thieves' [287]. Their amusement is to go with their women upon the seas with those small boats of theirs: those boats resemble *fucelere*,[137] but are narrower, and some are black, [some] white, and others red; at the side opposite the sail, they have a large piece of wood pointed at the top, with poles laid across it and resting on the water, in order that the boats may sail more safely [288].[138] The sail is made from palm leaves sewn together and is shaped like a lateen sail [289]. For rudders they use a certain blade like a baker's peel that has a piece of wood at the end [290]. They can change stern and bow at will, and those boats resemble dolphins that leap in the water from wave to wave [291]. Those thieves thought, according to the signs that they made, that there were no other people in the world but themselves [292].

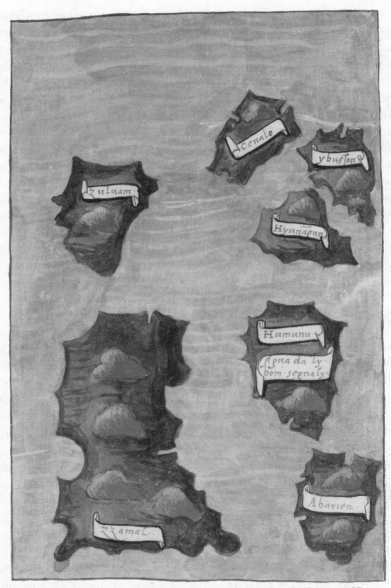

[Chart depicting ZZamal (Samar), Zuluam (Suluan), Cenalo (Dinaga), Ybuston (Ibusson), Hyunangan (Kabugan?), Humunu (Homonhon, with the scroll: 'The Watering Place of Good Signs'), and Abarien (Cabalian) (IV)][139

[50] At dawn on Saturday, 16 March 1521,[140] we came upon a high land at a distance of three hundred leagues from the Islands of Thieves, an island named Samar [293].[141] The following day, the captain-general desired to land on another island, which was uninhabited and lay to the right of the above mentioned island,[142] in order to be more secure, and to get water and have some rest [294]. He had two tents set up on the shore for the sick and had a sow slaughtered for them [295].

[51] On Monday afternoon, 18 March, after eating, we saw a boat coming toward us with nine men in it; therefore, the captain-general ordered that no one should move or say a word without his permission [296]. When those men reached the shore, their chief went immediately to the captain-general, giving signs of joy because of our arrival [297]. Five of the most ornately adorned of them remained with us, while the rest went to get some others who were fishing, and so they all came [298]. The captain-general, seeing that they were reasonable men, ordered food to be set before them, and gave them red caps, mirrors, combs, bells, ivory, bocasine,[143] and other things [299]. When they saw the captain's courtesy, they presented fish, a jar of palm wine, which they call *uraca*,[144] figs more than one span long,[145] and others that were smaller and more delicate, and two coconuts [300]. They had nothing else then, but made us signs with their hands that they would bring *umay* or rice, and coconuts and many other articles of food within four days [301].

[52] Coconuts are the fruit of the palm tree [302]. Just as we have bread, wine, oil, and milk, so these people get everything from those trees [303]. They obtain wine in the following manner: they make a hole in the heart of the tree at the top called *palmito*, from which distils a liquor that resembles white must; it is sweet but somewhat tart, and [is gathered] in canes [of bamboo] as thick as the leg and thicker [304]. They fasten the bamboo to the tree at evening for the morning, and in the morning for the evening [305]. That palm bears a fruit, namely, the coconut; this coconut is as large as a man's head or thereabouts [306]. Its outside husk is green and thicker than two fingers, and certain filaments are found in that husk, whence is made cord for binding together their boats [307]. Under that husk there is a hard shell, much thicker than the shell of the walnut, which they burn and from which they derive a powder that is useful to them [308]. Under

that shell there is a white marrowy substance one finger in thickness, which they eat fresh with meat and fish as we do bread; and it has a taste resembling the almond, and it could be dried and made into bread [309]. There is a clear, sweet water in the middle of that marrowy substance that is very refreshing, and when that water stands for a while after having been collected, it congeals and becomes like an apple [310]. When the natives wish to make oil, they take that coconut, and allow the marrowy substance and the water to putrefy; then they boil it and it becomes oil like butter [311]. When they wish to make vinegar, they allow only the water to putrefy, and then place it in the sun, and a vinegar results like [that made from] white wine [312]. Milk can also be made from it, for we made some: we scraped that marrowy substance and then mixed the scrapings with its own water, which we strained through a cloth, and so obtained milk like goat's milk [313]. Those palms resemble date palms, and although not smooth they are less knotty than date palms [314]. A family of ten persons can support itself on two trees, by utilizing one for eight days and then the other for eight days for the wine, for if they did otherwise, the trees would dry up; and they last one hundred years [315].[146]

[53] Those people became very familiar with us; they told us many things, their names and those of some of the islands that could be seen from that place [316]. Their island was called Suluan and it is not very large [317]. We took great pleasure with them, for they were very pleasant and conversable [318]. In order to show them greater honour, the captain-general took them to his ship and showed them all his merchandise: cloves, cinnamon, pepper, ginger, nutmeg, mace, gold, and all the things in the ship [319]. He had some mortars fired for them, which greatly frightened them, and they tried to jump out of the ship [320]. They made signs to us that the articles just mentioned grew in that place where we were going [321]. When they were about to retire they took their leave very gracefully and neatly, saying that they would return according to their promise [322]. The island where we were is called Homonhon; but since we found two springs there of the clearest water, we called it 'the watering-place of good signs,'[147] for there were the first signs of gold, which we found in those districts [323]. We found a great quantity of white coral there, and large trees with fruit a trifle smaller than the almond and resembling pine seeds, and also many

palms, some of them good and others bad [324]. There are many islands in that district, and therefore we called them 'the Archipelago of San Lazaro,' as they were discovered on the Sunday of St Lazurus;[148] they lie in ten degrees of latitude toward the Arctic Pole, and in a longitude of 161 degrees from the line of demarcation [325].

[54] At noon on Friday, 22 March, those men came as they had promised us in two boats with coconuts, sweet oranges, a jar of palm wine, and a cock,[149] in order to show us that there were fowls in that district [326]. They exhibited great signs of pleasure at seeing us; we purchased all those articles from them [327]. Their lord was an old man who was tattooed, and he wore two gold earrings in his ears, and the others many gold armlets on their arms and kerchiefs about their heads [328]. We stayed there eight days, and during that time our captain went ashore daily to visit the sick, and every morning gave them coconut water from his own hand, which comforted them greatly [329]. There are people living near that island who have holes in their ears so large that they can carry their arms in them [330]. Those people are Kaffirs, that is to say, heathen;[150] they go naked, with a cloth woven from the bark of a tree about their private parts, except some of the chiefs who wear cotton cloth embroidered with silk at the ends by means of a needle [331]. They are olive skinned, fat, and tattooed, and they anoint themselves with coconut and with beneseed oil as a protection against sun and wind; they have very black hair that falls to the waist, and they use daggers, knives, and spears ornamented with gold, large shields, *focine*,[151] javelins, and fishing nets that resemble *rizali* [332].[152] Their boats are like ours [333].

[55] On the afternoon of Holy Monday, the day of our Lady, 25 March [Feast of the Annunciation], while we were on the point of weighing anchor, I went to the side of the ship to fish, and, putting my feet upon a yard leading down into the storeroom, they slipped, for it was rainy, and consequently I fell into the sea, so that no one saw me, and when I was all but under, my left hand happened to catch hold of the clew garnet of the mainsail, which was dangling in the water [334]. I held on tightly, and began to cry out so lustily that the small boat came to rescue me [335]. I was aided, not, I believe, indeed, through my merits, but through the mercy of that font of

charity [the Virgin] [336]. That same day we shaped our course toward the west-south-west between four small islands, namely, Cenalo, Hiunanghan, Ibusson, and Abarien [337].[153]

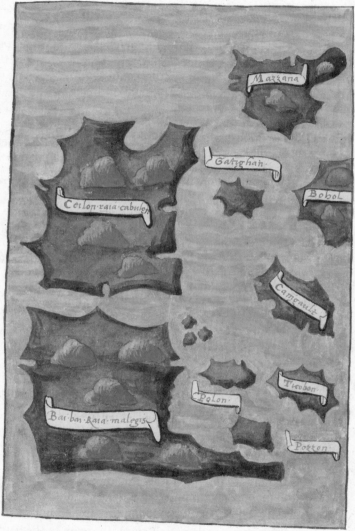

[The chart of Mazzana (Mazaua: Limasawa), Bohol, Ceilon (Leyte), Baibai (Baybay). Canighan (Canigao), Polon (Poro), Ticobon (Pacijan), and Pozzon (Pozon) (V)][154]

[56] On Thursday morning, 28 March, as we had seen a fire on an island the night before, we anchored near it [338].[155] We saw a small boat that the natives call *boloto* with eight men in it, approaching the flagship [339]. A slave[156] belonging to the captain-general who was a native of Sumatra, which was formerly called Taprobane, spoke to them,[157] and they immediately understood him [340]. They came alongside the ship, but were unwilling to come aboard, taking a position at some little distance [341]. When the captain saw that they would not trust us, he threw them a red cap and other things tied to a bit of wood [342]. They received them very gladly, and went away quickly to advise their king [343]. About two hours later we saw two *balanghai* coming (which are large boats and are so called by those people),[158] full of men [344]. Their king was in the larger of them, being seated under an awning of mats [345]. When the king came near the flagship, the slave spoke to him [346]. The king understood him, for in those districts the kings know more languages than the other people; he ordered some of his men to enter the ships [347]. But he always remained in his *balanghai*, at some little distance from the ship, until his own men returned; and as soon as they returned he departed [348]. The captain-general showed great honour to the men who entered the ship, and gave them some presents, and for this reason the king wished before his departure to give the captain a large bar of gold and a basketful of ginger; however, the latter thanked the king heartily but would not accept it [349]. In the afternoon we went in the ships [and anchored] near the dwellings of the king [350].

[57] The next day, Good Friday, the captain-general sent his slave, who acted as our interpreter, ashore in a small boat to say to the king that if he had any food that he should have it carried to the ships, for they would be well compensated by us, and that we had come to the island as friends and not as enemies [351].

[58] The king came with six or eight men in the same boat and entered the ship and he embraced the captain-general, to whom he gave three porcelain jars covered with leaves and full of raw rice, two very large giltheads,[159] and other things [352]. The captain-general, gave the king a garment of red and yellow cloth made in the Turkish

fashion, and a fine red cap; and to the king's men he gave to some knives and to others mirrors [353]. Then the captain-general had them served a meal, and had the king told through the slave that he desired to be *casi casi* with him, that is to say, brother [354].[160] The king replied that he wished to be the same to him [355]. Then the captain showed him cloth of various colours, linen, coral [ornaments], and many other articles of merchandise, and all the artillery, which he had discharged for him, and which greatly frightened some of the natives [356]. Then the captain-general had a man armed as a man of arms,[161] and placed him in the midst of three men armed with swords and daggers, who struck him on all parts of the body, at which the king was almost beside himself with wonder [357]. The king told him through the slave that one of those armed men was worth one hundred of his own men [358]. The captain-general answered that that was a fact, and that he brought with him two hundred men in each ship that were armed in that manner [359].[162] He showed the king cuirasses, swords, and bucklers, and had an assault made on a man [360]. Then he led the king to the deck of the ship, which is located above at the stern, and had his sea chart and compass brought, and he told the king through the interpreter how he had found the strait in order to come there to him, and how many moons had passed without seeing land, at which the king was astonished [361]. Lastly, he told the king that he would like, if it were pleasing to him, to send two of his men with him so that he might show them some of his things [362]. The king replied that he was agreeable; I went with one other [363].

[59] When I reached shore, the king raised his hands toward the sky and then turned toward the two of us; we did the same toward him as did all the others [364]. The king took me by the hand; one of his more notable men took my companion: and thus they led us under a bamboo covering, where there was a *balanghai*, as long as eighty of my palm lengths, and resembling a *fusta* [365].[163] We sat down upon the stern of that *balanghai*, constantly conversing with signs [366]. The king's men stood about us in a circle with swords, daggers, spears, and bucklers [367]. The king had a plate of pork

brought in and a large jar filled with wine [368]. At every mouthful, we drank a cup of wine [369]. The wine that was left [in the cup] at any time, although that happened but rarely, was put into a jar by itself [370]. The king's cup was always kept covered and no one else drank from it but the king and I [371]. Before the king took the cup to drink, he raised his clasped hands toward the sky, and then toward us; and when he was about to drink, he extended the fist of his left hand toward me (at first I thought that he was about to punch me) and then drank, and I did the same toward the king [372]. They all make those gestures one toward another when they drink [373]. We ate with such ceremonies and with other gestures of friendship [374]. I ate meat on Good Friday, for I could not do otherwise [375].

[60] Before the supper hour I gave the king many things I had brought [376]. I wrote down the names of many things in their language [377]. When the king and the others saw me writing, and when I told them their words, they were all astonished [378]. While engaged in that, it came time to eat: two large porcelain dishes were brought in, one full of rice and the other of pork with its gravy [379]. We ate with the same gestures and ceremonies; afterward, we went to the palace of the king that was built like a hayloft and was thatched with fig and palm leaves [380]. It was built up high from the ground on huge posts of wood so that it was necessary to enter it by means of ladders [381]. The king had us sit down there on a bamboo mat with our feet drawn up like tailors [382]. After a half-hour a platter of roast fish cut in pieces was brought in, with freshly gathered ginger, and wine [383]. The king's eldest son, who was the prince, came over to us, whereupon the king told him to sit down near us, so he did so [384]. Then two platters were brought in (one with fish and its sauce, and the other with rice), so that we might eat with the prince [385]. My companion became intoxicated as a consequence of so much drinking and eating [386]. They used the gum of a tree called *anime* [164] wrapped in palm or fig leaves for lights [387]. The king made us a sign that he was going to go to sleep; he left the prince with us, and we slept with the latter on a bamboo mat with pillows made of leaves [388]. When day dawned the king came and took me by the hand, and in that manner we went to where we had had supper, in order to have breakfast, but the boat

came to get us [389]. Before we left, the king kissed our hands with great joy, and he us [390]. One of his brothers, the king of another island, and three men came with us [391]. The captain-general kept him to dine with us, and gave him many things [392].

[61] Pieces of gold of the size of walnuts and eggs are found by sifting the earth in the island of that king who came to our ships [393]. All the dishes of that king are of gold and also some portion of his house, as the king himself told us [394]. According to their customs he was very grandly decked out, and the most handsome man that we saw among those people [395]. His hair was exceedingly black, and hung to his shoulders, with a silk veil on his head and two large golden earrings fastened in his ears; he wore a cotton cloth all embroidered with silk, which covered him from the waist to the knees; at his side hung a dagger, the handle of which was very long and all gold, and its scabbard of carved wood; he had three spots of gold on every tooth, and his teeth appeared as if bound with gold; he was perfumed with storax and benzoin;[165] he was olive-skinned and tattooed all over [396]. That island of his was called Butuan and Caraga [397].[166] When those kings wished to see one another, they both came to hunt in that island where we were [398]. The name of the first king is Rajah Colambu,[167] and the second Rajah Siaiu [399].[168]

[62] Early on the morning of Sunday, the last of March, and Easter Day, the captain-general sent the priest with many men to prepare for saying mass, and the interpreter went to tell the king that we were not going to land in order to dine with him, but to say mass; therefore the king sent us two slaughtered swine [400]. When the hour for mass arrived, we landed with about fifty men, without our body armour, but carrying our other arms, and dressed in our best clothes [401]. Before we reached the shore with our boats, six pieces were discharged as a sign of peace [402]. We landed; the two kings embraced the captain-general and placed him between them [403]. We went in marching order to the consecrated place, which was not far from the shore [404]. Before the mass began, the captain sprinkled the entire bodies of the two kings with musk water [405]. At the time of the offertory, the kings went forward to kiss the cross as we did, but they did not

make any offering [406]. When the body of Our Lord was elevated, they remained on their knees and worshipped Him with clasped hands [407]. The ships fired all their artillery at once when the body of Christ was elevated, the signal having been given from the shore with muskets [408].

[63] After the conclusion of mass, many of our men took Communion [409]. The captain-general arranged a fencing tournament, at which the kings were greatly pleased [410]. Then he had a cross brought and the nails and a crown, to which immediate reverence was made [411]. He told the kings through the interpreter that they were the standards given to him by the emperor his sovereign, so that wherever he might go he might set up those signs of his, and that he wished to set it up in that place for their benefit, for whenever any of our ships came, they would know that we had been there by that cross and would do nothing to displease them or harm their property, and if any of their men were captured, they would be set free immediately on that sign being shown; and it was necessary to set that cross on the summit of the highest mountain, so that on seeing it every morning, they might adore it, and if they did that, neither thunder, lightning, nor storms would harm them in the least [412].

[64] They thanked him heartily and [said] that they would do everything willingly [413]. The captain-general also had them asked whether they were Moors or heathen, or what was their belief, and they replied that they worshipped nothing, but that they raised their clasped hands and their face to the sky, and that they called their god Abba,[169] for which the captain was very glad [414]. Seeing that, the first king raised his hands to the sky, and said that he wished that it were possible for him to make the captain see his love for him [415]. The interpreter asked the king why there was so little to eat there, and the latter replied that he did not live in that place except when he went hunting and to see his brother, but that he lived in another island where all his family was [416]. The captain-general had him asked to declare whether he had any enemies, so that he might go with his ships to destroy them and to render them obedient to him [417]. The king thanked him and said that there were indeed two islands hostile to him, but that it was not the season to go there [418]. The captain told him that if God

would allow him to return to those districts again, he would bring so many men that he would make the king's enemies subject to him by force, and that he wanted to go to dinner, and that he would return afterward to have the cross set up on the summit of the mountain; they replied that they were content with this [419]. Having formed into a battalion, and firing the muskets, and after the captain had embraced the two kings, we took our leave [420].

[65] After dinner we all returned clad in our doublets, and went together with the two kings to the summit of the highest mountain there [421]. When we reached the summit, the captain-general told them that he was pleased to have sweated for them, for it could not but be of great use to them to have the cross there, and he asked them which was the best port in which to get provisions [422]. They replied that there were three, namely, Ceylon, Cebu, and Caraga,[170] but that Cebu was the largest and the one with most trade, and they offered of their own accord to give us pilots to show us the way [423]. The captain-general thanked them, and determined to go there for his unhappy destiny willed it thus [424].[171] After the cross was placed in position, each of us repeated a Pater Noster and an Ave Maria, and adored the cross; and the kings did the same [425].

[66] Then we descended through their cultivated fields, and went to the place where the *balanghai* was [426]. The kings had some coconuts brought in so that we might refresh ourselves [427]. The captain asked the kings for the pilots since he intended to depart the following morning, and [said] that he would treat them as if they were the kings themselves, and would leave one of us as hostage [428]. The kings replied that the pilots were at his command whenever he wished, but the first king changed his mind during the night [429]. In the morning when we were about to depart, he sent word to the captain-general, asking him for love of him to wait two days until he should have his rice harvested and other trifles attended to, asking the captain-general to send him some men to help him, so that it might be done sooner, and saying that he intended to act as our pilot himself [430]. The captain sent him some men, but the kings ate and drank so much that they slept the entire day; some said to excuse them that they were slightly sick [431]. Our men did nothing on that day, but they worked the next two days [432].

[67] One of those people brought us a bowlful of rice and also eight or ten figs fastened together to barter them for a knife that at the most was worth three *quattrini* [433].[172] The captain, seeing that that native cared for nothing but a knife, called him to look at other things, and he put his hand in his purse and wished to give him one real[173] for those things, but the native refused it [434]. The captain showed him a ducat but he would not accept that either [435]. Finally the captain tried to give him a doubloon worth two ducats,[174] but he would take nothing but a knife; and accordingly, the captain had one given to him [436].[175] When one of our men went ashore for water, one of them wanted to give him a pointed crown made of massy gold and large as a necklace for six strings of glass beads,[176] but the captain refused to let him barter, so that the natives should learn at the very beginning that we prized our merchandise more than their gold [437].[177]

[68] Those people are heathens; they go naked and painted; they wear a piece of cloth woven from a tree about their private parts; they are very heavy drinkers [438]. Their women are clad in tree cloth from their waist down, and their hair is black and reaches to the ground; they have holes pierced in their ears that are filled with gold [439]. Those people are constantly chewing a fruit (which they call *areca*[178] and resembles a pear): they cut that fruit into four parts, then wrap it in the leaves of a tree of theirs (which they call *betre*[179] and which resemble the leaves of the mulberry), and mix it with a little lime, and when they have chewed it thoroughly, they spit it out; it makes the mouth exceedingly red [440]. All the people in those parts of the world use it, for it is very cooling to the heart, and if they ceased to use it they would die [441]. There are dogs, cats, swine, fowls, goats, rice, ginger, coconuts, figs, oranges, lemons, millet, panicum, sorghum, wax, and much gold in that island [442]. It lies in a latitude of nine and two-thirds degrees toward the Arctic Pole, and in a longitude of 162 degrees from the line of demarcation, and it is twenty-five leagues from 'the watering-place of good signs'[180] and is called Mazaua [443].[181]

[69] We remained there seven days, after which we laid our course toward the northwest, passing among five islands, namely, Ceylon,

Bohol, Canigao, Baybay, and Gatighan [444].[182] In the last-named island of Gatighan there are bats as large as eagles [445].[183] As it was late we killed only one of them, which resembled chicken in taste [446]. There are doves, turtledoves, parrots, and certain black birds as large as domestic chickens that have a long tail [447].[184] The latter birds lay eggs as large as those of a goose, which they bury a cubit beneath the sand for the great heat it generates [448]. When the chicks are hatched, they push up the sand, and come out [449]. Those eggs are good to eat [450]. There is a distance of twenty leagues from Mazaua to Gatighan [451]. We set out westward from Gatighan, but the king of Mazaua could not keep up with us, and, consequently, we awaited him near three islands, namely, Polo, Ticobon, and Ponson [452].[185] When he caught up with us he was greatly astonished at the rapidity with which we sailed [453]. The captain-general had him come into his ship with several of his chiefs, at which they were pleased; thus did we go to Cebu [454]. From Gatighan to Cebu the distance is fifteen leagues [455]. *[Chart VI appears here in original.]*

[70] At noon on Sunday, 7 April, we entered the port of Cebu [456]. Passing by many villages, we saw many houses built upon logs [457].[186] On approaching the city, the captain-general ordered the ships to put out their flags; the sails were lowered and arranged as if for battle, and all the artillery was fired, which greatly frightened those people [458]. The captain sent a personal servant of his as ambassador to the king of Cebu with the interpreter [459].[187] When they reached the city, they found a vast crowd of people together with the king, all of whom had been frightened by the mortars [460]. The interpreter told them that this was our custom when arriving at such places, as a sign of peace and friendship, and we had discharged all our mortars to honour the king of the village [461]. The king and all of his men were reassured, and the king had us asked by his governor what we wanted [462]. The interpreter replied that his master was a captain of the greatest king and prince in the world, and that he was going to discover the Moluccas; nevertheless, he had come solely to visit the king and to buy food with his merchandise because of the good report he had had of him from the king of Mazaua [463]. The king told him that he was welcome, but that it was their custom for all ships entering their ports to pay tribute, and that it was but four days

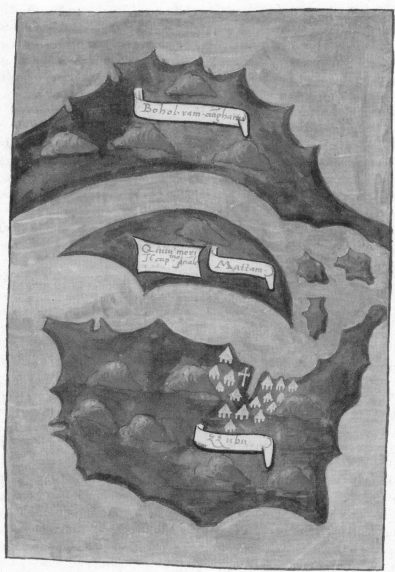

[The chart Zzubu (Cebu), Mattam (Mactan: 'Here the captain-general died'), and Bohol (VI)][188]

since a junk from Siam[189] laden with gold and slaves had paid him tribute; and as proof of his statement, the king pointed out to the interpreter a merchant from Siam, who had remained on the island to trade in gold and slaves [464].

[71] The interpreter told the king that, since his master was the captain of so great a king, he did not pay tribute to any lord in the world, and that if the king wished peace he would have peace, but if war, he would have war [465]. Thereupon, the Moor merchant said to the king 'Cata raia chita,' that is to say, 'Look well, sire, these men are the same who have conquered Calicut, Malacca, and all India Major [466].[190] If they are treated well, they will give good treatment, but if they are treated badly, they will deliver bad treatment and worse, as they have done to Calicut and Malacca [467].'

The interpreter understood it all and told the king that his master's king was more powerful in men and ships than the king of Portugal, that he was the king of Spain and emperor of all the Christians, and that if the king did not care to be his friend he would next time send so many men that they would destroy him [468]. The Moor related everything to the king, who said thereupon that he would confer with his men, and would answer the captain on the following day [469]. Then he had served a meal of many dishes, all made from meat and contained in porcelain platters, as well as many jars of wine [470]. After our men had eaten, they returned and told us everything [471]. The king of Mazaua, who was the most influential after that king and the lord of a number of islands, went ashore to speak to the king about the great courtesy of our captain-general [472].

[72] Monday morning, our notary, together with the interpreter, went to Cebu [473]. The king, accompanied by his chiefs, came to the open square where he had our men sit down near him; he asked the notary whether there were more than one captain in that company, and if the captain wished him to pay tribute to the emperor his master [474]. The notary replied in the negative, but that the captain wished only to trade with him and with no others [475]. The king said that he was satisfied, and that if the captain wished to become his friend, he should send him a drop of blood from his right arm, and he himself would do the same [to him] as a sign of the most sincere

friendship [476].[191] The notary answered that the captain would do it [477]. Thereupon, the king told him that all the captains who came to that place were used to giving presents to one another, and he asked whether our captain or he ought to begin [478]. The interpreter told the king that since he desired to maintain the custom, he should begin [479]. And so he began [480].

[73] Tuesday morning the king of Mazaua came to the ships with the Moor; he saluted the captain-general on behalf of the king [of Cebu], and said that the king of Cebu was collecting as much food as possible to give to him, and that after dinner he would send one of his nephews and two others of his chief men to make peace [481]. The captain-general had one of his men armed with his own equipment, and had the Moor told that we all fought in that manner [482]. The Moor was greatly frightened, but the captain told him not to be frightened for our weapons were soft toward our friends and harsh toward our enemies; and as handkerchiefs wipe off sweat so did our arms overthrow and destroy all our adversaries, and those who hate our faith [483]. The captain did that so that the Moor, who seemed more intelligent than the others, might tell it to the king [484].

[74] After dinner the king's nephew, who was the prince, came to the ships with the king of Mazaua, the Moor, the governor, the chief constable, and eight chiefs, to make peace with us [485]. The captain-general was seated in a red velvet chair, the principal men on leather chairs, and the others on mats upon the floor, and he asked them through the interpreter whether it was their custom to speak in secret or in public, and whether that prince and the king of Mazaua had authority to make peace [486]. They answered that they spoke in public, and that they were empowered to make peace [487]. The captain said many things concerning peace, and that he prayed God to confirm the peace in heaven [488]. They said that they had never heard anyone speak such words, but that they took great pleasure in hearing them [489]. The captain, seeing that they listened and answered willingly, began to advance arguments to induce them to accept the faith [490].

He asked them who would succeed to power after the death of the king [491]. He was answered that the king had no sons but only daughters, the eldest of whom was the wife of that nephew of his, who therefore was the prince, and that when the fathers and mothers grew old, they received no further honour, but their children commanded them [492]. The captain told them how God made the heaven, the earth, the sea, and everything else; how he had commanded us to honour our fathers and our mothers, and that whoever did otherwise was condemned to eternal fire; how we are all descended from Adam and Eve, our first parents; how we possess an immortal soul; and many other things pertaining to the faith [493].

[75] All joyfully entreated the captain to leave them two men, or at least one, to instruct them in the faith, and [said] that they would show them great honour [494]. The captain replied to them that he could not leave them any men then, but that if they wished to become Christians, our priest would baptize them, and that he would next time bring priests and friars who would instruct them in our faith [495]. They answered that they would first speak to their king, and that then they would become Christians [496]. We all wept with great joy [497]. The captain-general told them that they should not become Christians for fear or to please us, but of their own free wills; and that nothing would be done against those who wished to live according to their own law, but that the Christians would be better regarded and treated than the others [498]. All cried out with one voice that they were not becoming Christians through fear or to please us, but of their own free will [499]. Then the captain told them that if they became Christians, he would leave them a suit of armour, for so had his king commanded him, and that they could not have intercourse with their women without committing a very great sin, since they were heathen; and that he assured them that if they became Christians, the devil would no longer appear to them except in the last moment at their death [500]. They said that they did not know how to respond to the beautiful words of the captain, but that they placed themselves in his hands, and that he should treat them as his most faithful servants [501]. The captain embraced them weeping, and clasping one of the prince's hands and one of the king's between his own, said to them that, by his faith in God and to his sovereign, the emperor, and by the habit that he wore,[192] he promised them that he would give them perpetual peace with the king of Spain; they answered that they promised the same [502].

[76] After the conclusion of the peace, the captain had a meal served to them; then the prince and the king [of Mazaua] presented some baskets of rice, swine, goats, and fowls to the captain-general on behalf of their king, and asked him to pardon them, for such things were but little [to give] to one such as he [503]. The captain gave the prince a white cloth of the finest linen, a red cap, some strings of glass beads, and a gilded drinking cup made of glass (glass objects are greatly appreciated in those districts) [504]. He did not give any present to the king of Mazaua, for he had already given him a robe of Cambay,[193] besides other articles, and to the others he gave now one thing and now another [505]. Then he sent to the king of Cebu through me and one other a yellow and violet silk robe, made in Turkish style, a fine red cap, some strings of glass beads (having placed everything in a silver dish), and two cups gilded by hand [506].

[77] When we reached the city we found the king in his palace surrounded by many people, seated on a palm mat on the ground, with only a cotton cloth covering his private parts, and an embroidered scarf on his head, a necklace of great value hanging from his neck, and two large gold earrings fastened in his ears set round with precious gems [507]. He was fat and short, and tattooed with fire in various designs; from another mat on the ground he was eating turtle eggs that were in two porcelain dishes, and he had four jars full of palm wine in front of him covered with sweet-smelling herbs and arranged with four small reeds in each jar, by means of which he drank [508]. Having duly made reverence to him, the interpreter told the king that his master [Magellan] thanked him very warmly for his present, and that he sent this present not in return for his present but for the intrinsic love that he bore him [509]. We dressed him in the robe, placed the cap on his head, and gave him the other things; then kissing the beads and putting them upon his head, I presented them to him, and he doing the same [kissing them] accepted them [510]. Then the king had us eat some of those eggs and drink through those reeds [511]. The others, his men, told him in that place the words of the captain concerning peace and his exhortation to them to become Christians [512]. The king wished to have us stay to supper with him, but we told him that we could not stay then [513].

[78] Having taken our leave of him, the prince took us with him to his house, where four young girls were playing [instruments]: one, on a drum like ours, but resting on the ground; the second was striking two suspended metal discs alternately with a stick made thick at the end with palm cloth wrapped around it; the third, one large metal disc in the same manner; and the last, two small metal discs held in her hand, by striking one against the other, which gave forth a sweet sound [514]. They played so harmoniously that it appeared they had great knowledge of music [515]. Those girls were very beautiful and almost as white as our girls and as large; they were naked except for tree cloth hanging from the waist and reaching to the knees, and some were quite naked and had large holes in their ears with a small round piece of wood in the hole, which keeps the hole round and large, and they have long black hair, and wear a short cloth about the head, and are always barefoot [516]. The prince made us dance with three of them who were completely naked [517]. We took refreshments and then went to the ships [518]. Those metal discs are made of brass and are manufactured in the regions about the Sinus Magnus that is called China [519].[194] They are used in those regions as we use bells and are called *aghon* [520].[195]

[79] On Wednesday morning, since one of our men had died during the previous night, the interpreter and I went to ask the king where we could bury him [521]. We found the king surrounded by many men, of whom, after the due reverence was made, I asked where we could bury him [522]. He replied, 'If I and my vassals all belong to your sovereign, how much more ought the land [523].' I told the king that we would like to consecrate the place, and to set up a cross there [524]. He replied that he was quite satisfied and that he wished to worship the cross as we did [525]. The deceased was buried in the square with as much pomp as possible, in order to furnish a good example, and then we consecrated the place [526]. In the evening, we buried another man [527].[196] We carried a quantity of merchandise ashore, which we stored in a house that king took under his care as well as four men who were left to trade the goods by wholesale [528]. Those people live in accordance with justice, and have weights and measures; they love peace, ease, and quiet [529].

[80] They have wooden scales, the bar of which has a cord in the middle by which it is held; at one end is a bit of lead, and at the other marks as if for quarters, thirds, and pounds [530]. When they wish to weigh they take the scales, which have three wires like ours, and place them above the marks, and so weigh accurately [531]. They have very large measures without any bottom [532].[197] The youth play on pipes made like ours that they call *subin* [533]. Their houses are constructed of wood, and are built of planks and bamboo, raised high above the ground on large logs, and one must enter them by means of ladders, and they have rooms like ours [534]. Under the house they keep their swine, goats, and fowls [535]. Large sea snails, beautiful in appearance, are found there that kill the whales that swallow them alive [536]. When they are in the whale's body, they come out of their shells and eat the whale's heart [537]. Those people afterward find them alive near the dead whale's heart [538]. Those creatures have black teeth and skin and a white shell; the flesh is good to eat, and they are called *laghan* [539].[198]

[81] On Friday we showed those people a shop full of our merchandise, at which they were very much amazed [540].[199] For metals, iron, and other large merchandise they gave us gold; for the other smaller articles they gave us rice, swine, goats, and other food [541]. Those people gave us ten pieces of gold for fourteen pounds of iron (one piece being worth about one and one-half ducats) [542]. The captain-general did not wish to take too much gold, for there would have been some sailors who would have given all that they owned for a small amount of gold, and would have spoiled the trade forever [543].

[82] On Saturday, as the captain had promised the king to make him a Christian on Sunday, a platform was built in the consecrated square, which was adorned with hangings and palm branches for his baptism [544]. The captain-general sent men to tell the king not to be afraid of the pieces that would be discharged in the morning, for it was our custom to discharge them on major feast days without stones [545].

[83] On Sunday morning, 14 April, forty of us went ashore, two of whom were completely armed, and preceded the royal banner [546]. When we reached land all the artillery was fired: those people fled us here and there [547]. The captain and the king embraced; the

captain told the king that the royal banner was not taken ashore except with fifty men armed as were those two, and with fifty muske-teers, but so great was his love for him that he had thus brought the banner [548]. Then we all approached the platform joyfully [549]. The captain and the king sat in chairs of red and violet velvet, the chiefs on cushions, and the others on mats [550]. The captain told the king through the interpreter that he thanked God for inspiring him to become a Christian, and that [now] he would more easily con-quer his enemies than before [551]. The king replied that he wished to become a Christian, but that some of his chiefs did not wish to obey, because they said that they were as good men as he [552]. Then our captain had all the chiefs of the king called, and told them that, unless they obeyed the king as their king, he would have them killed and would give their possessions to the king [553]. They replied that they would obey him [554]. The captain told the king that he was going to Spain, but that he would return again with so many forces that he would make him the greatest king of those regions, as he had been the first to desire to become a Christian [555]. The king, lifting his hands to the sky, thanked the captain, and requested him to let some of his men remain [with him], so that he and his people might be better instructed in the faith [556]. The captain replied that he would leave two men to satisfy him, but that he would like to take two of the children of the chiefs with him, so that they might learn our language, who afterward on their return would be able to tell the others about Spain [557].

[84] A large cross was set up in the middle of the square; the cap-tain told them that if they wished to become Christians as they had declared on the previous days, they must burn all their idols and set up a cross in their place, they were to adore that cross daily with clasped hands, and every morning they were to make the sign of the cross (which the captain showed them how to make); and they ought to come hourly, at least in the morning, to that cross, and adore it kneeling; the intention that they had already declared, they were to confirm with good works [558]. The king and all the others wished to confirm all this [559]. The captain-general told the king that he was clad all in white to demonstrate his sincere love toward them; they replied that they knew not how to respond to his sweet words [560].

With these good words, the captain led the king by the hand to the platform in order to baptize him; he told the king that he would call him Don Carlo, after his sovereign the emperor; the prince, Don Fernando, after the emperor's brother;[200] the king of Mazaua, John; a chief, Fernando, after our chief, that is to say, the captain; the Moor, Christopher; and then the others, now one name, and now another [561].

Five hundred men were baptized before mass [562]. After the conclusion of mass, the captain invited the king and some of the other chiefs to dinner, but they refused [563]. They accompanied us, however, to the shore; the ships discharged all the mortars, and, embracing, the king and chiefs and the captain took leave of one another [564].

[85] After dinner the priest and some others of us went ashore to baptize the queen, who came with forty women [565]. We conducted her to the platform, and she was made to sit down upon a cushion, and the other women near her [566]. While the priest was dressing, I showed her an image of Our Lady, a very beautiful child Jesus made of wood, and a cross; thereupon, she was seized with contrition, and, weeping, asked for baptism [567]. We named her Juana, after the emperor's mother;[201] we called her daughter, the wife of the prince, Catherine, and the queen of Mazaua, Elizabeth; and to the others, gave each a different name [568]. Counting men, women, and children, we baptized eight hundred souls [569]. The queen was young and beautiful, and was entirely covered with a white and black cloth; her mouth and nails were very red, while on her head she wore a large hat of palm leaves in the manner of a parasol, with a crown about it of the same leaves, like the tiara of the pope; and she never goes any place without one of these crowns [570]. She asked us to give her the little child Jesus to keep in place of her idols; and then she went away [571].

[86] When it was late, the king and queen, accompanied by numerous persons, came to the shore; thereupon, the captain had many trombs of fire[202] and large mortars discharged, by which they were most highly delighted [572]. The captain and the king called one another brothers [573]. That king's name was Rajah Humabon [574]. Before that week had gone, all the persons of that island, and

some from the other islands, were baptized [575]. We burned one hamlet that was located in a neighbouring island, because it refused to obey the king or us [576].[203] We set up the cross there, for those people were heathens [577]. Had they been Moors, we would have erected there a column as a sign of greater harshness, for the Moors are much harder to convert than the heathens [578].

[87] The captain-general went ashore daily during those days to hear mass, and told the king many things regarding the faith [579]. One day, the queen came with great pomp to hear mass [580]. Three girls preceded her, each with one of her hats in their hands; she was dressed in black and white with a large silk scarf crossed with gold stripes thrown over her head and covering her shoulders; and she had on her hat on top of that [581]. A great number of women accompanied her who were all naked and barefoot, except that they had a small covering of palm-tree cloth before their privies, and a small scarf upon the head, and all with hair flowing free [582]. The queen, having made the due reverence to the altar, seated herself on a silk embroidered cushion [583]. Before the commencement of the mass, the captain sprayed her and some of her women with musk rosewater, at which they very were much delighted [584]. The captain, knowing that the queen was very much pleased with the child Jesus, gave it to her, telling her to keep it in place of her idols, for it was in memory of the son of God [585]. Thanking him heartily she accepted it [586].[204]

[88] Before mass one day, the captain-general had the king come clad in his silk robe, and the chief men of the city [587]. The king's brother and prince's father was named Bendara;[205] another of the king's brothers, Cadaio; and others were named Simiut, Sibnaia, Sisacai, Maghalibe, and many other names that I leave aside to avoid going on too long [588]. The captain made them all swear to be obedient to their king, and they kissed the captain's hand; then the captain had the king declare that he would always be obedient and faithful to the king of Spain, and the king so swore [589]. Thereupon, the captain drew his sword before the image of Our Lady, and told the king that when anyone so swore, he should prefer to die rather

than to break such an oath since he swore by that image by the life of the emperor his sovereign and by his habit[206] to be ever faithful [590]. After the conclusion of that the captain gave the king a red velvet chair, telling him that wherever he went he should always have it carried before him by one of his nearest relatives; and he showed him how it ought to be carried [591]. The king responded that he would do that willingly for love of him, and he told the captain that he was making a jewel to give to him, namely, two large earrings of gold to fasten in his ears, two armlets to put on his arms, above the elbows, and two other rings for the feet above the ankles, besides other precious gems to adorn the ears [592]. Those are the most beautiful ornaments that the kings of those districts can wear; they always go barefoot, and wear a cloth garment that hangs from the waist to the knees [593].

[89] One day the captain-general asked the king and the other people why they did not burn their idols as they had promised when they became Christians, and why they sacrificed so much flesh to them [594]. They replied that they were not doing it for themselves, but for a sick man who had not spoken now for four days, so that the idols might give him health [595]. He was the prince's brother, and the bravest and wisest man in the island [596]. The captain told them to burn their idols and to believe in Christ, and that if the sick man were baptized, he would immediately recover; and if that did not happen, they could behead him [the captain] [597]. Thereupon, the king replied that he would do it, for he truly believed in Christ [598]. We made a procession from the square to the house of the sick man with as much pomp as possible, where we found him unable to speak or to move [599]. We baptized him and his two wives, and ten maidens [600]. Then the captain had him asked how he felt [601]. He spoke immediately and said that by the grace of our Lord he felt very well [602]. That was a most manifest miracle [that happened] in our times [603]. When the captain heard him speak, he thanked God fervently; then he made the sick man drink some almond milk, which he had already had made for him [604]. Afterward he sent him a mattress, a pair of sheets, a coverlet of yellow cloth, and a pillow; and each day until he recovered his health, the captain sent him almond

milk, rosewater, oil of roses, and some sweet preserves [605]. Within five days, the sick man began to walk [606]. He had an idol that certain old women had concealed in his house burned in the presence of the king and all the people, and he had many shrines along the seashore destroyed, in which the consecrated meat was eaten [607]. The people themselves cried out 'Castile! Castile!' and destroyed those shrines; they said that if God would lend them life, they would burn all the idols that they could find, even if they were in the king's house [608]. Those idols are made of wood, and are hollow, and lack the back parts; their arms are open and their feet turned up under them with the legs open; they have a large face with four huge tusks like those of the wild boar, and are painted all over [609].[207]

[90] There are many villages in that island and their names, those of their inhabitants, and of their chiefs are as follows: Cinghapola, and its chiefs, Cilaton, Ciguibucan, Cimaningha, Cimatichat, and Cicanbul; another Mandani, and its chief, Apanoaan; another Lalan, and its chief, Theteu; another Lalutan, and its chief, Tapan; another Cilumai; and another, Lubucun [610].[208] All those villages rendered obedience to us, and gave us food and tribute [611]. Near that island of Cebu was an island called Mactan, which formed the port where we were anchored;[209] the name of its village was Mactan, and its chiefs were Cebu and Cilapulapu [612].[210] That city we burned was on that island and was called Bulaia [613].[211]

[91] In order that your most illustrious Lordship[212] may know the ceremonies that those people use in consecrating the swine, they first sound those large metal discs; then three large dishes are brought in; two with roses and with cakes of rice and millet, baked and wrapped in leaves, and roast fish; the other with cloth of Cambay and two palm flags [614]. One Cambay cloth is spread on the ground; then two very old women come, each with a bamboo trumpet in her hand [615]. When they have stepped upon the cloth they make obeisance to the sun; then they wrap the cloths about themselves [616]. One of them puts a kerchief with two horns on her forehead, and takes another kerchief in her hands, and dancing and blowing upon her trumpet, she thereby calls out to the sun [617]. The other takes one of the flags and dances and blows on her trumpet [618]. They dance and call out

thus for a little space, saying many things between themselves to the sun [619]. She with the kerchief takes the other flag and lets the kerchief drop, and both, blowing on their trumpets for a long time, dance about the bound hog [620]. She with the horns always speaks covertly to the sun, and the other answers her [621]. A cup of wine is presented to the one with the horns, and she dancing and repeating certain words, while the other answers her, and making pretense four or five times of drinking the wine, sprinkles it upon the heart of the hog; then she immediately begins to dance again [622]. A lance is given to the same woman; she, shaking it and repeating certain words, while both of them continue to dance, and making motions four or five times of thrusting the lance through the heart of the hog, with a sudden and quick stroke, thrusts it through from one side to the other [623]. The wound is quickly stopped with grass [624]. The one who has killed the hog, taking in her mouth a lighted torch, which has been lighted throughout that ceremony, extinguishes it [625]. The other one, after dipping the end of her trumpet in the blood of the hog, goes around marking with her finger with blood first the foreheads of their husbands, and then the others; but they never came to us [626]. Then they undress and go to eat the contents of those dishes, and they invite only women [to eat with them] [627]. The hair is removed from the hog by means of fire; thus, no one but old women consecrate the flesh of the hog, and they do not eat it unless it is killed in this way [628].

[92] Those people go naked, wearing but one piece of palm-tree cloth about their private parts [629]. The males, both young and old, have their penis pierced from one side to the other near the head, with a gold or tin bolt as large as a goose quill, and in both ends of the same bolt, some have what resembles a spur, with points upon the ends, and others [have] what resembles the head of a cart nail [630]. I very often asked many, both old and young, to see their penis, because I could not believe it [631]. In the middle of the bolt is a hole, through which they urinate [632]. The bolt and the spurs always hold firm [633]. They say that their women wish it so, and that if they did otherwise they would not have intercourse with them [634]. When the men wish to have intercourse with their women, the women themselves

take the penis, not in the regular way, and commence very gently to introduce it [into their vagina], with the spur on top first, and then the other part [635]. When it is inside it takes its regular position; and thus the penis always stays inside until it gets soft, for otherwise they could not pull it out [636]. Those people make use of that device because they are of a weak nature [637].[213] They have as many wives as they wish, but one of them is the principal wife [638].

[93] Whenever any of our men went ashore, both by day and by night, they invited him to eat and to drink [639]. Their viands are half cooked and very salty; they drink frequently and copiously from the jars through those small reeds, and one of their meals lasts for five or six hours [640]. The women loved us very much more than their own men [641]. All of the women from the age of six years and upward have their vaginas gradually opened because of the men's penises [642].

[94] They practice the following ceremonies when one of their chiefs dies: first, all the principal women of the place go to the house of the deceased [643]. The deceased is placed in the middle of the house in a coffin [644]. Ropes are placed about the box in the manner of a palisade, to which many tree branches are attached [645]. In the middle of each branch hangs a cotton cloth like a curtained canopy, and the most important women sit under those hangings, and are all covered with white cotton cloth; each one sits by a girl who fans her with a palm-leaf fan [646]. The other women sit about the room sadly [647]. Then there is one woman who cuts off the hair of the deceased very slowly with a knife [648]. Another, who was the principal wife of the deceased, lies down upon him, and places her mouth, her hands, and her feet upon those of the deceased: when the former is cutting off the hair, the latter weeps, and when the former finishes the cutting, the latter sings [649]. There are many porcelain jars containing fire about the room, and myrrh, storax, and bezoin, which make a strong scent through the house, are put on the fire [650]. They keep the body in the house for five or six days during those ceremonies; I believe that the body is anointed with camphor [651]. Then they bury the body within the coffin, which is shut by means of wooden nails in a kind of box and covered and enclosed by logs of wood [652].

[95] Every night about midnight in that city, a jet black bird as large as a crow was wont to come, and no sooner had it reached the houses than it began to screech, so that all the dogs began to howl; and that screeching and howling would last for four or five hours [653]. Those people would never tell us the reason for it [654].

[96] On Friday, 26 April, Zula, a chief of the island of Mactan, sent one of his sons to present two goats to the captain-general, and to say that he would send him all that he had promised, but that he had not been able to send it to him because of the other chief, Cilapulapu, who refused to obey the king of Spain;[214] he requested the captain to send him only one boatload of men on the next night, so that they might help him to fight against the other chief [655]. The captain-general decided to go there with three boatloads [656]. We begged him repeatedly not to go, but he, like a good shepherd, refused to abandon his flock [657]. At midnight, sixty of our men set out armed with corselets and helmets, together with the Christian king, the prince, some of the chief men, and twenty or thirty *balanghai*; three hours before dawn, we reached Mactan [658]. The captain did not wish to fight then, but sent a message to the natives by the Moor to the effect that if they would obey the king of Spain, recognize the Christian king as their sovereign, and pay us our tribute, he would be their friend; but that if they wished otherwise, they should expect to see how our lances wounded [659]. They replied that if we had lances, they had lances of bamboo and stakes hardened with fire; [they asked us] not to proceed to attack them at once, but to wait until morning, so that they might have more men [660]. They said that in order to induce us to go in search of them; for they had dug certain pitfalls between the houses in order that we might fall into them [661].

[97] When morning came, forty-nine of us leaped into the water up to our thighs, and walked through water for more than two cross-bow flights before we could reach the shore [662]. The boats could not approach nearer because of certain rocks in the water [663]. The other eleven men remained behind to guard the boats [664]. When we reached land, those men had formed in three divisions to the number of more than fifteen hundred persons [665]. As soon as they became aware of us, they charged down upon us with exceedingly

loud cries, two divisions on our flanks and the other on our front [666].[215] When the captain saw that, he formed us into two divisions, and thus did we begin to fight [667]. The musketeers and crossbowmen shot from a distance for about a half-hour, but uselessly; for they merely pierced their shields, which were made of thin wood, and their arms [668]. The captain cried to them, 'Cease firing, cease firing!' but his order was not at all heeded [669]. When the natives saw that we were shooting our muskets to no purpose, crying out, they determined to stand firm, and they redoubled their shouts when our muskets ran out of ammunition [670]. The natives would never stand still, but leaped here and there, covering themselves with their shields [671]. They shot very many arrows, bamboo spears (some of them tipped with iron); at the captain-general they launched pointed stakes hardened with fire, stones, and mud [672]. We could scarcely defend ourselves [673]. Seeing that, the captain-general sent some men to burn their houses in order to terrify them [674]. When they saw their houses burning, they were roused to greater fury [675]. Two of our men were killed near the houses, and we managed to burn twenty or thirty houses [676]. So many of them charged down upon us that they shot the captain through the right leg with a poisoned arrow; on that account, he ordered us to retreat slowly, but the men took to flight, except six or eight of us who remained with the captain [677]. The natives shot only at our legs because they were naked [678]. So many were the spears and stones that they hurled at us, that we could offer no resistance [679]. The mortars in the boats could not aid us since they were too far away, so we continued to retreat for more than a good crossbow flight from the shore, still fighting in water up to our knees [680]. The natives continued to pursue us, and picking up the same spear four or six times, hurled it at us again and again [681].

[98] Recognizing the captain, so many turned upon him that they knocked his helmet off his head twice, but he always stood firm like a good knight along with some others [682]. We fought thus for more than one hour, refusing to retreat farther; an Indian hurled a bamboo spear into the captain's face [683]. The latter immediately killed him with his lance, which he left in the Indian's body [684]. Then,

trying to lay hand on sword, he could draw it out only halfway, because he had been wounded in the arm with a bamboo spear [685]. When the natives saw that, they all hurled themselves upon him [686]. One of them wounded him on the left leg with a large *terciado*, which resembles a scimitar, only being larger; that caused the captain to fall face downward [687]. Immediately they rushed upon him with iron and bamboo spears and with their cutlasses, until they killed our mirror, our light, our comfort, and our true guide [688]. When they wounded him, he turned back many times to see whether we were all in the boats [689]. Thereupon, beholding him dead, we, wounded, retreated as best we could to the boats, which were already pulling off [690]. The Christian king would have aided us, but the captain charged him before we landed not to leave his *balanghai*, but to stay to see how we fought [691].[216] When the king learned that the captain was dead, he wept [692]. Had it not been for that unfortunate captain, not a single one of us would have been saved in the boats; for while he was fighting, the others retreated to the boats [693].[217]

[99] I hope through the efforts of your most illustrious Lordship[218] that the fame of so noble a captain will not become extinguished in our times [694]. Among the other virtues, he was more constant than anyone else in the greatest of storms;[219] he endured hunger better than all others; and more accurately than any man in the world did he chart and navigate, and that this was the truth was seen openly, for no other had had so much natural talent nor the boldness nor the knowledge to sail around the world, as he had almost already accomplished [695].[220]

[100] That battle was fought on Saturday, 27 April 1521 (the captain desired to fight on Saturday, because it was the day especially holy to him),[221] and eight of our men were killed with him in that battle, and four Indians who had become Christians and who had come afterward to aid us were killed by the mortars of the boats; of the enemy, only fifteen were killed, while many of us were wounded [696].

[101] After dinner, the Christian king sent a message with our consent to the people of Mactan, to the effect that if they would give us the captain and the other men that had been killed, we would give them as much merchandise as they wished [697]. They

answered that they would not give up such a man, as we had hoped they would, and that they would not give him up for all the riches in the world, but that they intended to keep him as a memorial [698].

[102] On Saturday, the day on which the captain was killed, the four men who had remained in the city to trade had our merchandise carried to the ships [699]. Then we chose two commanders, namely, Duarte Barbosa, a Portuguese and a relative of the captain,[222] and the Spaniard João Serrão [700].[223] As our interpreter, Enrique by name,[224] was slightly wounded, he would not go ashore any more to attend to our needs, but always stayed beneath a heavy blanket;[225] on that account, Duarte Barbosa, the commander of the flagship, cried out to him and told him that although his master, the captain, was dead, he was not therefore free: on the contrary, he (Barbosa) would see to it that when we should reach Spain, he should still be the slave of Dona Beatrice, the wife of the captain-general, and he threatened the slave that if he did not go ashore, he would be flogged [701]. The slave arose and, feigning to take no heed to those words, went ashore to tell the Christian king that we were about to leave very soon, but that if he would follow his advice, he could gain the ships and all our merchandise; accordingly, they arranged a plot [702].[226] The slave returned to the ship, where he showed himself to be more prudent[227] than before [703].

[103] On Wednesday morning, the first of May, the Christian king sent word to the commanders that the jewels that he had promised to send to the king of Spain were ready, and that he begged them and their other companions to come to dine with him that morning, when he would give them the jewels [704]. Twenty-four men went ashore, among whom was our astrologer, San Martin of Seville [705]. I could not go since I was all swollen from a wound from a poisoned arrow I had in the forehead [706]. João Carvalho and the constable[228] returned, and told us that they saw the man who had been cured by a miracle take the priest to his house; and for this reason they had left that place, because they suspected some evil [707]. Scarcely had they spoken those words when we heard loud cries and lamentations [708]. We immediately weighed anchor and, discharging many mortars into

the houses, drew in nearer to the shore; while discharging [our pieces], we saw João Serrão in his shirt bound and wounded, crying to us not to fire any more, for the natives would kill him [709]. We asked him whether all the others and the interpreter were dead [710]. He said that they were all dead except the interpreter [711]. He begged us earnestly to ransom him with some of the merchandise; but João Carvalho, his boon companion, [and others] would not allow the boat to go ashore, so that they might remain masters of the ships [712]. But João Serrão, still weeping, asked us not to set sail so quickly, for they would kill him, and he swore to God that on Judgment Day he would demand the soul of João Carvalho, his comrade [713]. We immediately departed; I do not know whether he died or survived [714].

[104] In that island are found dogs, cats, rice, millet, panicum, sorghum, ginger, figs, oranges, lemons, sugar cane, garlic, honey, coconuts, *chiacare*,²²⁹ gourds, flesh of many kinds, palm wine, and gold [715]. It is a large island, and has a good port with two entrances, one to the west and the other to the east northeast [716]. It lies in ten degrees of latitude toward the Arctic Pole, and in a longitude of one hundred and sixty-four degrees from the line of demarcation, and its name is Cebu [717]. We heard word of Molucca there before the death of the captain-general [718]. Those people play a violin with copper strings [719].

[105] Words of those heathen people:²³⁰

1] For man *lac*	14] For teeth *nipin*
2] For woman *paranpoan*	15] For gums *leghex*
3] For young woman *beni beni*	16] For tongue *dilla*
4] For married woman *babay*	17] For ears *delengan*
5] For hair *boho*	18] For throat *liogh*
6] For face *guay*	19] For neck *tangip*
7] For eyelids *pilac*	20] For chin *silan*
8] For eyebrows *chilei*	21] For beard *bonghot*
9] For eye *matta*	22] For shoulders *bagha*
10] For nose *ilon*	23] For the back *licud*
11] For jaws *apin*	24] For breast *dughan*
12] For lips *olol*	25] For body *tiam*

13] For mouth *baba*

27] For arm *botchen*

28] For elbow *sico*

29] For pulse *molanghai*

30] For hand *camat*

31] For the palm of the hand
palan

32] For finger *dudlo*

33] For fingernail *coco*

34] For navel *pusut*

35] For the male member *utin*

36] For testicles *boto*

37] For the female nature *billat*

38] For intercourse with women
tiam

39] For buttocks *samput*

40] For thigh *paha*

41] For knee *tuhud*

42] For shin *bassag bassag*[231]

43] For the calf of the leg *bitis*

44] For ankle *bolbol*

45] For heel *tiochid*

46] Fore sole of the foot *lapa
lapa*

47] For gold *balaoan*

48] For silver *pilla*

49] For brass *concach*

50] For iron *butan*

51] For sugar cane *tube*

52] For spoon *gandan*

53] For rice *bughax baras*

54] For honey *deghex*

55] For wax *talho*

56] For salt *acin*

57] For wine *tuba nio nipa*

58] For to drink *minuncubil*

59] For to eat *macan*

26] For armpit *ilot*

60] For hog *babui*

61] For goat *candin*

62] For chicken *monoch*

63] For millet *humas*

64] For sorghum *batat*

65] For panic grass *dana*

66] For pepper *manissa*

67] For cloves *chianche*[232]

68] For cinnamon *mana*

69] For ginger *luia*

70] For garlic *laxima*

71] For oranges *acsua*

72] For eggs *itlog*

73] For coconut *lubi*

74] For vinegar *zucha*

75] For water *tubin*

76] For water *claio*

77] For smoke *assu*

78] For to blow *tigban*

79] For balances *tinban*

80] For weight *tahil*[233]

81] For pearl *mutiara*

82] For mother of pearl *tipay*

83] For pipe (a musical instru-
ment) *subin*[234]

84] For disease of St Job
alupalan[235]

85] Bring me *palatin comorica*

86] For certain rice cakes *tinapai*

87] Good *maiu*

88] No *ti da le*

89] For knife *capal sundan*

90] For scissors *catle*

91] For to shave *chunthinch*

92] For a well-adorned man
pixao

93] For linen *balandan*
94] For the cloth with which they cover themselves *abaca*
95] For hawk's bell *colon colon*
96] For paternosters of all *tacle*
97] For comb *cutlei missamis*
98] For to comb *monssughud*
99] For shirt *sabun*
100] For sewing needle *daghu*
101] For to sew *mamis*
102] For porcelain *mobuluc*
103] For dog *aian ydo*
104] For cat *epos*
105] For their scarves *gapas*
106] For glass beads *balus*
107] For come here *marica*
108] For house *ilaga balai*
109] For timber *tatamue*
110] For the mats on which they sleep *tagichan*
111] For palm mats *bani*
112] For their leaf cushions *ulunan*
113] For wooden platters *dulan*
114] For their God *Abba*[236]
115] For sun *adlo*
116] For moon *songhot*
117] For star *bolan binthun*
118] For dawn *mene*
119] For morning *uema*
120] For large cup *tagha*
121] For big *bassal*
122] For bow *bossugh*
123] For arrows *oghon*
124] For shield *calassan*

125] For quilted garments used for fighting *baluti*
126] For their daggars *calix baladao*
127] For their cutlasses *campilan*
128] For spear *bancau*
129] For like *tuan*
130] For figs (bananas) *saghin*
131] For gourds *baghin*
132] For the cords of their violins *gotzap*
133] for river *tau*
134] For fishing net *pucat laia*
135] For small boat *sampan*
136] For large canes *cauaghan*
137] For the small ones *bonbon*
138] For their large boats *balanghai*[237]
139] For their small boats *boloto*[238]
140] For crabs *cuban*
141] For fish *icam yssida*
142] For coloured fish *panapsapan*
143] For another red fish *timuan*
144] For another (kind of fish) *pilax*
145] For another (kind of fish) *cimaluan*
146] For all the same *siama siama*
147] For a slave *bonsul*
148] For gallows *boll*
149] For ship *benaoa*
150] For a king or captain-general *raia*

Numbers:

151] One *uzza*	156] Six *onom*
152] Two *dua*	157] Seven *pitto*
153] Three *telo*	158] Eight *gualu*
154] Four *upat*	159] Nine *ciam*
155] Five *lima*	160] Ten *polo*

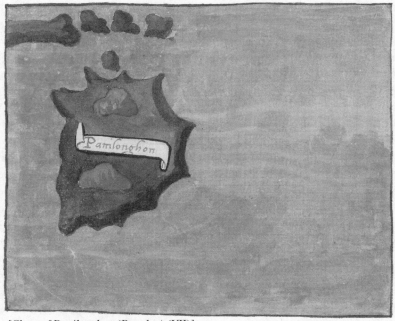

[Chart of Panilonghon (Panglao) (VII)]

[106] At a distance of eighteen leagues from that island of Cebu, at the head of the other island called Bohol, we burned in the midst of that archipelago the ship *Concepción,* for too few of us remained to man it,[239] and we supplied the two other ships with the best of its contents [721]. We laid our course toward south-south-west, coasting along the island called Panglao, in which there are black men like those of Ethio-

pia [722].²⁴⁰ Then we came to a large island,²⁴¹ whose king, in order to make peace with us, drew blood from his left hand, marking his body, face, and the tip of his tongue with it as a token of the closest friendship [723]. We did the same [724].²⁴² I went ashore alone with the king in order to see that island [725]. We had no sooner entered a river than many fishermen offered fish to the king [726]. Then the king removed the cloths that covered his private parts, as did some of his chiefs; and, singing, began to row [727]. Passing by many dwellings that were upon the river, we reached the king's house two hours after nightfall [728]. The distance from the beginning of the river where our ships were to the king's house was two leagues [729].

When we entered the house, they came to meet us with many torches of cane and palm leaves [730]. These torches were of the *anime*, of which mention was made above [731].²⁴³ While the supper was being prepared, the king with two of his chiefs and two of his beautiful women drank a large jar of palm wine without eating anything [732]. I, excusing myself as I had supped, would only drink but once [733]. In drinking they observed all the same ceremonies that the king of Mazaua did [734]. Then the supper was brought in, consisting of rice and very salty fish, served in porcelain dishes: they ate their rice as if it were bread [735]. They cook the rice in the following manner [736]. They first put a large leaf in an earthen jar like our jars, so that it lines all of the jar; then they add the water and the rice, and after covering it, allow it to boil until the rice becomes as hard as bread; then they take it out in pieces [737]. Rice is cooked this way throughout those districts [738]. When we had eaten, the king had a reed mat and another of palm leaves, and a leaf pillow brought in so that I might sleep on them [739]. The king and his two women went to sleep in a separate place, while I slept with one of his chiefs [740].

[107] When day came and until the dinner was brought in, I walked about that island [741]. I saw many articles of gold in those houses but little food [742]. After that we dined on only rice and fish [743]. At the conclusion of dinner, I asked the king by signs whether I could see the queen; he replied that he was willing [744]. We went together to the summit of a lofty hill, where the queen's house was located [745]. When I entered the house, I made a bow to the queen, and she did the

same to me [746]. I sat down beside her, as she was making a sleeping mat of palm leaves [747]. In the house there was hanging a number of porcelain jars and four metal discs for playing upon, one of which was larger than the second, while the other two were still smaller [748]. There were many male and female slaves who served her [749]. Those houses are constructed like those already mentioned [750]. Having taken our leave, we returned to the king's house, where the king had us immediately served with refreshments of sugar cane [751].

[108] The most abundant product of that island is gold (they showed me certain large valleys, making me a sign that the gold there was as abundant as the hairs of their heads), but they have no iron with which to dig it, nor do they care to go to the trouble [to get it] [752]. That part of the island belongs to the same land as Butuan and Caraga, and lies toward Bohol, and is bounded by Mazaua [753]. As we shall return to that island again, I shall say nothing further [now] [754].[244]

[109] In the afternoon, I desired to return to the ships, and the king and the other chief men wished to accompany me, and therefore we went in the same *balanghai* [755]. As we were returning along the river, I saw, on the summit of a hill at the right, three men hanging from one tree, the branches of which had been cut away [756]. I asked the king what was the reason for that, and he replied that they were malefactors and robbers [757]. Those people go naked as do the others mentioned above [758]. The king's name is Rajah Calanao [759]. The harbour is an excellent one, and rice, ginger, swine, goats, fowls, and other things are to be found there; it lies in a latitude of eight degrees toward the Arctic Pole and in a longitude of 167 degrees from the line of demarcation, and it is fifty leagues from Cebu, and it is called Kipit [760].[245] Two days' journey from there to the north-west is found a large island called Luzon,[246] where six or eight junks belonging to the Lequian[247] people go yearly [761]. *[Chart VIII appears here in original.]*

[110] Leaving there and laying our course west-south-west, we cast anchor at a not very large and almost uninhabited island [762]. The people of that island are Moors and were banished from an island called Borneo [763]. They go naked as do the others; they have blow-pipes and small quivers at their side, full of arrows and a poisonous herb; they have daggers whose hafts are adorned with gold and

[Chart of Caghaiam (Cagayan (VIII)]

precious gems, spears, bucklers, and small cuirasses of buffalo horn [764]. They called us 'holy beings' [765]. Little food was to be found in that island, but [there were] immense trees [766]. It lies in a latitude of seven and one-half degrees toward the Arctic Pole, and is forty-three leagues from Kipit, and its name is Cagayan [767].[248]

[111] About twenty-five leagues west-north-west of the above island we found a large island, where rice, ginger, swine, goats, fowls, figs one-half cubit long and as thick as one's arm (they are excellent, and certain others are one span and less in length and are much better than all the others),[249] coconuts, potatoes, sugar cane, and roots resembling turnips in taste are found, and rice cooked under the fire in bamboos or in wood (this kind lasts better than that cooked in earthen pots) [768]. We could well call that land 'the promised land' because we suffered great hunger before we found it [769]. We were often on the point of abandoning the ships and going ashore in order that we might not die of hunger [770]. The king made peace with us by cutting himself slightly in the breast with one of our knives and, upon bleeding, touching the tip of his tongue and his forehead in token of the truest peace, and we did the same [771]. That island lies in a latitude of nine and one-third degrees toward the Arctic Pole, and a longitude of 171 and one-third degrees from the line of demarcation and is called Palawan [772].[250]

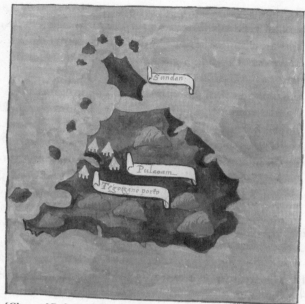

[Chart of Pulaoan (Palawan), Teggozzano porto, and Sundan (IX)]

[112] Those people of Palawan go naked like the others [773]. Almost all of them cultivate their fields; they have blowpipes with wooden arrows more than a span in length with harpoon points, and others tipped with fish-bones, and poisoned with an herb; while others are tipped with points of bamboo like harpoons and are poisoned [774]. At the end of the arrow they attach a little piece of soft wood, instead of feathers [775]. At the end of their blowpipes they fasten a bit of iron like a spearhead; and when they have shot all their arrows they fight with that [776]. They place a value on brass rings and chains, bells, knives, and still more on copper wire for binding their fish hooks [777]. They have large and very tame cocks, which they do not eat because of a certain veneration that they have for them [778]. Sometimes they make them fight with one another, and each one puts up a certain amount on his cock, and the prize goes to him whose cock is the victor [779].[251] They have distilled rice wine, which is stronger and better than that made from the palm [780].

[113] Ten leagues southwest of that island,[252] we came to an island that, as we coasted by, seemed to us to grow very high [781]. After entering the port, the holy body [i.e., St Elmo's fire] appeared to us through the pitchy darkness [782]. There is a distance of fifty leagues from the beginning of that island to the port [783].[253]

[114] On the following day, 9 July, the king of that island sent to us a very beautiful *prau*,[254] whose bow and stern were worked in gold [784]. At the bow flew a white and blue banner surmounted with peacock feathers [785]. Some men were playing on pipes and drums [786]. Two *almadies* came with that *prau* (*praus* resemble fustas, while the *almadies*[255] are their small fishing boats) [787]. Eight old men, who were chiefs, entered the ships and took seats in the stern upon a carpet; they presented us with a painted wooden jar full of betel and *areca* (the fruit they chew continually), and jasmine and orange blossoms, a covering of yellow silk cloth, two cages full of fowls, a couple of goats, three jars full of distilled rice wine, and some bundles of sugar cane; they did the same to the other ship and, embracing us, took their leave [788]. The rice wine is as clear as water, but so strong that many of our men got drunk drinking it, and they call it *arach* [789].[256]

[115] Six days later the king again sent three *praus* with great pomp [790]. Musical instruments playing and drums and brass discs beating, they encircled the ship and saluted us with those cloth caps of theirs that cover only the top of their heads [791]. We saluted them by firing our mortars without [loading with] stones [792]. Then they gave us a present of various kinds of food, made only of rice; some were wrapped in leaves and were made in somewhat longish pieces, some resembled sugarloaves, while others were made in the manner of tarts with eggs and honey [793]. They told us that their king was willing to let us get water and wood, and to trade at our pleasure [794]. Upon hearing this, seven of us entered their *prau* bearing a present to their king, which consisted of a green velvet robe made in the Turkish manner, a violet velvet chair, five cubits of red cloth, a cap, a gilded drinking glass, a covered glass vase, three quires of paper, and a gilded writing case; to the queen [we took] three cubits of yellow cloth, a pair of silvered shoes, and a silvered needle case full of needles; [we took] three cubits of red cloth, a cap, and a gilded

drinking-glass to the governor; to the herald who came in the *prau* we gave a robe of red and green cloth, made in the Turkish fashion, a cap, and a quire of paper; and to the other seven chief men, one a bit of cloth, and to another a cap, and to all of them a quire of paper; then we immediately departed [for the land] [795].

[116] When we reached the city,[257] we remained about two hours in the *prau*, until the arrival of two elephants with silk trappings and twelve men, each of whom carried a porcelain jar covered with silk in which to carry our presents [796]. Then we mounted the elephants while those twelve men preceded us afoot with the presents in the jars [797]. In this way we went to the house of the governor, where we were given a supper of many kinds of food [798]. During the night we slept on cotton mattresses, whose lining was of taffeta, and the sheets of Cambay [799].

[117] The next day we stayed in the house until noon; then we went to the king's palace upon elephants, with our presents in front as on the preceding day [800]. All the streets from the governor's to the king's house were full of men with swords, spears, and shields, for such were the king's orders [801]. We entered the courtyard of the palace mounted on the elephants; we went up a stairway accompanied by the governor and other chiefs and entered a large hall full of many nobles, where we sat down upon a carpet with the presents in the jars near us [802]. At the end of that hall there is another hall, higher but somewhat smaller, adorned with silk hangings, and where two windows opened with two brocade curtains, through which light entered the hall [803]. There were in that hall three hundred foot soldiers with naked rapiers at their thighs to guard the king [804]. At the end of the small hall was a large window from which a brocade curtain was drawn aside [805]. Behind it, we saw the king seated at a table with one of his young sons, chewing betel [806]. There were only women behind him [807].

[118] Then a chief told us that we could not speak to the king, and that if we wished anything, we were to tell it to him, so that he could communicate it to one of higher rank, and the latter would communicate it to a brother of the governor who was stationed in the smaller hall, and this man would communicate it by means of a speaking tube through a hole in the wall to one who was inside with the king [808]. The chief taught us the manner of making three obeisances to the

king with our hands clasped above our head, raising first one foot and then the other and then kissing the hands toward him [809]. And so we did [810]. This is the method of the royal obeisance [811]. We told the king that we came from the king of Spain, and that the latter desired to make peace with him and asked only for permission to trade [812]. The king had told us that since the king of Spain desired to be his friend, he was very willing to be his, and said that we could take water and wood, and trade at our pleasure [813]. Then we gave him the presents, on receiving each of which he nodded slightly [814].

To each one of us was given some brocaded and gold cloth and silk, which were placed upon our left shoulders, where they were left but a moment [815]. They presented us with refreshments of cloves and cinnamon [816]. Then the curtains were drawn and the windows closed [817]. The men in the palace were all attired in cloth of gold and silk, which covered their private parts, and they carried daggers with gold hafts adorned with pearls and precious gems, and had many rings on their hands [818].

[119] We returned upon the elephants to the governor's house, seven men carrying the king's presents to us and always preceding us [819].

When we reached the house, they gave each one of us presents, placing them upon our left shoulders, and we gave each of those men a couple of knives for his trouble [820]. Nine men came to the governor's house with a like number of large wooden trays from the king [821]. Each tray contained ten or twelve porcelain dishes full of veal, capons, chickens, peacocks, and other animals, and fish [822]. We ate on the ground seated upon a palm mat from thirty or thirty-two different kinds of meat besides the fish and other things [823]. At each mouthful of food we drank a small cupful of their distilled wine from a porcelain cup the size of an egg [824]. We ate rice and other sweet food with gold spoons like ours [825]. In our sleeping quarters there during those two nights, two torches of white wax were kept constantly alight in two rather tall silver candlesticks, as well as two large lamps full of oil with four wicks apiece and two men to snuff them continually [826].

We rode upon elephants back to the seashore, where we found two *praus* that took us back to the ships [827].

[120] That city is entirely built in salt water, except the houses of the king and certain chiefs, and it contains between twenty and twenty-five thousand hearths [828].²⁵⁸ The houses are all constructed of wood and built up from the ground on tall pillars [829]. When the tide is high the women go in boats through the settlement selling articles necessary to maintain life [830]. There is a large brick wall in front of the king's house with towers like a fort, in which were mounted fifty-six bronze pieces and six of iron [831]. During the two days of our stay there, many pieces were discharged [832]. That king is a Moor and his name is Rajah Siripada; he was forty years old and fat [833]. No one serves him except women who are the daughters of chiefs [834]. He never goes outside of his palace, unless when he goes hunting [835]. No one is allowed to talk with him except through the speaking tube [836]. He has ten scribes who write down his deeds on very thin tree bark; these scribes are called *xiritoles* [837]. ²⁵⁹

[121] On Monday morning, 29 July, we saw more than one hundred *praus* divided into three squadrons and a like number of *tunguli* (which are their small boats) coming toward us [838].²⁶⁰ Upon catching sight of them, imagining that there was some trickery afoot, we hoisted our sails as quickly as possible, slipping an anchor in our haste [839]. We were especially concerned that we might be caught in between certain junks that had anchored behind us on the preceding day [840]. We immediately turned upon the latter, capturing four of them and killing many persons [841]. Three or four of the junks sought flight by beaching [842]. In one of the junks that we captured was the son of the king of the island of Luzon [843]. He was the captain-general of the king of Brunei, and came with those junks from a large city named Laoe, which is located at the end of that island [Borneo] toward Java Major,²⁶¹ which he had destroyed and sacked because it refused to obey the king [of Brunei] but [obeyed] the king of Java Major instead [844]. João Carvalho, our pilot, released that captain and the junks without our consent, for a certain sum of gold, as we learned afterward [845]. Had the pilot not given up the captain to the king, the latter would have given us whatever we had asked, for that captain was exceedingly feared throughout those regions, especially by the heathens, as the latter are very hostile to that Moorish king [846].

[122] In that same port there is another city inhabited by heathens, which is larger than that of the Moors, and built like the latter in salt water; on that account, the two peoples have daily combats together in that same harbour [847]. The heathen king is as powerful as the Moorish king, but is not so haughty, and could be converted easily to the Christian faith [848].

When the Moorish king heard how we had treated the junks, he sent us a message by one of our men who was ashore to the effect that the *praus* were not coming to do us any harm, but that they were going to attack the heathens, and as a proof of that statement, the Moors showed him some heads of men who had been killed, which they declared to be the heads of heathens [849].

We sent a message to the king, asking him to please allow two of our men who were in the city for purposes of trade and the son of João Carvalho, who had been born in the country of Verzin, to come to us, but the king refused [849]. That was the result of João Carvalho's letting the above captain go [851].[262]

We kept sixteen of the most important men [of the captured junks] to take them to Spain, and three women in the queen's name, but João Carvalho claimed the latter for himself [852].

[123] Junks are their ships, and they are made in the following manner: the bottom part stands about two spans above the water and is of planks fastened with wooden pegs, which are very well made [853]. Above that they are entirely made of very large bamboo, and one of those junks carries as much cargo as a ship [854]. On both sides they use bamboos as counterweights; their masts are made of bamboo, and the sails are made of the bark of trees [855]. Their porcelain is a sort of exceedingly white earth that is left for fifty years under the earth before it is worked, for otherwise it would not be fine [856]. The father buries it for the son [857]. If [poison][263] is placed in a dish made of fine porcelain, the dish immediately breaks [858].

The money used by the Moors in those regions is of bronze pierced in the middle in order that it may be strung, and on only one side of it are four characters, which are letters of the great king of China; and they call that money *picis* [859].[264] They gave us six porcelain dishes for one *cathil*[265] (which is equivalent to two of our pounds) of quicksilver; one hundred *picis* for one quire of writing paper; one small porcelain vase for 160 *cathils* of metal; one porcelain vase for three knives; one *bahar* (which is equivalent to 203 cathils) of wax for 160 *cathils* of bronze; one *bahar*[266] of salt for eighty *cathils* of bronze; one *bahar* of anime to caulk the ships (for no pitch is found in those regions) for forty *cathils* of metal [860]. Twenty *tahils* make one *cathil* [861]. There the people highly esteem metal, quicksilver, glass, cinnabar, wool cloth, linens, and all our other merchandise, although iron and spectacles more than all the rest [862]. Those Moors go naked like the others [863]. They drink quicksilver: the sick man drinks it to cleanse himself, and the well man to preserve his health [864].

[124] The king of Brunei has two pearls as large as two hen's eggs, and they are so round that they will not stand still on a table; I know that for a fact, for when we carried the king's presents to him, signs were made for him to show them to us [865]. He said that he would show them next day [866]. Afterward some chiefs said that they had seen them [867].[267]

[125] Those Moors worship Muhammad, and his law states: do not eat pork; wash the buttocks with the left hand and do not to use that hand to eat; do not cut anything with the right hand; sit down to urinate; do not kill fowls or goats without first addressing the sun; cut off the tops of the wings of hens with the little bits of skin that stick up from under the wings and the feet and then split them down the middle; wash the face with the right hand, but do not clean the teeth with the fingers; and do not eat anything that has been killed unless by them [868]. They are circumcised like the Jews [869].

[126] Camphor, a kind of balsam, is produced in that island, and it seeps between the wood and the bark, and the drops are as small as [grains of] wheat bran [870]. If it is exposed it gradually evaporates; those people call it *capor* [871].[268] Cinnamon, ginger, mirabolans, oranges, lemons, jackfruit, watermelons, cucumbers, gourds, turnips, cabbages, scallions, cows, buffaloes, swine, goats, chickens, geese, deer, elephants, horses, and other things are found there [872]. That island is so large that it takes three months to sail round it in a prau [873]. It lies in a latitude of five and one-fourth degrees toward the Arctic Pole, and in a longitude of 176 and two-thirds degrees from the line of demarcation, and its name is Borneo [874].[269]

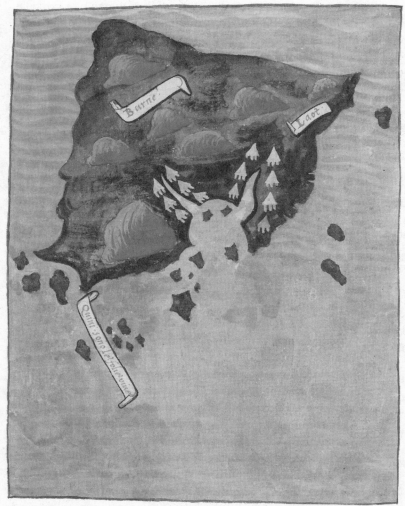

[Chart of Burne (Borneo), Loat (Loac?), and the scroll: 'Where the living leaves are.' (X)]

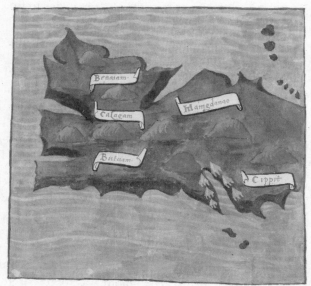

[Chart of Mindanao (XI)]

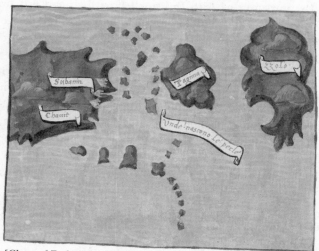

[Chart of Zzolo (Jolo), Subanin, Tagima (Basilan), Cavit (Cavite) and the scroll: 'Where the pearls are born' (XII)][270]

[127] Leaving that island, we turned back[271] in order to find a suitable place to caulk the ships, for they were leaking [875]. One ship ran on to some shoals of an island called Bibalon,[272] because of the carelessness of its pilot, but by the help of God we freed it [876]. A sailor of that ship incautiously snuffed a candle into a barrel full of gunpowder [877]. He quickly snatched it out without any harm [878]. Then pursuing our course, we captured a prau laden with coconuts on its way to Borneo [879]. Its crew sought refuge on a small island [880]. While we were capturing this one, three other praus escaped behind certain islets [881].

[128] At the head of Borneo between it and an island called Cimbonbon, which lies in [a latitude of] eight degrees and seven minutes, is a perfect port for repairing ships;[273] consequently, we entered it, but as we lacked many things for repairing the ships, we remained there for forty-two days [882].[274]

During that time, each one of us laboured hard, one at one thing and one at another, but our greatest labour was to go barefoot into the woods for firewood [883]. In that island there are wild boars, of which we killed one that was going by water from one island to another [by pursuing it] with the small boat; its head was two and one-half span long, and its teeth were large [884]. There are large crocodiles there, both on land and sea, oysters and shellfish of various kinds; among the last named we found two, the flesh of one of which weighed twenty-six pounds, and the other forty-four [885].[275] We caught a fish that had a head like that of a hog and two horns; its body consisted entirely of one bone, and on its back it resembled a saddle; and it was small [886].[276] There are also found trees that produce leaves [887]. When they fall they are living and walk about [888]. Those leaves are very similar to those of the mulberry, but are not so long [889]. On both sides near the stem they have two feet [890]. The stem is short and pointed [891]. They have no blood, but if one touches them they run away [892]. I kept one of them for nine days in a box [893]. When I opened the box, that leaf went round and round it [894]. I believe those leaves live on nothing but air [895].[277]

[129] Having left that island,[278] that is, the port, we met at the head of the island of Palawan[279] a junk that was coming from Borneo, in

which was the travelling governor of Palawan [896]. We made them a signal to haul in their sails, and as they refused to haul them in, we captured the junk by force and sacked it [897]. [We told] the governor [that] if [he] wished his freedom, he was to give us, inside of seven days, four hundred measures of rice, twenty swine, twenty goats, and 150 fowls [898]. Then he presented us with coconuts, figs, sugar canes, jars full of palm wine, and other things [899]. Seeing his liberality, we returned some of his daggers and harquebuses to him [900]. Then we gave him a flag, a yellow damask robe, and fifteen cubits of cloth; to his son, a cloak of blue cloth; to a brother of the governor, a robe of green cloth and other things [901].

[130] We parted from the governor as friends, and we turned our course back between the island of Cagayan[280] and the port of Kipit [902].[281] We laid our course east by south in order that we might find the islands of Molucca, and we passed by certain reefs near which we found the sea to be full of grass, although the depth was very great [903]. When we passed through them, it seemed as though we were entering another sea [904]. Leaving Kipit to the east, we found two islands, Jolo and Taghima,[282] which lie toward the west, and near which pearls are found [905]. The two pearls of the king of Brunei were found there, and the king got them, as was told us, in the following manner [906]. That king took to wife a daughter of the king of Jolo, who told him that her father had those two pearls [907]. The king determined to get possession of them by whatever means [908]. Going one night with five hundred praus, he captured the king and two of his sons, and took them to Brunei [909]. If the king of Jolo wished to regain his freedom, he had to surrender the two pearls to him [910].[283]

[131] Then we laid our course east by north between two settlements called Cavite and Subanin, and an inhabited island called Monoripa,[284] located ten leagues from the reefs [911]. The people of that island make their dwellings in boats and do not live elsewhere [912]. In those two settlements of Cavite and Subanin, which are located in the island of Butuan and Caraga, is found the best cinnamon to be had anywhere [913]. Had we stayed there two days, those people would have laden our ships for us, but as we had a wind favourable for passing a point and certain islets which were near that island, we did not wish to delay; while

under sail, we bartered two large knives that we had taken from the governor of Palawan for seventeen pounds [of cinnamon] [914]. The cinnamon tree grows to a height of three or four cubits, and is as thick as the fingers of the hand, and it has but three or four small branches [915]. Its leaves resemble those of the laurel; its bark is the cinnamon [916]. It is gathered twice per year [917]. The wood and leaves give off as strong an aroma as the cinnamon when they are green [918]. Those people call it *caiumana*: *caiu* means 'wood', and *mana*, 'sweet', hence, 'sweet wood' [919].[285]

[132] Laying our course toward the north-east, and going to a large city called Magindanao,[286] which is located in the island of Butuan and Caraga,[287] so that we might gather information concerning Molucca, we captured by force a *biguiday* (a vessel resembling a prau) and killed seven men [920]. It contained only eighteen men, who were as well built as any whom we had seen in those regions, and all of them were chiefs of Magindanao [921]. Among them was one who told us that he was a brother of the king of Magindanao, and that he knew the location of Molucca [922]. Following his directions we discontinued our course toward the north-east, and took that toward the south-east [923].

At a cape of that island of Butuan and Caraga, and near a river, are found hairy men who are very great fighters and archers [924]. They use swords one span in width, and eat only raw human hearts with the juice of oranges or lemons; those people are called *Benaian*, 'the hairy' [925].[288] When we took our course toward the south-east, we lay in a latitude of six degrees and seven minutes toward the Arctic Pole, and thirty leagues from Cavite [926]. *[Chart XIII appears here in original.]*

[133] Sailing toward the south-east, we found four islands, [namely,] Ciboco, Birahan Batolach, Sarangani, and Candighar.[289] One Saturday night, 26 October, while coasting by Birahan Batolach, we were assaulted by a furious storm; thereupon, praying God, we lowered all the sails [928]. Immediately our three saints appeared to us and chased away all the darkness [929]. St Elmo remained for more than two hours on the maintop, like a torch; St Nicholas on the mizzentop; and St Clara on the foretop [930]. We promised a slave to St Elmo, St Nicholas, and St Clara; we gave alms to each of them [931].

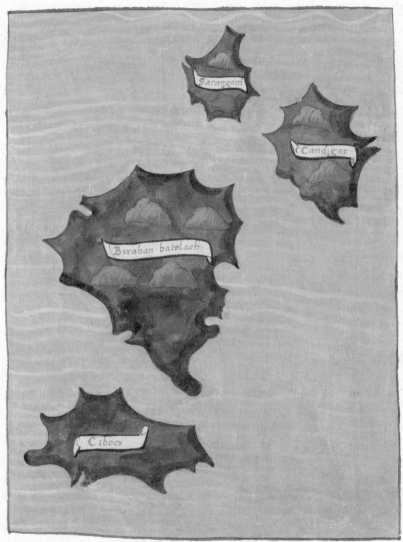

[Chart of the islands of Ciboco (Sibago), Birahan batolach (Batukali?); Sarangani, Candigar (Balut?) (XIII)]

[**134**] Then continuing our voyage, we entered a harbour between the two islands of Sarangani and Candighar, and anchored to the eastward near a settlement of Sarangani, where gold and pearls are found [932]. Those people are heathens and go naked as the others [933]. That harbour lies in a latitude of five degrees nine minutes, and is fifty leagues from Cavite [934].

[**135**] Remaining one day in that harbour, we captured two pilots by force, in order that they might show us the way to Molucca [935]. Then laying our course south-south-west, we passed among eight islands, some inhabited and others not, which were situated in the manner of a street, and their names are Cheava, Caviao, Cabiao, Camanuca, Cabaluzao, Cheai, Lipan, and Nuza;[290] finally, we came to an island at their end, which was very beautiful to look at [936]. As we had a contrary wind, so that we could not double a point of that island, we sailed here and there near it; consequently, one of the men whom we had captured at Saranghai, together with the brother of the king of Magindanao who took with him his small son, escaped during the night by swimming to that island, but the boy was drowned, for he was unable to hold tightly to his father's shoulders [937]. Being unable to double the said point, we passed below the island, where there were many small islands [938]. That island has four kings, [namely,] Rajah Matandatu, Rajah Lalagha, Rajah Bapti, and Rajah Parabu: they are heathens [939]. The island lies in a latitude of three and one-half degrees toward the Arctic Pole and is twenty-seven leagues from Sarangani; its name is Sanghihe [940].[291] *[Charts XIV and XV appear here in original.]*

[**136**] Continuing the same course, we passed near six islands, [namely,] Kima, Karakitang, Para, Zangalura, Siau (which is ten leagues from Sanghihe, has a high but not large mountain, and its king is named Rajah Ponto),[292] and Paghinzara[293] (which is located eight leagues from Siau, has three high mountains, and its king is named Rajah Babintau): all of these islands are inhabited by heathens [941]. To the east of Kima is the island of Talaud [942].[294] Then we found twelve leagues to the east of Paghinzara two islands, not very large, but inhabited, called Zoar and Meau [943].[295]

After passing those two islands, on Wednesday, 6 November, we discovered four lofty islands fourteen leagues east of the two

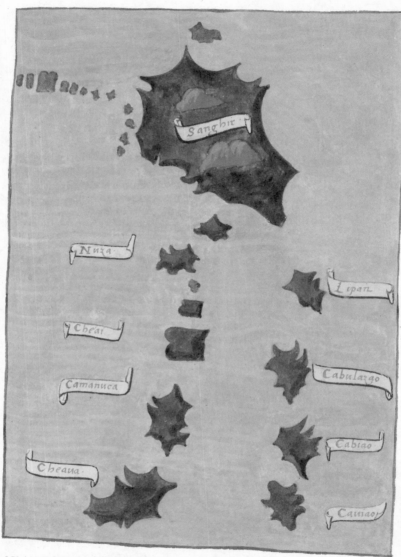

[Chart of the island of Sanghir (Sanghihe), Nuza (?), Lipan (Lipang), Cheai (?),
Cabulzago (Kawalusu), Camanuca (Memanuk), Cabiao (Kamboling?), Cheva (?),
Caviao (Kawio) (XIV)]

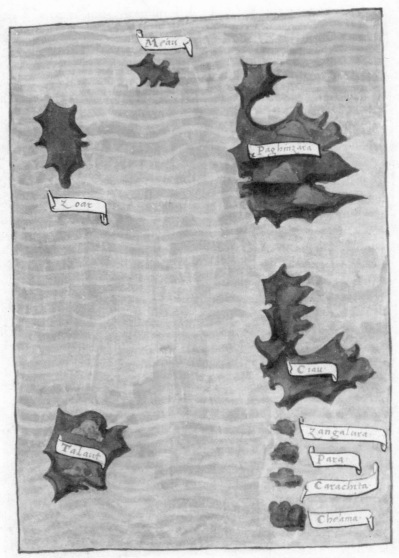

[*Chart of the archipelago of Paghinzara including Paghinzara, Ciau (Siau),*
Zangalura (Sanggeluhang), Para, Carachita (Karakitang), Cheama (Kima),
Meau (Maju), Zoar (Tifore) (XV)]

[above-mentioned islands] [944]. The pilot, who still remained with us, told us that those four islands were Molucca; therefore, we thanked God and as an expression of our joy discharged all our artillery [945]. It was no wonder that we were so glad, for we had passed twenty-seven months less two days in our search for Molucca [946]. Among all those islands, even to Molucca, the shallowest bottom that we found was at a depth of one or two hundred fathoms, which contradicts the assertion of the Portuguese that that region could not be navigated because of the numerous shoals and the dark sky as they have imagined [947]. *[Charts XVI and XVII appear here in original.]*

[**137**] Three hours before sunset on Friday, 8 November, 1521,[296] we entered into a harbour of an island called Tidore, and anchoring near the shore in twenty fathoms we fired all our artillery [948]. The next day, the king came to the ships in a prau, and circled about them once [949]. We immediately went to meet him in a small boat, in order to show him honour [950]. He made us enter his prau and seat ourselves near him [951]. He was seated under a silk awning, which sheltered him on all sides [952]. In front of him was one of his sons with the royal sceptre, and two persons with two gold jars to pour water on his hands, and two others with two gilded caskets filled with their betel [953].[297]

The king told us that we were welcome there,[298] and that he had dreamt some time ago that some ships were coming to Molucca from remote parts; and that for more assurance he had determined to consult the moon, whereupon he had seen the ships were coming, and that we were they [954].[299] Upon the king entering our ships all kissed his hand [955]. Then we led him to the poop, and in order to enter there, he would not stoop, but climbed in [through a small door] from above [956].[300] We had him sit down in a red velvet chair, and we clothed him in a yellow velvet robe made in the Turkish fashion [957]. In order to show him greater honour, we sat down on the ground near him [958].

[**138**] Then when all were seated, the king began to speak and said that he and all his people desired to always be the most loyal friends and vassals to our king of Spain, that he received us as his children, and that we could go ashore as if in our own houses; for from that

[*Chart of the island of Tarenate (Ternate), Giailonlo (Gilolo: Halmahera), Maitara (Mutir) with the scroll: 'All the islands represented in this book are in the other hemisphere of the world at the antipodes' (XVI)*]

[*Chart of the islands of Molucca including Pulongha, Tadore (Tidore), Mare, Mutir (Motir), and Machiam (Makiam) with the scroll: 'Cavi gomode, that is, the Clove tree' (XVII)*][301]

time forward, his island was to no longer be called Tidore, but Castile, because of the great love that he bore our king, his lord [959]. We made him a present that consisted of the robe, the chair, a piece of delicate linen, four cubits of scarlet cloth, a piece of brocaded silk, a piece of yellow damask, some Indian cloth embroidered with gold and silk, a piece of white *berania*³⁰² (the linen of Cambay), two caps, six strings of glass beads, twelve knives, three large mirrors, six pairs of scissors, six combs, some gilded drinking cups, and other articles; to his son we gave an Indian cloth of gold and silk, a large mirror, a cap, and two knives; and to each of nine other principal men, a silk cloth, caps, and two knives; and to many others caps or knives, giving presents until the king told us to stop [960].

[139] After that he declared to us that he had nothing else except his own life to send to the king his sovereign, and that we were to approach nearer to the city, and that whoever came to the ships at night, we were to kill with our muskets [961]. In leaving the poop, the king would never bend his head [962]. When he took his leave we discharged all our artillery [963]. That king is a Moor and about forty-five years old, well built, of a regal bearing, and an excellent astrologer [964]. At that time he was clad in a shirt of the most delicate white stuff with the ends of the sleeves embroidered in gold, and in a cloth that reached from his waist to the ground, and he was barefoot [965]. Around his head he wore a silk scarf and over that a crown of flowers; and he was called Rajah Sultan Manzor [966].³⁰³

[140] On Sunday, 10 November, that king desired us to tell him how long it was since we had left Spain, and what pay and *quintalada*³⁰⁴ the king gave to each of us; he requested us to give him a signature of the king and a royal banner, for then and thenceforth he would arrange it that his island and another called Ternate³⁰⁵ [provided that he were able to crown as king one of his grandsons, named Calonaghapi]³⁰⁶ would both belong to the king of Spain; and for the honour of his king he was ready to fight to the death, and when he could no longer resist, he would go to Spain with all his family in a junk that he was having built new, carrying the royal signature and banner; and therefore he was the king's servant for a long time [967]. He begged us to leave him some men so that he might constantly be

reminded of the king of Spain and did not ask for merchandise because the latter would not remain with him [968]. He told us that he would go to an island called Batjan,[307] in order sooner to furnish the ships with cloves, for there were not enough dry cloves in his island to load the two ships [969]. As that day was Sunday, it was decided not to trade [970]. The festive day of those people is our Friday [971].

[141] In order that your most illustrious Lordship may know the islands where cloves grow, they are five, [namely,] Ternate, Tidore, Motir, Makian and Batjan.[308] Ternate is the chief one, and when its king was alive, he ruled nearly all the others [973]. Tidore, the one where we were, has a king [974]. Motir and Makian have no king but are ruled by the people, and when the two kings of Ternate and of Tidore engage in war, those two islands furnish them with men [975]. The last island is Batjan, and it has a king [976]. That entire province where cloves grow is called Molucca [977].

[142] At that time it was not eight months since one Francisco Serrão, a Portuguese and the captain-general of the king of Ternate against the king of Tidore, had died in Ternate [978]. He had done so well that he had constrained the king of Tidore to give one of his daughters to wife to the king of Ternate, and almost all the sons of the chiefs as hostages, and the above-mentioned grandson of the king of Tidore was born to that daughter [979].[309] Peace having been made between the two kings, when Francisco Serrão came one day to Tidore to trade cloves, the king of Tidore had him poisoned with those betel leaves of theirs, and he lived only four days [980].[310] His king wished to have him buried according to his religion, but three Christians who were his servants would not consent to it [981]. He left a son and a daughter, both young, born by a woman whom he had taken in Java Major, and two hundred *bahars* of cloves [982]. Serrão was a close friend and a relative of our faithful captain-general, and was the cause of inciting the latter to undertake that enterprise, for when our captain was at Malacca [Melaka], he had written to him several times that he was in Ternate [983].[311] As Don Manuel, then king of Portugal, refused to increase our captain-general's pension by only a single testoon[312] per month for his merits, he went to Spain, where he had obtained everything he could think to ask for from his sacred Majesty [984]. Ten days after the death of Francisco Serrão, the king

of Ternate, by name, Rajah Abuleis, having expelled his son-in-law, the king of Batjan, was poisoned by his daughter, the wife of the latter king, under pretext of trying to bring about peace between the two kings [985]. The king lingered but two days, and left nine principal sons, whose names are Chechili Momuli, Tidoree Vunighi, Chechili de Roix, Cili Manzur, Cili Pagi, Chialin, Chechilin Cathara, Vaiechu Serich, and Calanoghapi [986].[313]

[143] On Monday, 11 November, one of the sons of the king of Ternate, Chechili de Roix, came to the ships clad in red velvet with two praus; his men were playing upon the above-mentioned metal discs and he refused to enter the ship at that time [987]. He had [charge of] the wife and children, and the other possessions of Francisco Serrão [988]. When we found out who he was, we sent a message to the king, asking him whether we should receive Chechili de Roix, since we were in the king's port [989]. He replied to us that we could do as we pleased [990]. The son of the king, seeing that we were hesitating, moved off somewhat from the ships [991]. We went to him with the boat in order to present him an Indian cloth of gold and silk, and some knives, mirrors, and scissors [992]. He accepted them somewhat haughtily, and immediately departed [993]. He had a Christian Indian with him named Manuel, the servant of one Pedro Alfonso de Lorosa, a Portuguese who went from Bandan to Ternate,[314] after the death of Francisco Serrão [994]. As the servant knew how to speak Portuguese, he came aboard our ship, and told us that, although the sons of the king of Ternate were at enmity with the king of Tidore, they were always at the service of the king of Spain [995]. We sent a letter to Pedro Alfonso de Lorosa, through his servant, [telling him] that he could come without any fear [996].

[144] Those kings have as many women as they wish, but only one chief wife, whom all the others obey [997]. The king of Tidore had a large house outside of the city, where two hundred of his chief women lived with a like number of women to serve them [998]. When the king eats, he sits alone or with his chief wife in a high place like a gallery from which he can see all the other women who sit about the gallery; and he orders her who best pleases him to sleep with him

that night [999]. After the king has finished eating, if he orders those women to eat together, they do so, but if not, each one goes to eat in her chamber [1000]. No one is allowed to see those women without permission from the king, and if anyone is found near the king's house by day or by night, he is put to death [1001]. Every family is obliged to give the king one or two of its daughters [1002]. That king had twenty-six children – eight sons and the rest daughters [1003].

[145] Next to that island there is a very large island, called Gilolo,[315] which is inhabited by Moors and heathens [1004]. Two kings are found there among the Moors; one of them, as the king told us, had had 600 children, and the other 525 [1005]. The heathens do not keep so many women; nor do they live under so many superstitions, but adore for all that day the first thing that they see in the morning when they go out of their houses [1006]. The king of those heathens, called Rajah Papua, is exceedingly rich in gold, and lives in the interior of the island [1007]. Reeds as thick around as the leg and filled with water that is very good to drink grow on the flinty rocks in the island of Gilolo:[316] we bought many of them from those people.

[146] On Tuesday, 12 November, the king had a house built for us for our merchandise in the city in one day [1009]. We carried almost all of our goods there, and left three of our men to guard them, and we immediately began to trade in the following manner: for ten cubits of red cloth of very good quality, they gave us one *bahar* of cloves, which is equivalent to four quintals and six pounds (one quintal is one hundred pounds); for fifteen cubits of cloth of not very good quality, one *bahar*; for fifteen hatchets, one *bahar*; for thirty-five glass drinking cups, one *bahar* (the king getting them all); for seventeen *cathils* of cinnabar,[317] one *bahar*; for seventeen *cathils* of quicksilver, one *bahar*; for twenty-six cubits of linen, one *bahar*; for twenty-five cubits of finer linen, one *bahar*; for 150 knives, one *bahar*; for fifty pairs of scissors, one *bahar*; for forty caps, one *bahar*; for ten pieces of Gujarat cloth,[318] one *bahar*; for three of those gongs of theirs, two *bahars*; for one quintal of bronze, one *bahar* [1010]. All the mirrors were broken, and the few good ones the king wished for himself [1011]. Many of those things [that we traded] were from those junks we had captured [1012]. Our haste to return to Spain made us dispose of our merchandise at better

bargains [to the natives] than we should have done [1013]. Daily so many boatloads of goats, fowls, figs [bananas], coconuts, and other kinds of food were brought to the ships that we were amazed [1014].

[147] We supplied the ships with good water, which issues forth hot [from the ground], but if it stands for the space of an hour outside its spring, it becomes very cold [1015]. The reason therefore being that it comes from the mountain of cloves, which is quite the opposite from the assertion made in Spain that it is necessary to carry water to Molucca from distant parts [1016].[319]

[148] On Wednesday, the king sent his son, named Mossahap, to Motir for cloves, so that they might supply us more quickly [1017]. On that day we told the king that we had captured certain Indians [1018]. The king thanked God heartily, and asked us to do him the kindness to give them to him, so that he might send them back to their land, with five of his own men, in order that they might make the king of Spain and his fame known [1019]. Then we gave him the three women who had been captured in the queen's name for the reason just given [1020].

[149] The next day, we gave the king all the prisoners, except those from Borneo, for which he thanked us fervently [1021]. Thereupon, he asked us, in order thereby to show our love for him, to kill all the swine that we had in the ships, in return for which he would give us an equal number of goats and fowls [1022]. We killed them in order to show him favour, and hung them up under the deck [1023]. When those people happened to see them they covered their faces in order that they might not look upon them or catch their odour [1024].

[150] In the afternoon of that same day, Pietro Alfonso, the Portuguese,[320] came in a prau, and he had not disembarked before the king sent to summon him and told him banteringly to answer us truly in whatever we should ask him, even if he did come from Ternate [1025]. He told us that he had been sixteen years in India, but ten in Molucca, for it was as many years since Molucca had been discovered secretly; it was a year less fifteen days since a large ship had arrived at that place from Malacca and had left laden with cloves, but it had been obliged to remain in Bandan for some months because of

bad weather; the ship's captain was Tristão de Meneses, a Portuguese, and when he asked the latter what was the news back in Christendom, he was told that a fleet of five ships had left Seville to discover Molucca in the name of the king of Spain under the command of Ferdinand Magellan, a Portuguese, and that the king of Portugal, angered that a Portuguese should be opposed to him, had sent some ships to the Cape of Good Hope, and a like number to the Cape of Santa Maria at the mouth of the Rio de la Plata, where the cannibals live, in order to prevent their passage, but Magellan had not been found [1026]. Then the king of Portugal had heard that the captain had passed into another sea, and was on his way to Molucca [1027]. He immediately wrote directing his chief captain of India, one Diogo Lopes de Sequeira,[321] to send six ships to Molucca, but the latter did not send them because the Grand Turk was coming to Molucca and he was obliged to send sixty sail to oppose him at the Strait of Mecca in the land of Jiddah,[322] where they found only a few galleys that had been beached on the shore of the strong and beautiful city of Aden, all of which they burned [1028]. After that the chief captain sent a large galleon with two tiers of guns to Molucca to oppose us, but it was unable to proceed or turn back because of certain shoals and currents of water near Molucca, and contrary winds (the captain of that galleon was Francisco Faria, a Portuguese) [1029].[323] It was but a few days since a caravel with two junks had been in that place to gather information about us [1030]. The junks went to Batjan for a cargo of cloves with seven Portuguese [1031]. As those Portuguese did not respect the women of the king and of his subjects, although the king told them often not to act so, and since they refused to discontinue, they were put to death [1032]. When the men in the caravel heard that, they immediately returned to Malacca, abandoning the junks with four hundred *bahars* of cloves and sufficient merchandise to purchase one hundred *bahars* more [1033]. Every year a number of junks sail from Malacca to Bandan for mace and nutmeg, and from Bandan to Molucca for cloves [1034]. Those people sail in three days in those junks of theirs from Molucca to Bandan, and in fifteen days from Bandan to Malacca [1035]. The king of Portugal had enjoyed Molucca already for ten years secretly, so that the king of Spain might not learn of it [1036].[324] That Portuguese remained with us until three in the morning, and told us many other things [1037]. We plied him so well, promising to pay him well, that he promised to return to Spain with us [1038].[325]

[151] On Friday, 15 November, the king told us that he was going to Batjan to get the cloves abandoned there by the Portuguese [1039]. He asked us for two presents so that he might give them to the two governors of Motir in the name of the king of Spain, and passing in between the ships, he desired to see how we fired our musketry, crossbows, and the culverins,[326] which are larger than a harquebus [1040]. He shot three times with a crossbow, for it pleased him more than the muskets.

[152] On Saturday, the Moorish king of Gilolo came to the ships with a considerable number of praus, and to some of the men we gave some green damask silk, two cubits of red cloth, mirrors, scissors, knives, combs, and two gilt drinking cups [1042]. That king told us that since we were friends of the king of Tidore, we were also his friends, for he loved that king as one of his own sons; and whenever any of our men would go to his land, he would show him the greatest honour [1043]. That king is very aged and is feared among all those islands, for he is very powerful; his name is Rajah Iussu [1044].

That island of Gilolo is so large that it takes four months to circumnavigate it in a prau [1045].

[153] On Sunday morning that same king came to the ships and desired to see how we fought and how we discharged our guns, and he took the greatest pleasure in it and then immediately departed [1046]. We were told that he had been a great fighter in his youth [1047].

[154] That same day, I went ashore to see how the clove grows [1048]. The clove tree is tall and as thick as a man's body or thereabout [1049]. Its branches spread out somewhat widely in the middle, but at the top they have the shape of a summit [1050]. Its leaves resemble those of the laurel, and the bark is olive coloured [1051]. The cloves grow at the end of the twigs, ten or twenty in a cluster [1052]. Those trees have generally more cloves on one side than on the other, according to the weather conditions [1053]. When the cloves sprout they are white, when ripe, red, and when dried, black [1054]. They are gathered twice per year, once at the nativity of our Saviour, and the other at the nativity of St John the Baptist;[327] for the climate is more moderate at those two

seasons, but more so at the time of the Nativity of our Savior [1055]. When the year is very hot and there is little rain, those people gather three or four hundred *bahars* [of cloves] in each of those islands [1056]. Those trees grow only in the mountains, and if any of them are planted in the lowlands near the mountains they do not survive [1057]. The leaves, the bark, and the green wood are as strong as the cloves [1058]. If the latter are not gathered when they are ripe, they become large and so hard that only their husk is good [1059]. No cloves are grown in the world except in the five mountains of those five islands, except that some are found in Gilolo and in a small island between Tidore and Motir, by name Mareh,[328] but they are not good [1060]. Almost every day we saw a mist descend and encircle now one and now another of those mountains, on account of which those cloves become perfect [1062]. Each of those people possesses clove trees, and each one watches over his own trees although he does not cultivate them [1063].

[155] Some nutmeg trees are found in that island: the tree resembles our walnut tree, and has leaves like it [1064]. When the nut is gathered it is as large as a small quince, with the same sort of down, and it is of the same color [1065]. Its first rind is as thick as the green rind of our walnut [1066]. Under that there is a thin layer, under which is found the mace, which is a brilliant red and is wrapped about the rind of the nut, and within that is the nutmeg [1067].

The houses of those people are built like those of the others, but are not raised so high from the ground, and are surrounded with bamboos like a hedge [1068].

The women there are ugly and go naked like the others, [covered only] with those cloths made from the bark of trees [1069]. Those cloths are made in the following manner: they take a piece of bark and leave it in the water until it becomes soft, and then they beat it with bits of wood and [thus] make it as long and as wide as they wish [1070]. It becomes like a veil of raw silk, and has certain threads within it that appear as if woven [1071]. They eat wooden bread made from a tree resembling the palm, which is made as follows: they take a piece of that soft wood from which they take certain long black thorns, and then they pound the wood, and so make the bread [1072]. They eat that bread almost only while at sea, and they call it *saghu*,[329] [1073]. The men there go naked as do the others [of those regions], but they are so jealous of their wives that they do not wish us to go ashore with our drawers exposed; for they assert that their women imagine that we are always in readiness [1074].

[156] A number of boats came from Ternate daily laden with cloves, but, as we were awaiting the king, we did not barter for anything except food [1075]. The men who came from Ternate complained a great deal because we refused to trade with them [1076].

[157] On Sunday night, 24 November, and toward Monday, the king came with metal discs a-sounding and passed between the ships, [at which] we discharged many pieces [1077]. He told us that cloves would be brought in quantity within four days [1078].

[158] Monday, the king sent us 791 *cathils* of cloves, without reckoning the tare (the tare is to take the spices for less than they weigh, for they become drier daily) [1079]. As those were the first cloves that we had laden in our ships, we fired many pieces [1080]. Cloves are called *ghomode*[330] there; in Sarangani, where we captured the two pilots, *bongalavan*; and in Malacca, *chianche* [1081].[331]

[159] On Tuesday, 26 November, the king told us that it was not the custom of any king to leave his island, but that he had left [his] for the love that he bore the king of Castile, and so that we might go to Spain sooner and return with so many ships that we could avenge the murder of his father, who was killed in an island called Buru and then thrown into the sea [1082].[332] He told us that it was the custom, when the first cloves were laden in the ships or in the junks, for the king to make a feast for the crews of the ships, and to pray to their god that he would lead those ships safe to their port; he also wished to do it because of the king of Batjan and one of his brothers, who were coming to visit him [1083]. He had the streets cleaned [1084].

Some of us imagining that some treachery was afoot, because three Portuguese in the company of Francisco Serrão had been killed in the place where we took in water, by certain of those people who had hidden in the thickets, and because we saw those Indians whispering with our prisoners, declared in opposition to some who wished to go to the feast that we ought not go ashore for feasts, for we remembered that other so unfortunate one [1085].[333]

In the end it was concluded that we should send a message to the king asking him to come soon to the ships, for we were about to depart and we would give him the four men whom we had promised him, besides some other merchandise [1086].

[**160**] The king came immediately and entered the ships, telling some of his men that he entered them as securely as into his own houses [1087]. He told us that he was greatly astonished at our intention to depart so soon, since the limit of time for lading the ships was thirty days; and that he had not left the island to do us any harm, but to supply the ships with cloves sooner; and that we should not depart then for that was not the season for sailing among those islands, both because of the many shoals found about Bandan and because we might easily meet some Portuguese ships [in those seas]; however, if it were our determination to depart then, we should take all our merchandise, for all the kings roundabout would say that the king of Tidore had received so many presents from so great a king, and had given nothing in return; and that they would think that we had departed only for fear of some treachery, and would always call him a traitor [1088]. Then he had his Koran brought, and first kissing it and placing it four or five times upon his head, and saying certain words to himself as he did so (which they call *zambahean*),[334] he declared in the presence of all, that he swore by Allah and by the Koran that he had in his hand, that he would always be a faithful friend to the king of Spain [1089]. He spoke all those words nearly in tears [1090]. In return for his good words, we promised to wait another fifteen days [1091]. Thereupon, we gave him the signature of the king and the royal banner [1092]. None the less, we heard afterward on good authority that some of the chiefs of those islands had proposed to him to have us killed because it would give the greatest pleasure to the Portuguese, and that the latter would forgive those of Batjan, but the king had replied that he would not do it under any circumstances since he had recognized the king of Spain and had made peace with him [1093].

[**161**] After dinner on Wednesday, 27 November, the king had an edict proclaimed that all those who had cloves could bring them to the ships [1094]. All that and the next day, we bartered for cloves like mad [1095].

[162] On Friday afternoon, the governor of Makian came with a considerable number of praus [1096]. He refused to disembark, for his father and one of his brothers who had been banished from Makian were living in Tidore [1097].[335]

[163] The next day, our king and his nephew, the governor, entered the ships [1098]. As we had no more cloth, the king sent to have three cubits of his brought and gave it to us, and we gave it with other things to the governor [1099]. At his departure we discharged many pieces [1100]. Afterwards the king sent us six cubits of red cloth, so that we might give it to the governor [1101]. We immediately presented it to the latter, and he thanked us heartily for it, telling us . that he would send us a goodly quantity of cloves [1102]. That governor's name is Humar, and he was about twenty-five years old [1103].

[164] On Sunday, 1 December, that governor departed [1104]. We were told that the king of Tidore had given him some silk cloth and some of those metal discs so that he might send the cloves quicker [1105].

[165] On Monday, the king went off the island to get cloves [1106].

[166] On Wednesday morning, since it was the feast of St Barbara,[336] and because the king came, all the artillery was discharged [1107]. At night the king came to the shore, and asked to see how we fired our rockets and firebombs, at which he was highly delighted [1108].

[167] On Thursday and Friday, we bought many cloves both in the city and in the ships: for four cubits of Frisian cloth, they gave us one *bahar* of cloves; for two brass chains, worth one *marcello*,[337] they gave us one hundred pounds of cloves [1109]. Finally, when we had no more merchandise, one man gave his cloak, another his doublet, and another his shirt, besides other articles of clothing, in order that they might have their share[338] in the cargo [1110].

[168] On Saturday, three of the sons of the king of Ternate and their three wives, the daughters of our king, and Pietro Alfonso, the Portuguese, came to the ships [1111]. We gave each of the three brothers a gilt glass drinking cup, and scissors and other things to the women [1112]. Many pieces were discharged at their departure [1113]. Then we sent ashore many things to the daughter of our king, now the wife of the king of Ternate, as she refused to come to the ships with the others [1114]. All those people, both men and women, always go barefoot [1115].

[169] On Sunday, 8 December, as it was the feast of the Immaculate Conception, we fired many pieces, rockets, and firebombs [1116].

[170] On Monday afternoon, the king came to the ships with three women, who carried his betel for him (no one except the king can take women with him) [1117]. Afterwards the king of Gilolo came and wished to see us fight together again [1118].

[171] Several days later, our king told us that he was like a child at the breast who knew his dear mother was departing and was leaving him alone;[339] he would be especially disconsolate because now he had become acquainted with us and enjoyed some of the products of Spain, and our return would be far in the future [1119]. He earnestly entreated us to leave him some of our culverins for his defence and advised us to sail only by day when we left, because of the numerous shoals amidst those islands [1120].

We replied to him that if we wished to reach Spain we would have to sail day and night [1121]. Thereupon, he told us that he would pray daily to his god for us, asking him to conduct us in safety, and he told us that the king of Batjan was about to come to marry one of his brothers to one of his [the king of Tidore's] daughters [1122]. He asked us to invent some entertainment in token of joy; but that we should not fire the large pieces, because they would do great damage to the ships as they were laden [1123].

[172] During that time, Pietro Alfonso, the Portuguese, came with his wife and all his other possessions to remain in the ships [1124].

[173] Two days later, Chechili de Roix, son of the king of Ternate, came in a well-manned prau and asked the Portuguese to come down into it for a few moments [1125]. The Portuguese answered that he would not come down, for he was going to Spain with us [1126]. The king's son tried to enter the ship, but we refused to allow him to come aboard [1127]. He was a close friend to the Portuguese captain of Malacca, and had come to seize the Portuguese, and he severely scolded those who lived near the Portuguese because they had allowed the latter to go without his permission [1128].

[174] On Sunday afternoon, 15 December, the king of Batjan and his brother came in a prau with three tiers of rowers at each side [1129]. In all, there were 120 rowers who carried many banners made of white, yellow, and red parrot feathers, sounding loudly the metal

discs (for the rowers kept time in their rowing to those sounds); he brought two other praus filled with girls to present them to his betrothed [1130]. When they passed near the ships, we saluted them by firing pieces, and they in order to salute us went round the ships and the port [1131]. Our king came to congratulate him, since it is not the custom for any king to disembark on the land of another king [1132]. When the king of Batjan saw our king coming, he rose from the carpet on which he was seated and took his position at one side of it [1133]. Our king refused to sit down upon the carpet, but on its opposite side, and so no one occupied the carpet [1134]. The king of Batjan gave our king five hundred *patols*[340] because our king was giving his daughter as wife to the former's brother [1035]. The said *patols* are cloths of gold and silk manufactured in China and are highly esteemed by them [1136]. Whenever one of those people dies, the other members of his family dress themselves in those cloths in order to show the dead man more honour [1137]. They give three *bahars* of cloves for one of those cloths or thereabouts, according to their value [1138].

[175] On Monday our king sent a banquet to the king of Batjan, brought by fifty women all clad in silk garments from the waist to the knees [1139]. They went two by two with a man between each pair [1140]. Each of them bore a large tray filled with other small dishes that contained various kinds of food [1141]. The men carried nothing but the wine in large jars [1142]. Ten of the oldest women acted as mace bearers [1143]. Thus did they go as far as to the prau where they presented everything to the king, who was sitting upon the carpet under a red and yellow canopy [1144]. As they were returning, those women captured some of our men and it was necessary to give them some little trifle in order to regain their freedom [1145]. After that our king sent us goats, coconuts, wine, and other things [1146]. That day[341] we put new sails on the ships, upon which there was a cross of St James of Galicia,[342] with an inscription that read: 'This is the sign of our good fortune' [1147].

[176] On Tuesday, we gave our king certain artillery pieces resembling harquebuses, which we had captured in those Indies, and some of our culverins, together with four barrels of powder [1148]. At that place we took aboard eighty casks of water in each ship [1149]. Five

days previously, the king had sent one hundred men to cut wood for us at the island of Mareh,[343] because we were to pass by there [1150]. On that day,[344] the king of Batjan and many of his men came ashore to make peace with us [1151]. Four men with drawn daggers in their hands walked before the king [1152]. In the presence of our king and all the others, he said that he would always be at the service of the king of Spain, and that he would hold in his name the cloves left by the Portuguese until the arrival of another of our fleets, and he would never give them to the Portuguese without our consent [1153].

He sent to the king of Spain a slave, two *bahars* of cloves (he sent ten, but the ships could not carry them as they were so heavily laden), and two extremely beautiful dead birds as presents [1154]. Those birds are as large as stock doves, and have a small head and a long beak; their legs are a span in length and as thin as a reed, and they have no wings, but in their stead long feathers of various colours, like large plumes; their tail resembles that of a stock dove; all the rest of the feathers except the wings are of a tawny colour; they never fly except when there is wind [1155].

The people told us that those birds came from the terrestrial paradise, and they call them *bolon diuata*, that is to say, 'birds of God' [1156].[345]

Each one of the kings of Molucca wrote to the king of Spain [to say] that they desired to be always his true subjects [1157]. The king of Batjan was about seventy years old, and he observed the following custom: whenever he was about to go to war or to undertake any other important thing, he first had it done to him two or three times by one of his servants whom he kept for no other purpose [1158].[346]

[177] One day our king sent to tell our men who were living in the house with the merchandise not to go out of the house by night, because of certain of his men who anoint themselves and roam abroad by night, and they appear to follow no leader [1159].[347] When any of them meets any other man, he touches the latter's hand and rubs a little of the ointment on him [1160]. The man falls sick very soon, and dies within three or four days; and when such persons meet three or four together, they do nothing else than to deprive them of their senses; [the king said] that he had had many

of them hanged [1161]. When those people build a new house, before they move in they make a fire around it and hold many feasts; then they fasten to the roof of the house a trifle of everything found in the island so that such things may never be wanting to the inhabitants [1162]. Ginger is found throughout those islands: we ate it green like bread [1163]. Ginger is not a tree, but a small plant that puts forth from the ground certain shoots a span in length that resemble reeds, and whose leaves resemble those of the reed, except that they are narrower [1164]. Those shoots are worthless, but the roots form the ginger, and it is not so strong green as dry [1165]. Those people dry it in lime, for otherwise it would not keep [1166].

[178] On Wednesday morning, as we desired to depart from Molucca, the king of Tidore, the king of Gilolo, the king of Batjan, and a son of the king of Ternate all came to accompany us to the island of Mareh [1167]. The ship *Victoria* set sail, and stood out a little awaiting the ship *Trinidad*, but the latter, not being able to weigh anchor, suddenly began to leak in the bottom [1168]. Thereupon, the *Victoria* returned to its anchorage, and we immediately began to lighten the *Trinidad* in order to see whether we could repair it [1169]. We heard that the water was rushing in as through a pipe, but we were unable to find where it was coming in [1170]. All that day and the next, we did nothing but work the pump, but to no avail [1171]. When our king heard about it, he came immediately to the ships, and went to considerable trouble to locate the leak [1172]. He sent five of his men into the water to see whether they could discover the hole [1173]. They remained more than half an hour underwater, but were quite unable to find the leak [1174]. The king, seeing that he could not help us and that the water was increasing by the hour, almost in tears, said that he would send to the head of the island for three men, who could remain underwater a long time [1175].

[179] Our king came with the three men early on Friday morning, and he immediately sent the men into the water with their hair hanging loose so that they could locate the leak by that means [1176]. They stayed a full hour under water but were quite unable to locate it [1177]. When the king saw that he could be of no assistance, he asked us weeping 'who will go to Spain to my sovereign, and give him news

of me' [1178]. We answered him that the *Victoria* would go there in order not to lose the east winds that were beginning to blow, while the other ship, as it was being refitted, would await the west winds and then go to Darien,[348] which is located on the other side of the sea in the country of Yucatan [1179].

The king told us that he had 225 carpenters who would do all the work, that he would treat all who remained there as if they were his sons, and that they would not need to work except for two of them needed to direct the carpenters in their work [1180]. He spoke those words so earnestly that he made all of us weep [1181]. We, of the ship *Victoria*,[349] worried that the ship might break open, as it was too heavily laden, lightened it of sixty quintals of cloves, which we had carried into the house where the other cloves were [1182]. Some of the men from our ship wanted to remain there, since they feared that the ship would not survive the voyage to Spain, but they feared dying of hunger even more [1183].

[180] On the feast of St Thomas, Saturday, 21 December, our king came to the ships and assigned us the two pilots whom we had paid to conduct us out of those islands; they said that it was the proper time to leave then, but as our men were still writing letters to Spain, we did not leave until noon [1184]. When that hour came, the ships bid one another farewell amid the discharge of the cannon, and it seemed as though they were bewailing their last goodbye [1185]. Our men [who were to remain] accompanied us in their boats a short distance, and then with many tears and embraces we departed [1186]. The king's governor accompanied us as far as the island of Mareh [1187]. We had no sooner arrived at that island than four praus laden with wood appeared, and in less than one hour, we stowed it aboard the ship and then immediately laid our course toward the south west [1188]. João Carvalho[350] stayed there with fifty-three of our men [1189]. We were forty-seven men and thirteen Indians [1190]. This island of Tidore has a bishop,[351] and he who then exercised that office had forty wives and a multitude of children [1191].

[181] Throughout those islands of Molucca are found cloves, ginger, sago (which is their wood bread), rice, goats, geese, chickens, coconuts, figs [bananas], almonds larger than ours, sweet and tasty

pomegranates, oranges, lemons, potatoes, honey produced by bees as small as ants, which make their honey in the trees, sugar cane, coconut oil, beneseed oil, watermelons, wild cucumbers, gourds, a refreshing fruit as large as cucumbers called *comulicai*,[352] another fruit, like the peach, called *guave*,[353] and other kinds of food [1192]. One also finds there parrots of various kinds, and among the other varieties, some white ones called *cathara*, and some entirely red called *nori*;[354] one of those red ones is worth one *bahar* of cloves, and that class speaks with greater distinctness than the others [1193]. Those Moors have lived in Molucca for about fifty years; heathens lived there before, but they did not value the cloves [1194]. There are still some of the latter, but they live in the mountains where the cloves grow [1195].

[182] The island of Tidore lies in a latitude of twenty-seven minutes toward the Arctic Pole, and in a longitude of 161 degrees from the line of demarcation; it is nine and one-half degrees south of the first island of the archipelago called Samar, and extends north by east and south by west; Ternate lies in a latitude of two-thirds of a degree toward the Arctic Pole; Motir lies exactly under the equinoctial line; Makian lies in one quarter degree toward the Antarctic Pole, and Batjan also toward the Antarctic Pole in one degree [1196].[355] Ternate, Tidore, Motir, and Makian are four lofty and peaked mountains where the cloves grow [1197]. When one is in those four islands, he cannot see Batjan, but it is larger than any of those four islands; its clove mountain is not so sharp as the others, but it is larger [1198].

Words of those Moors [1199]:[356]

1] For their God *Alla*	9] For their devout men *mossai*
2] For Christians *naceran*	10] For their ceremonies
3] For Turk *rumno*[357]	*zambahehan de ala meschit*
4] For Moor *isilam*	11] For father *bapa*
5] For heathen *caphre*	12] For mother *mama ambui*
6] For their mosque *mischit*	13] For son *anach*
7] For their priests *maulana*,	14] For brother *saudala*
catip, mudin	15] For brother of so-and-so
8] For their wise men *horan pandita*	*capatin muiadi*[358]

16] For cousin *saudala sopopu*
17] For grandfather *niny*
18] For father-in-law *minthua*
19] For son-in-law *minanthu*
20] For man *horan*
21] For woman *poranpoan*
22] For hair *lambut*
23] For head *capala*
24] For forehead *dai*
25] For eye *matta*
26] For eyelashes *quilai*
27] For eyelids *cenin*[359]
28] For nose *idon*
29] For mouth *mulut*
30] For lips *bebere*
31] For teeth *gigi*
32] For gums *issi*
33] For tongue *lada*
34] For palate *langhi*
35] For chin *aghai*
36] For beard *ianghut*
37] For moustache *missai*
38] For jaw *pipi*[360]
39] For ear *talingha*
40] For throat *laher*
41] For neck *tundun*
42] For shoulders *balachan*[361]
43] For breast *dada*
44] For heart *atti*
45] For teat *sussu*
46] For stomach *parut*
47] For body *tundunbutu*
48] For penis *botto*
49] For vagina *bucchij*
50] For intercourse with women *amput*
51] For buttocks *buri*
52] For things *taha*
53] For leg *mina*
54] For the shinbone of the leg *tula*
55] For its calf *tilor chaci*[362]
56] For ankle *buculali*
57] For heel *tumi*
58] For foot *batis*
59] For the sole of the foot *empachaqui*
60] For fingernail *cuchu*
61] For arm *langhan*
62] For elbow *sichu*
63] For hand *tanghan*
64] For large finger of the hand (thumb) *idum tanghan*
65] For the second finger *tungu*
66] For the third *geri*
67] For the fourth *mani*
68] For the fifth *calinchin*
69] For rice *bugax*[363]
70] For coconut in Molucca and Borneo *biazzao*
71] For coconut in Luzon *nior*
72] For coconut in Java Major *calambil*[364]
73] For banana *pizan*[365]
74] For sugar cane *tubu*[366]
75] For potatoes *gumbili*
76] For roots (like turnips) *ubi*
77] For jackfruit *mandicai sicui*[367]
78] For cucumbers *antimon*
79] For gourd *labu*[368]
80] For cow *lambu*
81] For hog *babi*

82] For buffalo *carbau*
83] For sheep *birj*
84] For she-goat *cambin*
85] For cock *sambunghan*[369]
86] For hen *aiambatina*
87] For capon *gubili*
88] For egg *talor*
89] For gander *itich*
90] For goose *ansa*
91] For bird *bolon*
92] For elephant *gagia*
93] For horse *cuda*
94] For lion *hurimau*[370]
95] For deer *roza*
96] For dog *cuiu*[371]
97] For bees *haermadu*
98] For honey *gulla*
99] For wax *lelin*[372]
100] For candle *dian*
101] For its wick *sumbudian*
102] For fire *appi*
103] For smoke *asap*
104] For ashes *abu*
105] For cooked *azap*[373]
106] For well cooked *lambech*
107] For water *tubi*
108] For gold *amax*
109] For silver *pirac*
110] For precious gems *premata*
111] For pearls *mutiara*
112] For quicksilver *raza*
113] For copper *tumbaga*
114] For iron *baci*
115] For lead *tima*
116] For their metal discs
     agun[374]

117] For cinnabar *galuga*
     sadalinghan
118] For silver *soliman davas*[375]
119] For silk cloth *cain sutra*
120] For red cloth *cain mira*
121] For black cloth *cain ytam*
122] For white cloth *cain pute*
123] For green cloth *cain igao*
124] For yellow cloth *cain cunin*
125] For cap *cophia*
126] For knife *pixao*
127] For scissors *guntin*
128] For mirror *chiela min*
129] For comb *sisir*
130] For glass bead *manich*
131] For bell *girin girin*
132] For ring *sinsin*
133] For cloves *ghianche*[376]
134] For cinnamon *caiumanis*
135] For pepper *lada*
136] For long pepper *sabi*
137] For nutmeg *buapala gosoga*
138] For copper wire *cauot*
139] For dish *pinghan*
140] For earthen pot *priu*
141] For pot *manchu*
142] For wooden dish *dulan*
143] For shell *calumpan*
144] For their measures *socat*[377]
145] For land *buchit*[378]
146] For mainland *buchit tana*
147] For mountain *gonun*
148] For rock *batu*
149] For island *polau*
150] For a point of land (a cape)
     banium buchit

151] For river *songhai*

152] For what is this called?
*apenamaito?*379

153] For coconut oil *mignach*

154] For beneseed oil *lana lingha*

155] For salt *garan, sira*

156] For musk and its animal
*castori*380

157] For the wood eaten by the
castori *comaru*

158] For leech *linta*

159] For civet *iabat*

160] For the cat that makes the
civet *mozan*

161] For rhubarb *calama*

162] For demon *saytan*

163] For world *bumi*

164] For wheat *gandun*

165] For to sleep *tidor*

166] For mats *tical*

167] For cushion *bantal*

168] For pain *sachet*

169] For health *bay*381

170] For brush *cupia*

171] For fan *chipas*

172] For their cloths *chebun*

173] For their shirts *baiu*

174] For their chests
*pati, alam*382

175] For year *tuan*

176] For month *bullan*

177] For day *alli*

178] For night *mallan*

179] For afternoon *malamarj*

180] For noon *tamhahari*

181] For morning *patan patan*383

182] For sun *matahari*

183] For moon *bulan*

184] For half-moon *tanam
patbulan*

185] For stars *bintan*

186] For sky *langum*

187] For thunder *gunthur*

188] For merchants *sandagar*

189] For city *naghiri*

190] For castle *cuta*

191] For house *ruma*

192] For to sit *duodo*

193] For sit down, sir *duodo,
orancaia*

194] For sit down, good fellow
duodo, horanbai et anan

195] For lord *tuan*

196] For boy *cana cana*

197] For one of their pupils
lascar

198] For slave *alipin*

199] For yes *ca*

200] For no *tida*

201] For to understand *thao*

202] For to not understand
tida taho

203] For do not look at me
tida liat

204] For look at me *liat*

205] For to be one and the same
thing *casi casi, siama siama*

206] For to kill *mati*

207] For to eat *macan*

208] For spoon *sandoch*

209] For prostitute *sondal*384

210] For large *bassal*

211] For long *pongian*

212] For small *chechil*

213] For short *pandach*

214] For to have *ada*

215] For not to have *tida hada*

216] For listen, sir *tuan, diam*[385]

217] For where did the junk go?
dimana aiun?

218] For sewing needle *ialun*

219] For to sew *banan*

220] For sewing thread
pintal banan[386]

221] For woman's headdress
dastar capala

222] For king *raia*

223] For queen *putli*

224] For wood *caiu*

225] For to work *caraiar*

226] For to take recreation
buandala

227] For the vein of the arm
where one is bled *urat
paratanghan*

228] For the blood of the arm
dara carval

229] For good blood *dara*

230] When they sneeze they say:
ebarasai[387]

231] For fish *ycam*

232] For polypus *calabutan*

233] For meat *dagin*

234] For sea snail *cepot*

235] For little *serich*

236] For half *satanha sapanghal*

237] For cold *dinghin*

238] For hot *panas*

239] For far *iau*

240] For truth *benar*

241] For lie *dusta*

242] For to steal *manchiuri*

243] For scab *codis*

244] For take *na*

245] Give to me *ambil*

246] For fat *gamuch*

247] For thin *golos*

248] For hair *tundun capala*

249] How many *barapa*

250] Once *satu chali*

251] One cubit *dapa*

252] For to speak *catha*

253] For here *sini*

254] For there *sana datan*

255] Good day *salamalichum*

256] For the answer [to good
day] *alichum salam*

257] Sirs, may good fortune
attend you *mali horancaia
macan*[388]

258] I have eaten already
suda macan

259] Fellow, get out of the way!
pandan, chita horan!

260] For to wake up
banunchan[389]

261] Good evening *sabalchaer*[390]

262] For the answer [to good
evening] *chaer sandat*

263] For to give *minta*

264] To strike someone *bripocol*

265] For iron fetters *balanghu*

266] Oh, what a smell! *bossochini!*

267] For young man *horan muda*

268] For old man *tua*
269] For scribe *xiritoles*391
270] For writing paper *cartas*
271] For to write *mangurat*
272] For pen *calam*
273] For ink *dauat*
274] For ink bottle *padautan*
275] For letter *surat*
276] I do not have it *guala*
277] Come here *camarj!*
278] What do you want?
   appa mau?
279] Who sent you? *appa ito?*
280] For seaport *labuan*
281] For galley *gurap*
282] For ship *capal*
283] For the bow *allon*
284] For the stern *biritan*
285] For to navigate *belaiar*
286] For the ship's mast *tian*
287] For yard [of a ship] *laiar*
288] For the rigging *tamira*
289] For sail *leier*
290] For the maintop *sinbulaia*
291] For the anchor rope *danda*
292] For anchor *sau*
293] For boat *sanpan*392
294] For oar *daiun*
295] For mortar [cannon] *badil*
296] For wind *anghin*
297] For sea *laut*393
298] Fellow, come here *horan,*
   itu datan!
299] For their dagger *calyx, golog*
300] For their dagger hilt
   daganan

301] For sword *padan, gole*
302] For blowpipe *sumpitan*
303] For their arrows *damach*
304] For poisonous herb *ypu*
305] For quiver *bolo*
306] For bow (weapon) *bossor*
307] For its arrows *anac paan*
308] For cats *cochin, puchia*
309] For rat *ticug*
310] For lizard *buaia*394
311] For shipworms *capan, lotos*
312] For fish-hook *matacauir*
313] For fish bait *unpan*
314] For fishing line *tunda*
315] For to wash *mandi*
316] Not to be afraid *iangan tacut*
317] Fatigue *lala*
318] A sweet kiss *sadap, manis*395
319] For friend *saudara*
320] For enemy *saubat*
321] It is certain *zonghu*
322] For to barter *biniaga*
323] I have not *auis*
324] To be a friend *pugna*
325] Two things *malupho*
326] If *oue*
327] Pimp *zoroan, pagnoro*
328] To give pleasure *mamani*
329] To be horrified *amala*396
330] For madman *gila*
331] For interpreter *giorobaza*
332] How many languages do you
   know? *barapa bahasa tau?*
333] Many *bagna*
334] The language of Malacca
   chiaramalaiu

335] Where is so and so? *dimana horan?*
336] For flag *tonghol*
337] Now *sacaran*
338] In the morning *hozoch*
339] The next day *luza*
340] Yesterday *calamarj*
341] For hammer *palmo colbasi*
342] For nail *pacu*
343] For mortar *lozon*
344] For pestle *atan*
345] For to dance *manarj*
346] For to pay *baiar*
347] For to call *panghil*
348] Unmarried *ugan*
349] Married *suda babini*
350] All one *samua*
351] For rain *ugian*
352] For drunken man *moboch*
353] For skin *culit*
354] For snake *ullat*
355] For to fight *guzar*
356] Sweet *manis*
357] Bitter *azon*
358] How are you? *appa giadi*397
359] Well *bay*
360] Poorly *sachet*
361] Bring me that *biriacan!*
362] This man is lazy *giadi hiat horan itu*
363] Enough *suda*
The winds:
364] For the north *iraga*
365] For the south *salatan*
366] For the east *timor*

367] For the west *baratapat*
368] For the north-west *utara*
369] For the south-west *berdaia*
370] For the north-east *bardaut*
371] For the south-east *tunghara*
Numbers:398
372] One *satus*
373] Two *dua*
374] Three *tiga*
375] Four *ampat*
376] Five *lima*
377] Six *anam*
378] Seven *tugu*
379] Eight *duolappan*
380] Nine *sambilan*
381] Ten *sapolo*
382] Twenty *duapolo*
383] Thirty *tigapolo*
384] Forty *ampatpolo*
385] Fifty *limapolo*
386] Sixty *anampolo*
387] Seventy *tuguppolo*
388] Eighty *dualapanpolo*
389] Ninety *sambilampolo*
390] One hundred *saratus*
391] Two hundred *duaratus*
392] Three hundred *tigaratus*
393] Four hundred *anamparatus*
394] Five hundred *limaratus*
395] Six hundred *anambratus*
396] Seven hundred *tugurattus*
397] Eight hundred *dualapanratus*
398] Nine hundred *sambilanratus*
399] One thousand *salibu*
400] Two thousand *dualibu*

401] Three thousand *tigalibu*
402] Four thousand *ampatlibu*
403] Five thousand *limalibu*
404] Six thousand *anamlibu*
405] Seven thousand *tugu libu*
406] Eight thousand *dualapanlibu*
407] Nine thousand *sanbilanlibu*
408] Ten thousand *salacza*
409] Twenty thousand *dualacza*
410] Thirty thousand *tigalacza*
411] Forty thousand *ampatlacza*
412] Fifty thousand *limalacza*
413] Sixty thousand *anamlacza*
414] Seventy thousand *tugulacza*
415] Eighty thousand *dualapanlacza*
416] Ninety thousan *sambilanlacza*
417] One hundred thousand *sacati*

418] Two hundred thousand *duacati*
419] Three hundred thousand *tigacati*
420] Four hundred thousand *ampatcati*
421] Five hundred thousand *limacati*
422] Six hundred thousand *anamcati*
423] Seven hundred thousand *tugucati*
424] Eight hundred thousand *dualapancati*
425] Nine hundred thousand *sambilancati*
426] One million [literally: ten times one hundred thousand] *saiuta*

All the hundreds, the thousands, the tens of thousands, the hundreds of thousands, and the millions are joined with the numbers *satus*, *dua*, etc. [1200].

[183] Proceeding on our course we passed amidst these islands: Caioan, Laigoma, Sico, Giogi, and Caphi (in the island of Caphi is found a race as small as dwarfs, who are amusing people: these are the pigmies,399 and they have been subjected by force to our king of Tidore), Laboan, Tolimau, Titameti, Batjan, of which we have already spoken, Latalata, Tabobi, Maga, and Batutiga [1201].400 Passing outside the latter on its western side, we laid our course west-south-west, and discovered many islets toward the south; since the Moluccan pilots told us to abandon ourselves to the winds, we found ourselves amongst many islands and shoals [1202]. We turned our course south-east, and encountered an island that lies in a latitude of two degrees toward the Antarctic Pole, and fifty-five leagues from Molucca, called Sulach [1203].401

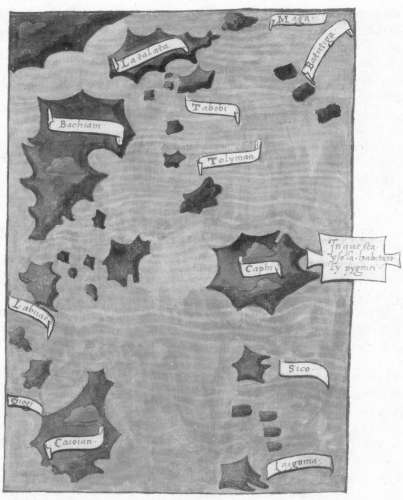

*[Chart of Maga, Batutiga, Caphi (Gafi), Sico, Laigoma, Caioian (Kajoa),
Giogi (Goraitji?), Labuac (Labuha), Bachiam (Batjan), Tolyman (Tolimau),
Tabobi, Latalata and the scroll next to Caphi: 'In this island live the Pygmies'
(XVIII)]*

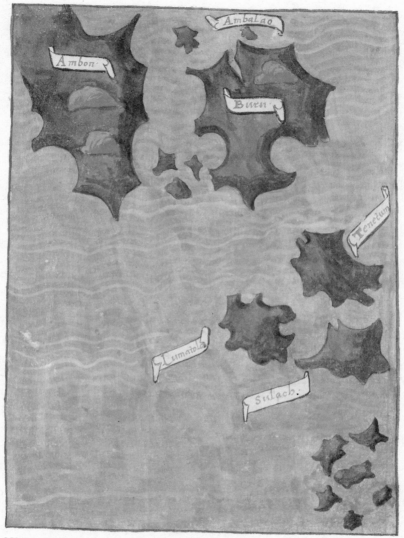

[Chart of the islands of Ambalao (Ambelou), Buru, Tenetum, Lumatola (Lifamatola), Sulach (Sula Besi), and Ambon (Amboina) (XIX)][402]

[184] Its inhabitants are heathens, and have no king; they eat human flesh, go naked, both men and women, only wearing a bit of bark two fingers wide covering their private parts [1204]. There are many islands thereabout where they eat human flesh; the names of some of them are as follows: Silan, Noselao, Biga, Atulabaou, Leitimor, Tenetun, Gondia, Pailarurun, Manadan, and Benaia [1205]. Then we coasted along two islands called Lamatola and Tenetun [1206]. *[Chart XIX appears here in original.]*

[185] Lying about ten leagues from Sulach,[403] in that same course, we encountered a very large island where one finds rice, swine, goats, fowls, coconuts, sugar cane, sago, a food made from one of their varieties of figs [Bananas] called *chanali*, *chiacare* (these are called *nangha*:[404] *chiacare* are a fruit resembling the cucumber: they are knotty on the outside, and inside they have a certain small red fruit like the apricot; it contains no stone, but has instead a marrowy substance resembling a bean but larger and having a delicate taste like chestnuts), and a fruit like the pineapple, yellow outside and white inside, that when cut is like a pear, but more tender and much better and called *connilicai* [1207].[405]

The inhabitants of that island go naked as do those of Solach; they are heathens and have no king [1208]. That island lies in a latitude of three and one-half degrees toward the Antarctic Pole, and is seventy-five leagues from Molucca, and its name is Buru [1209].[406] Ten leagues east of the above island is a large island that is bounded by Gilolo and that is inhabited by Moors and heathens [1210]. The Moors live near the sea, and the heathens in the interior, and the latter eat human flesh [1211]. The products mentioned are produced in that island, and [that island] is called Amboina [1212].[407] Between Buru and Amboina are found three islands surrounded by reefs, called Vudia, Cailaruri, and Benaia [1213].[408] Near Buru, and about four leagues to the south, is a small island called Ambelou [1214].[409] *[Chart XX appears here in original.]*

[186] About thirty-five leagues to the south by west of the above island of Buru is found Bandan [1215]. Bandan consists of twelve islands [1216].[410] Mace and nutmeg grow in six of them, and their names are as follows: Zoroboa, the largest of them all, and the others, Chelicel, Samianapi, Pulae, Pulurun, and Rosoghin [1217]. The other six are as follows: Unuveru, Pulaubaracan, Lailaca, Manucan, Man,

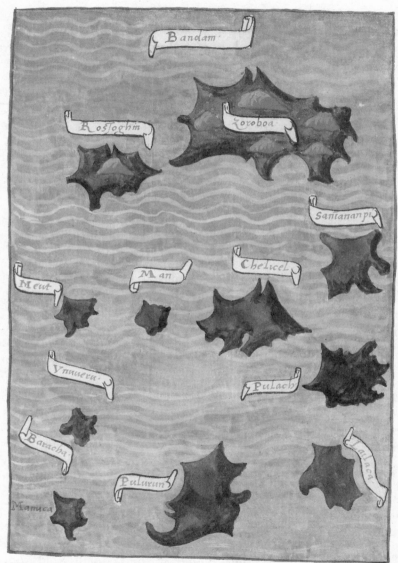

[Chart of Bandan including the islands of Bandam, Zoroboa, Samianapi, Chelicel, Pulach (Ai), Lailaca, Puluran (Rhun), Manuca (Manucan), Baracha, Unuveru, Meut, Man, Rosoghin (Rosengain) (XX)]

and Meut [1218]. Nutmeg is not found in them, but only sago, rice, coconuts, figs, and other fruits; those islands are located near one another [1219]. Their inhabitants are Moors and they have no king [1220]. Bandan lies in a latitude of six degrees toward the Antarctic Pole, and in a longitude of 163 and one-half degrees from the line of demarcation, and as it was somewhat outside of our course, we did not go there [1221]. *[Chart XXI appears here in original.]*

[187] Leaving the above-mentioned island of Buru, and taking the course toward the south-west by west, we reached, [after sailing through] about eight degrees of longitude, three islands, quite near together, called Zolot, Nocemamor, and Galiau [1222].[411] While sailing amidst them, we were struck by a fierce storm, which caused us to vow a pilgrimage to Our Lady of Guidance,[412] and running before the storm, we landed at a lofty island,[413] but before reaching it we were greatly worn out by the violent gusts of wind that came from the mountains of that island, and the great currents of water [1223]. The inhabitants of that island are savage and bestial, eat human flesh, and have no king; they go naked, wearing only that bark as do the others, except that when they go to fight they wear certain pieces of buffalo hide before, behind, and at the sides, which are ornamented with small shells, boars' tusks, and tails of goat skins fastened before and behind [1224]. They wear their hair done up high and held by certain long reed pins that they pass from one side to the other, which keep the hair high; they wear their beards wrapped in leaves and thrust into small bamboo tubes (a ridiculous sight); they are the ugliest people who live in those Indies [1225]. Their bows and arrows are of bamboo, and they have a kind of a sack made from the leaves of a tree in which their women carry their food and drink [1226]. When those people caught sight of us, they came to meet us with bows, but after we had given them some presents, we immediately became their friends [1227].

[188] We remained there fifteen days in order to caulk the sides of the ship [1228]. In that island are found fowls, goats, coconuts, wax (of which they gave us fifteen pounds for one pound of old iron), and pepper, both long and round [1229]. The long pepper resembles the first blossoms of the hazelnut in winter [1230]. Its plant resembles

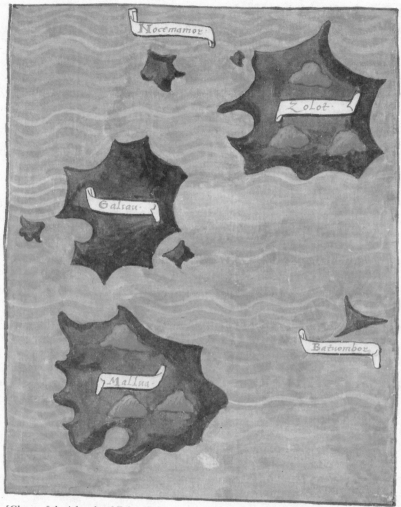

[Chart of the islands of Zolot (Solor, Batuombor, Mallua (Alor), Galiau (Lmblen?),
Nocemamor (Nobokamor) (XXI)]

ivy, and it clings to trees like that plant; but its leaves resemble those of the mulberry; it is called *luli* [1231]. The round pepper grows like the former, but in ears like Indian corn, and is shelled off; it is called *lada* [1232].[414] The fields in those regions are full of this [last variety of] pepper, planted to resemble arbours [1233]. We captured a man in that place so that he might take us to some island where we could lay in provisions [1234]. That island lies in a latitude of eight and one-half degrees toward the Antarctic Pole, and a longitude of 169 and two-thirds degrees from the line of demarcation; and is called Malua [1235].

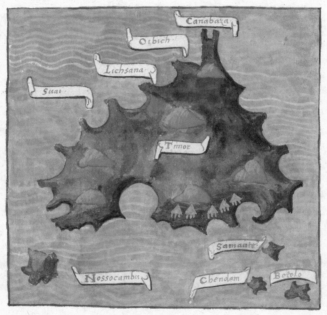

[Chart of the island of Timor, Botolo, Chendam, Samante, Nossocambu, and the capes on Timor including Suai, Lichsana (Líquicá?), Oibich, Canabaza (XXII)]

[189] Our old pilot from Molucca told us that there was an island nearby called Arucheto,[415] the men and women of which are not taller than one cubit, but who have ears as long as themselves: with

one of them they make their bed and with the other they cover themselves [1236].[416] They go shaven close and quite naked, run swiftly, and have shrill voices; they live in caves underground, and subsist on fish and a substance that grows between the wood and the bark [of a tree], which is white and round like preserved coriander and is called *ambulon*; however, we did not go there because of the strong currents of water, and the numerous shoals [1237].

[190] On Saturday, 25 January 1522, we left the island of Malua,[417] and on Sunday, the twenty-sixth, we reached a large island[418] that lies five leagues to the south-south-west of Malua [1238]. I went ashore alone to speak to the chief of a city called Amabau[419] to ask him to furnish us with food [1239]. He told me that he would give us buffaloes, swine, and goats, but we could not come to terms because he asked many things for one buffalo [1240]. Inasmuch as we had but few things, and hunger was constraining us, we retained in the ship a chief and his son from another village called Balibo;[420] he, for fear lest we kill him, immediately gave us six buffaloes, five goats, and two swine, and to complete the number of ten swine and ten goats [which we had demanded], they gave us one [additional] buffalo, for thus we had placed the condition [of their ransom] [1241]. Then we sent them ashore very well pleased with linen, Indian cloth of silk and cotton, hatchets, Indian knives, scissors, mirrors, and knives [1242].

[191] That chief to whom I went to talk had only women to serve him [1243]. All the women go naked like the other women [of the islands], and in their ears they wear small earrings of gold, with silk tassels hanging from them; on their arms they wear many gold and brass armlets as far as the elbow [1244]. The men go as the women, except that they fasten certain gold articles, round like a trencher, about their necks, and wear bamboo combs adorned with gold rings in their hair; some of them wear the necks of dried gourds in their ears in place of gold rings [1245].

[192] In that island is found white sandalwood (and nowhere else),[421] ginger, buffaloes, swine, goats, fowls, rice, figs [bananas], sugar cane, oranges, lemons, wax, almonds, beans, and other things, and

parrots of various colours [1246]. On the other side of the island are four brothers, who are the kings of that island [1247]. Where we were, there were towns and some of their chiefs [1248]. The names of the four settlements of the kings are as follows: Oibich, Lichsana, Suai, and Cabanaza [1249].⁴²² Oibich is the largest [1250]. There is a quantity of gold found in a mountain in Cabanaza, according to the report given us, and its inhabitants make all their purchases with little bits of gold [1251]. All the sandalwood and wax that is traded by the inhabitants of Java and Malacca is traded for in that region: there we found a junk from Luzon,⁴²³ which had come there to trade in sandalwood [1252].

Those people are heathens, and when they go to cut the sandalwood, the devil (according to what they told us) appears to them in various forms, and tells them that if they need anything they should ask him for it; as a result of that apparition, they become ill for some days [1253].

The sandalwood is cut at a certain time of the moon, for otherwise it would not be good [1254]. The merchandise valued in exchange for sandalwood there is red cloth, linen, hatchets, iron, and nails [1255].

[193] That island is inhabited in all parts, and extends for a long distance east and west, but is not very broad north and south; it lies in a latitude of ten degrees toward the Antarctic Pole, and in a longitude of 174 and one-half degrees from the line of demarcation, and is called Timor [1256]. The disease of St Job was to be found in all of the islands that we encountered in that archipelago, but more in that place than in others; it is called *for franchi*, that is to say, 'the Portuguese disease' [1257].⁴²⁴ *[Chart XXIII appears here in original.]*

[194] A day's journey from there toward the west-north-west, we were told that we would find an island where quantities of cinnamon grow, by name Ende⁴²⁵ (its inhabitants are heathens and have no king), and that there are also many islands in the same course, one following the other, as far as Java Major⁴²⁶ and the Cape of Malacca, and the names of those islands are as follows: Ende, Tanabutun, Crevochile, Bimacore, Aranaran, Main, Sumbava, Lomboch, Chorum, and Java Major (those inhabitants do not Call it Java but Jaoa) [1258].⁴²⁷ The largest cities are located in Java, and are as follows: Majapahit (when its king was alive, he was the most powerful in all

[Chart depicting 'Laut chidol, that is, the Great sea' (XXIII)]

those islands, and his name was Rajah PatiYunus); Sunda, where considerable pepper grows; Daha; Demak; Gaghiamada; Minutaranghan; Japara; Sedan; Tuban; Gresik; Surubaya; and Bali [1259].[428] Also, we were told that Java Minor is the island of Madura, and is located near to Java Major, [being only] one-half league away [1260].

[195] We were told also that when one of the chief men of Java dies, his body is burned [1261]. His principal wife adorns herself with garlands of flowers and has herself carried on a chair through the entire village by three or four men, and, smiling and consoling her relatives, who are weeping, she says: 'Do not weep, for I am going to sup with my dear husband this evening, and to sleep with him this night [1262].' Then she is carried to the fire where her husband is being burned, and, turning toward her relatives and again consoling them, she throws herself into the fire where her husband is being burned, and if she did not do this, she would not be considered an

honourable woman or a true wife to her dead husband [1263]. [429] When the young men of Java are in love with any gentlewoman, they fasten certain little bells between their penis and the foreskin, go beneath their sweetheart's window, and, making a pretence of urinating and shaking their penis, they make the little bells ring and continue to ring them until their sweetheart hears the sound; the sweetheart descends immediately, and they take their pleasure, always with those little bells, for their women take great pleasure in hearing those bells ring inside [1264]. Those bells are covered, and the more they are covered the louder they sound [1265].

Our oldest pilot told us that in an island called Ocoloro, which lies below Java Major, there are only women, and that they become pregnant from the wind, and when they give birth, if the offspring is a male, they kill it, but if it is a female they rear it; if men go to that island, they kill them if they can [1266].[430]

[196] They also told us that a very huge tree is found below Java Major toward the north, in the gulf of China (which the ancients call Sinus Magnus), in which live birds called *garuda*, which are so large that they carry a buffalo or an elephant to the place of that tree called *puzathaer*, and the tree is called *caiu paunganghi*, and its fruit *bua paunganghi*: the latter is larger than a cucumber [1267]. The Moors of Borneo whom we had in our ship told us that they had seen them, for their king had had two of them sent to him from the kingdom of Siam [1268]. No junk or other boat can approach to within three or four leagues of the place of the tree, because of the great whirlpools in the water round about it [1269]. The first time that anything was learned of that tree was [from] a junk that was driven by the winds into the whirlpool and beaten to pieces [1270]. The entire crew was drowned except a little boy, who, hanging on to a plank, was miraculously driven near that tree, and he climbed up into the tree without being aware of it, where he placed himself under the wing of one of those birds [1271]. The next day, the bird having gone ashore and having seized a buffalo, the boy came out from under the wing as best he could [1272]. The story was learned from him, and then the people nearby knew that the fruit they found in the sea came from that tree [1273].[431]

[197] The Cape of Malacca lies in one and one-half degrees toward the Antarctic Pole [1274].[432] Along the coast east of that cape are many villages and cities, and the names of some of them are as follows: Singapore, which is located on the cape; Panhang, Calantan, Pattani, Bradlun, Benan, Lagon, Khiri Khan, Chumpon, Pranburi, Cui, Rat Buri, Bangha,[433] Iudia[434] (which is the city where the king of Siam, by name Siri Zacabedera, lives), Iandibum, Lanu, and Langhonpifa [1275].[435] Those cities are built like ours, and are subject to the king of Siam [1276]. On the shores of the rivers of that kingdom of Siam live, as we were told, large birds that will not eat of any dead animal that may have been carried there, unless another bird comes first to eat its heart, after which they eat it [1277]. Next to Siam is found Camogia[436] (whose king is called Saret Zacabedera), then Chiempa[437] (whose king is Rajah Brahaun Maitri) [1278].

Rhubarb, collected in the following manner, grows there: twenty or twenty-five men assemble and go together into the forests [1279]. Upon the approach of night, they climb trees, both to see whether they can catch the scent of the rhubarb, and also for fear of the lions, elephants, and other wild beasts; the wind bears to them the odour of the rhubarb from the direction in which it is to be found [1280]. When morning dawns they go in that direction from which the wind has come, and seek the rhubarb until they find it [1281]. The rhubarb is a large rotten tree; and unless it has become rotten, it gives off no odour [1282]. The best part of that tree is the root, although the wood is also rhubarb, which is called *calama* [1283]. Next is found Cochi[438] (whose king is called Rajah Seribumnipala) [1284].

[198] After that country is found Great China, whose king, the greatest in all the world, is called Santhoa Rajah,[439] and has seventy crowned kings subject to himself, and some of the latter have ten or fifteen kings subject to them [1285]. His port is called Guantau;[440] among the multitude of other cities, there are two principal ones called Namchin and Comlaha[441] where the above king lives [1286]. He keeps four of his principal men near his palace, one toward the west, one toward the east, one toward the south, and one toward the north [1287]. Each one of those four men gives audience only to those who come from his own quarter [1288]. All the kings and lords

of greater and upper India obey that king; and in token that they are his true vassals, each one has an animal that is stronger than a lion, and called *chinga*,[442] carved in marble in the middle of his square [1289]. That *chinga* is the seal of the said king of China, and all those who go to China must have that animal carved in wax [or] on an elephant's tooth, for otherwise they would not be allowed to enter his harbour [1290].

When any lord is disobedient to that king, he is ordered to be flayed, and his skin dried in the sun and salted, and then the skin is stuffed with straw or other substance, and placed head downward in a prominent place in the square, with the hands clasped above the head, so that he may be seen then to be performing *zonghu*, that is, obeisance [1291].

That king never allows himself to be seen by anyone, and when he wishes to see his people, he rides about the palace on a skilfully made peacock, a most elegant contrivance, accompanied by six of his principal women clad like himself; after which he enters a serpent called *nagha*,[443] which is as rich a thing as can be seen and is kept in the greatest court of the palace [1292]. The king and the women enter it so that he may not be recognized among his women [1293]. He looks at his people through a large glass that is in the breast of the serpent; he and the women can be seen, but one cannot tell which is the king [1294]. The latter is married to his sisters, so that the blood royal may not be mixed with others [1295].

Near his palace are seven encircling walls, and in each of those circular places are stationed ten thousand men for the guard of the palace [who remain there] until a bell rings [1296]. Then ten thousand other men come for each circular space; they are changed in this manner each day and each night [1297].

Each circle of the wall has a gate: at the first stands a man with a large hook in his hand, called *satu horan* with *satu bagan*; in the second, a dog, called *satu hain*; in the third, a man with an iron mace, called *satu horan* with *pocum bicin*; in the fourth, a man with a bow in his hand, called *satu horan* with *anac panan*; in the fifth, a man with a spear, called *satu horan* with *tumach*; in the sixth, a lion, called *satu horimau*; in the seventh, two white elephants, called two *gagia pute* [1298].

That palace has seventy-nine halls that contain only women who serve the king, and torches are always kept lighted [1299]. It takes an entire day to visit the palace [1300]. In the upper part of it are four halls, where the principal men go sometimes to speak to the king: one is ornamented with copper, both below and above; one all with silver; one all with gold; and the fourth with pearls and precious gems [1301]. When the king's vassals take him gold or any other precious things as tribute, they are placed in those halls, and they say: 'Let this be for the honour and glory of our Santhoa Rajah [1302].' All the above and many other things were told us by a Moor who said that he had seen them [1303].

[199] The inhabitants of China are white and wear clothes, and they eat at tables as we do; they have the cross, but it is not known for what purpose [1304]. Musk is produced in that country of China: its animal is a cat like the civet cat, and it eats nothing except a sweet wood as thick as the finger called *chamaru* [1305]. When the Chinese wish to make the musk, they attach a leech to the cat, which they leave fastened there, until it is well distended with blood; then they squeeze the leech out into a dish and put the blood in the sun for four or five days [1306]. After that they sprinkle it with urine, and as often as they do that they place it in the sun, and thus it becomes perfect musk [1307]. Whoever owns one of those animals has to pay a certain sum to the king [1308]. Those grains that seem to be grains of musk are of kid's flesh crushed with a little musk [1309]. The real musk is of the aforesaid blood, and if the blood turns into grains, it evaporates [1310]. The musk and the cat are called *castori* and the leech *lintha* [1311].[444]

[200] Many peoples are to be found as one follows the coast of that country of China, which are as follows: the Chienchii[445] inhabit islands where pearls and cinnamon grow; the Lechii[446] live on the mainland (above their port stretches a mountain, so that all the junks and ships which desire to enter that port must unstep their masts) [1312]. The king on the mainland [is called] Moni:[447] he has twenty kings under him and is subordinate to the king of China; his city is called Baranaci; the great Oriental Cataio (Cathay) is located there [1313]. Han [is] a cold, lofty island[448] where copper, silver, pearls, and

silk are produced, whose king is called Rajah Zotru [1314]. The king of Miliaula is called Rajah Chetisirimiga [1315]. The king of Guio is Rajah Sudacali [1316]. All three of the above places are cold and are located on the mainland [1317]. Trengganu and Tringano [are] two islands where pearls, copper, silver, and silk are produced, and whose king is Rajah Rrom [1318]. Bassi Bassa [is] on the mainland [1319]. Then [follow] two islands, Sumbdit and Pradit,449 which are very rich in gold, and whose inhabitants wear a large gold ring around their legs at the ankle [1320]. On the mainland, near that point, lives a race of men in some mountains who kill their fathers and mothers as age comes on, so that they may suffer no more pain [1321]. All the peoples of those places are heathens [1322].

[201] On Tuesday night as it drew near Wednesday, 11 February 1522, we left the island of Timor and took to the great open sea called Laut Chidol,450 and, laying our course toward the west-south-west, to the north on our right hand, we left the island of Zamatra (formerly called Traprobana)451 for fear of the king of Portugal; [as well as] Pegu, Bengala, Uriza, Chelin (where the Malabars live, who are subject to the king of Narsingha), Calicut (subject to the same king), Cambaia (where the Guzerati live), Cananor, Goa, Ormuz, and all the rest of the coast of India Major [1323].452 Six different classes of people inhabit India Major: *Nairi, Panichali, Irauai, Pangelini, Macuai*, and *Poleai* [1324]. The *Nairi* are the chiefs, and the *Panichali* are the townspeople (those two classes of men consort together); the *Irauai* gather the palm wine and figs; the *Pangelini* are the sailors; the *Macuai* are the fishermen; the *Poleai* are the farmers and harvest the rice [1325]. These last always live in the country, although they enter the city at times, and when anything is given them, it is laid on the ground, and then they take it [1326]. When they go through the streets they call out *Po! po! po!* that is 'Beware of me! [1327]' It happened, as we were told, that a *Nair* once had the misfortune to be touched by a *Polea*, for which the *Nair* immediately had himself killed so that he would not remain with that disgrace [1328].453

[202] In order that we might double the Cape of Good Hope, we descended to forty-two degrees on the side of the Antarctic Pole [1329]. We were nine weeks near that cape with our sails hauled down

because we had the west and northwest winds on our bow quarter and because of a most furious storm [1330].454 That cape lies in a latitude of thirty-four and one-half degrees, and is sixteen hundred leagues from the Cape of Malacca, the largest and most dangerous cape in the world [1331].

Some of our men, both sick and well, wished to go to a Portuguese settlement called Mozambique, because the ship was leaking badly, because of the severe cold, and especially because we had no other food than rice and water; for as we had no salt, our provisions of meat had putrefied [1332]. Some others, however, who were more protective of their honour than of their life, decided to go to Spain dead or alive [1333]. Finally, by God's help, we doubled that cape on 6 May at a distance of five leagues: had we not approached so closely, we could never have doubled it [1334].

[203] Then we sailed north-west for two months continually, without taking on any fresh food or water [1335]. Twenty-one men died during that short time: when we cast them into the sea, the Christians went to the bottom face upward, while the Indians always went down face downward [1336]. Had not God given us good weather we would all have starved to death [1337]. Finally, constrained by our great distress, we went to the islands of Cape Verde [1338].

[204] Wednesday, 9 July, we reached one of those islands called Santiago, and immediately sent the boat ashore for food, with the story for the Portuguese that we had lost our foremast under the equinoctial line (although we had lost it upon the Cape of Good Hope), and when we were re-stepping it, our captain-general had gone to Spain with the other two ships [1339]. With those good words, and with our merchandise, we got two boatloads of rice [1340]. We charged our men when they went ashore in the boat to ask what day it was [1341]. They told us that it was Thursday for the Portuguese: we were greatly surprised for it was Wednesday for us, and we could not see how we had made a mistake [1342]. For since I had always been healthy, I had written down every day without any interruption [1343]. However, as was told us later, it was no error, but as the voyage had been made continually toward the west and we had returned to the same place as does the sun, we had made that gain of twenty-four hours, as is clearly seen [1344].455 The boat having

returned to the shore again for rice, thirteen men and the boat were detained, because one of them, as we learned afterward in Spain, told the Portuguese that our captain was dead, as well as others, and that we were not going to Spain [1345]. Fearing lest we also be taken prisoners by certain caravels, we hastily departed [1346].[456]

[205] On Saturday, 6 September 1522, we entered the bay of San-lùcar with only eighteen men, and the majority of them sick [1347]. All the rest, of the sixty men who left Molucca, had died of hunger, had deserted at the island of Timor, or had been put to death for crimes [1348].

From the time we left that bay [of Sanlùcar][457] until the present day [of our return], we had sailed 14,460 leagues, and furthermore had completed the circumnavigation of the world from east to west [1349].

[206] On Monday, 8 September, we cast anchor near the quay of Seville, and discharged all our artillery [1350].

[207] Tuesday, we all went in shirts and barefoot, each holding a candle, to visit the shrine of Santa Maria de la Victoria, and that of Santa Maria de Antigua [1351].

[208] Leaving Seville, I went to Valladolid, where I presented to his sacred Majesty, Don Carlo,[458] neither gold nor silver, but things worthy to be very highly esteemed by such a sovereign [1352]. Among other things, I gave him a book, written by my hand, concerning all the matters that had occurred from day to day during our voyage [1353]. I left there as best I could and went to Portugal, where I spoke with King Dom João[459] of what I had seen [1354]. Passing through Spain, I went to France, where I made a gift of certain things from the other hemisphere to the mother of the most Christian king, Don Francis, Madame the Regent [1355].[460] Then I came to Italy, where I devoted myself forever, and these my poor labours, to the famous and most illustrious Lord Philippe de Villiers l'Isle-Adam, the most worthy Grand Master of Rhodes [1356].

The Knight
Antonio Pigafetta

Notes

1 Philippe Villiers de l'Isle-Adam (1464–1534) was the forty-third Grand
   Master of the Order of the Knights of St John (called Knights of Malta
   after 1530). Elected Grand Master of the Order on 22 January 1521,
   Villiers de l'Isle-Adam led a heroic but unsuccessful defence of Rhodes
   against a siege by the Ottoman emperor Suleiman I, 'the Magnificent.'
   The Grand Master subsequently sought refuge in Italy, and in 1524 the
   Order was settled in the city of Viterbo by Clement VII. A general chapter
   of the Order was held there in June of 1527, when it was decided to accept
   the island of Malta, which had been offered by Charles V, a gift which was
   confirmed by letters-patent of Charles V in 1530. For a contemporary
   account of the Siege of Rhodes, see 'A relation of the siege and taking
   of the citie of Rhodes …,' an English translation from a French original
   by Sir Thomas Dockwra in Richard Hakluyt's *The Principal Navigations*
   (Glasgow: J. MacLehose and Sons, 1903–5), 1–160.
2 Charles V, Habsburg king of Spain from 1516 (Charles I), was emperor
   of the Holy Roman Empire between 1519 and 1556.
3 Francesco Chiericati (1480–1539) was born in Vicenza, the son of Belpi-
   etro of the Vicentine family of the Chiericati courts and of Mattea Corradi, daughter of Andrea Corradi of Austria, a Mantuan noble who was
   related to the Gonzaga. Chiericati's good relations with the Gonzaga and
   the court of Mantua continued throughout his life. Chiericati studied in
   Padua, Bologna, and finally Siena, where he completed degrees in civil
   and ecclesiastical law. At Bologna, he enjoyed the protection of Federico
   Fregoso, archbishop of Salerno, one of the principal participants in the
   conversations of Baldassare Castiglione's *The Courtier* (*Il cortegiano*). In
   1511, the year Fregoso was killed, Chiericati obtained the protection of
   Sigismondo Gonzaga, who was then papal legate to the Marches, and

became an apostolic protonotary. Upon moving to Rome, Chiericati became Latin secretary of Cardinal Matthäus Schiner, and at this time began his diplomatic career. He accompanied Schiner when he was named legate for Lombardy and Germany between January 1512 and the death of Julius II on 21 February 1513. That same year, Chiericati passed into the service of Cardinal Adriano Castellesi, and between 1514 and 1515 he accomplished on his behalf several important diplomatic missions. In his role as a secretary to Castellesi, Chiericati was present in December 1515 at the congress of Bologna between Leo X and Francis I, and immediately thereafter obtained the papal ambassadorship to England, which lasted from 1515 to 1517. Upon his return to Rome, Chiericati passed into the service of Cardinal Giulio de' Medici (the future Clement VII), and was sent to Spain in December 1518 on a private mission by Pope Leo X, especially to promote a crusade against the Turks; two years later he went to Portugal as a papal ambassador. During the missions in Spain and Portugal, Chiericati became greatly interested in the recent geographical discoveries and the voyage reports that were circulating. His house in Barcelona became a meeting place where literature and the latest geographical discoveries were discussed. In Zaragoza and Barcelona, Chiericati had come to know Cardinal Florenz, the future Pope Adrian VI (1469–1523), who, upon becoming pope on 31 August 1522, immediately named Chiericati bishop of Teramo, in the Abruzzi, and sent him upon his most important mission as ambassador to Germany for the Diet of Nuremburg. There he presented the pope's pleas for united action against the Turks and for enforcement of the Edict of Worms against Luther. While in Nuremburg he also received copy of Pigafetta's journal, which he highly recommended, together with its author, to Isabella d'Este. Under Pope Clement VII, Chiericati's diplomatic role declined, although he took part in embassies to Prussia and Muscovy. He survived the Sack of Rome in 1527 and was sent to collect money from Italian princes to ransom the pope. In 1536, Chiericati entered the service of Cardinal Ercole Gonzaga, at whose side he passed the last three years of his life. He died on 5 December 1539 in Bologna while returning to Mantua. Chiericati's friends and associates included Silvestro Gigli, Egidio Antonini of Viterbo, and Paolo Giovio, and he was a correspondent of Erasmus. See the article on Francesco Chiericati.

A. Foa, *Dizionario biografico degli italiani* (Rome: Istituto della Enciclopedia Italiana, 1960), 24:674–89.

4 Leo X: Giovanni de' Medici, pope between 1513 and 1521.

5 The five ships were the *Victoria, Santiago, S. Antonio, Concepción,* and *Trinidad*. The *Victoria* was the only one to complete the circumnavigation; the *Santiago* was shipwrecked along the South American coast while searching for the strait (cf. 180); the *S. Antonio* deserted immediately after the discovery of the strait (cf. 207), the *Concepción,* following the death of Magellan, was burned by the crew, grown too few to man it (cf. 721); the *Trinidad,* the captain's ship, had to be abandoned in the Moluccas (cf. 1183). The list of the ships and their equipment was published by Navarrete (415–29). The most detailed information on the ships and their equipment is found in J.T. Medina, 'Los compañeros de Magallanes,' in *El descubrimiento del Océano Pacifico: Hernando de Magallanes y sus compañeros* (Santiago, Chile: Imprenta Universitaria, 1920); L. Diaz-Trechuelo, 'La organizacíon del viaje magallánico: financiacíon, enganches, acopios y preparativos,' in *A viagem de Fernão de Magalhães e a Questão das Molucas: Actas do II Colóquio luso-espanhol de história ultramarina* (Lisbon: Junta de investigações cientificas do Ultramar, 1975), 265–314; F.H.H. Guillemard, *The Life of Ferdinand Magellan and the First Circumnavigation of the Globe* (London: George Philip and Son, 1890), 142–46.

6 Magellan had been decorated with a knighthood and commandery in the Order of Santiago by Charles I in the presence of the Royal Council in July 1518. See Guillemard, 114.

7 Chiericati, with Pigafetta in his retinue, followed Charles's court from Zaragoza to Barcelona in January 1519. Pigafetta must have left Barcelona in early May in order to have arrived in Seville three months before Magellan's preparations were completed (10 August).

8 Pope Clement VII: Giulio de' Medici (1478–1534) assumed the papacy on 18 November 1523. Pigafetta was summoned to Rome very soon after Clement's election, for he writes to Federico Gonzaga from there on 2 February 1524 (see the introduction).

9 In the province of Viterbo, twenty-six miles southeast of that city.

10 Of the other captains, Juan de Cartagena (*S. Antonio*), Gaspar Quesada (*Concepción*), and Luis de Mendoza (*Victoria*) were Spanish; only João Serrão (*Santiago*) was Portuguese. The pilots, whom Pigafetta does not

mention, were all Portuguese. Of the expedition's 270–80 men, at least thirty-seven were Portuguese. Peter Martyr observes: 'There exists between Castillians and the Portuguese an inveterate hatred, and Magellan sought under every pretext and on divers occasions to kill a number of Castillians who refused to obey him.' *De orbe novo: The Eight Decades of Peter Martyr d'Anghera*, trans. F.A. MacNutt (1912; repr. New York: B. Franklin, 1970) 2:152.

11 The instructions for the conduct of the voyage, from which Pigafetta extracts a few items here, were issued to Magellan in a royal *cédula* of 8 May 1519, and contained seventy-four articles. See Guillemard, 127–30. French ms. 5650 gives a slightly different version of this passage: 'Finally, most illustrious Lordship, after all provisions had been made and the ships were in readiness, the captain-general, a wise and virtuous man, and one mindful of his honor, would not commence his voyage without first making some good and suitable rules, such as it is the approved custom to make for those who go to sea, although he did not entirely declare the voyage that he was about to make lest those men, through astonishment and fear, should refuse to accompany him on the so long voyage that he had determined upon. In consideration of the furious and violent storms that reign on the Ocean Sea where he was about to sail, and in consideration of another reason also, namely, that the masters and captains of the other ships in his fleet had no liking for him (the reason for which I know not, unless because he, the captain-general, was a Portuguese, and they Spaniards or Castilians, who have for a long while been biased and ill-disposed toward one another, but who, in spite of that, rendered him obedience), he made his rules such as follow, so that his ships might not go astray and become separated from one another during storms at sea. He published those rules and gave them in writing to every master in the ships and ordered them to be inviolably observed and kept, unless for urgent and legitimate excuse, and the proof that any other action was impossible.' J.A.R. Robertson, *Magellan's Voyage around the World by Antonio Pigafetta* (Cleveland: Arthur H. Clark, 1906), 2:202.

12 Spanish for 'lantern.'

13 From the Spanish *estrenque*, denoting a large rope made from Spanish grass hemp.

14 In ancient military language, the second of the four quarters into which the night was divided (*prima, modorra, modorrilla,* and *alba*) for the changing of the guard.

15 Columns or groups; from the Venetian *colonello.*

16 The French manuscript includes a long explanation of the signals and watches while the Ambrosiana manuscript is much abridged. Therefore, at least for this passage, the Italian could not have served as a model for the French versions. The passage from Ms Fr. 5650, which serves to clarify the meaning of the Italian in this case, is as follows: 'In addition to the said rules for carrying on the art of navigation as is fitting, and in order to avoid the dangers that may come upon those who do not have watches set, the said captain, who was skilled in the things required and in navigation, ordered three watches to be set. The first was at the beginning of the night; the second at midnight; and the third toward daybreak, which is commonly called the 'diane' [i.e., 'morn'] or otherwise the 'star of dawn.' The above-named watches were changed nightly: that is to say, that he who had stood first watch stood second the day following, while he who had stood second, stood third; and thus did they continue to change nightly. The said captain ordered that his rules, both those of the signals and of the watches, be thoroughly observed, so that their voyage might be made with the greatest of safety. The men of the said fleet were divided into three divisions: the first was that of the captain; the second that of the pilot or boatswain's mate; and the third that of the master. The above rules having been instituted, the captain-general determined to depart, as follows.' Robertson, 2: 230–4. This system of watches like the division of crew into three companies was prescribed in rules laid in the *cédula* of 8 May 1519. See note 11.

17 The stores and equipment carried by the fleet are detailed by Guillemard, 329–336. For crew lists, see Robertson, 205–16.

18 There were 239 according to the lists published by Martin Fernández de Navarette, *Colección de las viajes y descrubimientos que hicieron por mar los Españoles,* vol. 2 (Madrid, 1837), 421–7, but others joined the expedition before departure and in the Canaries so that, in the end, somewhere between 260 and 280 embarked on the voyage (Luzzana Caraci-Pozzi, *Notizie,* 527).

19 The Puerto de las Muelas, in Seville Harbour.

20 The Roman name for the river, Baetis, was superseded by the Moorish Guadalquivir (Wâd-el-Kebir, the Great River).

21 Coria del Rio, on the right bank of the river.

22 The distance given is far too short for the distance between Sanlúcar de Barrameda and Cape St Vincent, which is over one hundred miles. The source of the error is unknown.

23 Otherwise known as the Fortunate Islands, which Ptolemy had placed at the farthest point west of the inhabited world. See Amerigo Vespucci, *Letters for a New World*, ed. Luciano Formisano (New York: Marsilio, 1992), 3, 19–20, 46, 59. That Pigafetta makes no mention of their classical denomination, as Vespucci and many other writers of the period typically did, is sign of a relative lack of humanistic background and of the vernacular character of Pigafetta's courtly perspective. See note 51.

24 Guillemard conjectures that this is Punta Roxa, located at the south end of Tenerife (148).

25 The first of a series of marvels that make up Pigafetta's account of the passage over. By way of contrast, the first acts of insubordination of Juan de Cartagena (who eventually took part in the mutiny of St Julian), which occurred during the passage over, go unreported by Pigafetta. See Guillemard, 152–3. The Vicentine instead invokes here one of the classic Atlantic marvels ('Your illustrious Lordship must know'), which had typically served rhetorically to mark the passage from Old World to the New: the miraculous tree of Hierro. Guillemard notes that 'both in Madeira and the Canaries the laurel and other heavy-foliaged evergreens condense upon abundant water from the daily mists' (149). Nevertheless, the tree's status as a literary topos seems paramount here, also since the expedition did not in fact stop at Hierro. The passage is perhaps best considered alongside other treatments in the tradition, including those of Niccolò Scillacio, Peter Martyr, Bartolomè de Las Casas, Fernandez de Oviedo, and especially Girolamo Benzoni's, which was illustrated by a noteworthy engraving by Theodor de Bry in his *Historia Americae*.

26 A somewhat gratuitous jab at the ancients? Amoretti suggests that the ancients believed that it never rained in the tropics, which rendered them uninhabitable Carlo Ampretti, *Primo Viaggio intorno al globo terracqueo* (Milan: G. Galeaggi, 1800), 12. The Yale Beinecke MS differs, and

presents an explanatory gloss: 'Which was a thing very strange and uncommon, in the opinion of the old people and of those who had sailed there several times before.' See R.A. Skelton, *Magellan's Voyage: A Narrative Account of the First Circumnavigation by Antonio Pigafetta*, 2 vols. (New Haven, CT: Yale University Press, 1969), 41.

27 Following the African coast south and south-east, from the Canaries to Sierra Leone, Magellan took sixty days to reach the equator. He was delayed by the equatorial calms in the doldrums. Why Magellan did not sail southwest from the Canaries, as was the usual route, has been the subject of much speculation. The most plausible explanation is that Magellan was seeking to avoid Portuguese convoys he might have encountered by following the normal route to Brazil. This variation in the route was responsible for the first friction between Magellan and his Spanish captains, particularly Juan de Cartagena, captain of the *S. Antonio*, who challenged Magellan and demanded a council. Magellan answered simply that he should follow the flagship.

28 Sharks. From the Spanish *tiburón*.

29 St Elmo's fire is the popular name for the atmospheric electricity that gathers in the form of a star or brush about the masthead of ships and on the rigging. St Elmo is the Spanish form of the name of St Erasmus, bishop of Formia, in Campania, who was widely venerated as the patron of sailors on the Mediterranean. The phenomenon is also called fire of 'St Elias,' 'St Clara,' 'St Nicolas,' and 'composite,' 'composant,' and 'corposant' (i.e., *corpus sanctum*). The phenomenon is a recurring theme in Pigafetta's narrative (cf. 38, 106, 782, 930–1) and may represent a Rhodian motif deriving from earlier sailing experience on the part of Pigafetta. The Knights of Rhodes had forts in both Rhodes and eventually in Malta named for St Elmo.

30 The Yale Beinecke MS adds (most likely an interpolated gloss, since the Ambrosiana MS has quite a different rhetorical effect): 'Be it noted that whenever this fire which represents the said St Anselm appears and descends on a ship (which is in a storm at sea), the ship never perishes.' Skelton, *Magellan's Voyage* 42.

31 The storm petrel (*Hydrobates pelagicus*), which is found along all the Atlantic coasts and on some of the Pacific. The tale was current among sailors according to Robertson who cites other sources (1: 220).

32 *Stercorarius parasiticus,* called also the jaeger, and by sailors 'boatswain,' 'teaser,' and 'dung-hunter.' The last name derived from the belief that the bird fed upon the dung of gulls and terns, when in reality it pursues the latter birds and compels them to disgorge the fish they have swallowed.

33 The flying fish is either a species of *Exocoetus,* or the *Scomberesox saurus* of Europe and America, both of which feed in large schools and jump from the water to escape their enemies. The theme of so many birds gathered as to seem an island is yet another topos of travel narratives of the period.

34 Brazil. *Verzino* (from the Arabic *wars*) is in the Italian name for Brazil wood (*Cesalpina sappan*); the Spanish and Portuguese from *brasil,* deriving from *brasa,* meaning 'live coals' and reflecting the colour of this valuable dye-wood, led to the name of the country: Brazil.

35 The sense, here corrupted, is presumably: 'Verzin extends southward to twenty-three and one-half degrees south.'

36 At eight degrees and twenty-one minutes south latitude, the most eastern headland of South America, now Cabo Branco, to the north of Recife.

37 The pineapple.

38 The tapir, according to most authorites, including M.D. Busnelli, *Anta* was a Spanish term from the Arabic, which indicated a species of African antelope. 'Per una lettera del *Primo viaggio intorno al mondo* di Antonio Pigafetta,' in *Studi di lessicografia italiana* 4 (1982): 25; R. Dozy, *Glossaire des mots espagnols et portugais dérivés de l'arabe* (Leiden: Brill, 1969), 195. I.L. Caraci and M. Pozzi observe however that the term may refer to the guanaco since Albo calls animals clearly identifiable as guanacos '*antas.*' *Scopritori e viaggiatori,* 532.

39 A common rhetorical motif in Vespucci: 'and if I am prolix, I beg your pardon.' 'Soderini Letter,' *Letters,* 58.

40 French ms. 5650 reads: 'And for a king of cards, of the kind which are used to play with in Italy, they gave me five fowls.' The four suites of Italian playing cards are called *spade* (swords), *bastoni* (clubs), *danari* (literally, money; translated here as diamonds), and *coppe* (cups).

41 This is the common Americanist theme of unequal exchange, as Columbus first reported in the 'Letter Announcing the Discovery': 'so it was found that a sailor for a strap received gold to the weight of two and a half *castellanos.'* In *The Four Voyages of Columbus,* ed. Cecil Jane (Mineola, NY: Dover, 1988), 8. The motif of the Indian who thinks he got the better of

the deal is Vespuccian: 'And when I gave a bell to an Indian, he gave me
157 pearls, later valued at a thousand ducats, and do not suppose he
deemed this a poor sale, because the moment he had the bell, he put it in
his mouth and went off in the forest, and I never saw him again: I think
he feared that I might change my mind.' 'Ridolfi Fragment,' *Letters From a
New World*, ed. Luciano Formisano (New York: Marsilio, 1995), 43.

42 Landfall was made 29 November: they coasted south-west past Cape Frio
and entered the harbour of Rio de Janeiro on St Lucy's Day, 13 December 1519, naming it after the saint. The name Rio de Janeiro probably
derives from the expedition of Vespucci, who arrived there in January
of 1502.

43 Cf. Columbus's 'Letter Announcing the Discovery': 'as a result of that
voyage, I can say that this island is larger than England and Scotland
together' (12).

44 Manuel I (1495–1521). The Portuguese Pedro Alvarez Cabral reached
the coast of Brazil in 1500. By the Treaty of Tordesillas (1494), Brazil
belonged to Portugal. See the other narratives of Brazil antecedent to
Pigafetta's including those of Vespucci, Vaz de Caminha, and Giovanni da
Empoli. According to Guillemard, 'It is unnecessary to dwell on Pigafettas's evidently hearsay or borrowed account of the Indians and their customs.' *Life of Magellan*, 154. Indeed, even a cursory consideration of Vaz
de Caminha's account of his encounters with the Guaraní Indians, when
compared with Pigafetta's, is enough to reveal the stereotypical character
of the latter. For an exemplary reading of Vaz de Caminha's narrative, see
Valeria Bertolucci Pizzorusso, 'Uno spettacolo per il Re: l'infanzia di
Adamo nella "Carta"' di Pero Vaz de Caminha,' *Quaderni Portoghesi* 4
(1978): 49–81.

45 Cf. Vespucci: 'They are people who live many years. And I have found one
of the oldest men who by such stone signs explained to me that he had
lived seventeen hundred lunar months, which by my reckoning must be
132 years, counting thirteen moons for every year.' *Letters*, 33.

46 Cf. Peter Martyr: 'Thus they call the heavens *tueri*, a house *boa*, gold *cauni*'
(I, 66). The index to Ramusio includes an entry for 'Boia an Indian word
which means house among the inhabitants to the island of Juana.' Gian
Battista Ramusio, *Navigationi e Viaggi: Venice 1563–1606*, 3 vols. (Amsterdam: Ghentrum Orbis Terrarum, 1970), 3:5. Columbus had misunderstood

bohío to be the name of Haiti, 'when it was really, as Las Casas explains, the Arawak word for "house" or "home"; the palm-thatched huts of the peasantry are still called *bohíos* in Cuba.' Samuel E. Morison, *Admiral of the Ocean Sea* (Boston: Little, Brown 1942), 250. In any case, the word emerges from the earliest narratives and appears to be more frequently associated with the islands than with the mainland as here.

47 The hanging beds or hammocks of the Arawaks are described repeatedly in the early narratives, for example, by Columbus in his *Diario* (Wednesday, 17 October, and Saturday, 13 November): 'That day many dugouts or canoes came to the ships to trade things of cotton thread and the nets which they slept, which are hammocks.' *The* Diario *of Christopher Columbus's First Voyage to America*, ed. O. Dunn and J.E. Kelley Jr (Norman: University of Oklahoma Press, 1989), 131. The use of the word here is probably a gloss added by Las Casas. Peter Martyr and Vespucci describe the hammock but never use the Indian term; Skelton claims that 'the word was introduced into European languages by the records of this voyage' (152). Pigafetta's use of the word may well be the first in an Italian text.

48 Skelton calls this '[a]nother word brought back to Europe by Magellan's men' (142), but the word had been appearing since Columbus's 'Letter Announcing the Discovery': 'In all the island they have very many canoes' (10). It is reported in Peter Martyr, Michele de Cuneo, Vespucci, and was a stereotypical Americanist theme by the time Pigafetta wrote. The origin for the Spanish *canoa* was the Arawak *kanawa*. See Formisano's observations in the glossary of Vespucci's *Lettere di viaggio*, ed. L. Formisano (Milan: Mondadori, 1985), 230 and Gianfranco Folena, 'Le prime immagini dell'America nel vocabolario italiano,' in *Bollettino dell'Atlante Linguistico Mediterraneo* 13–15 (1971–3): 673–92.

49 The Italian reads *d'uno solo arburo ma schize*. '*Schize*' in the Venetian dialect means flattened or crushed. Robertson had read and translated *maschize* as one word, that is, *massiccio* or massive, huge.

50 Cf. Giuliano Dati's *L'invenzione delle nuove insule di Channaria indiane*, ed. T.J. Cachey, Jr, and L. Formisano (Chicago: Newberry Library, 1989), octave LI, 26: 'These people go from one island to another in certain boats found on this island, made of a single tree-trunk, which are called canoes. They are long and narrow, and seem almost to fly to whoever is placed within them, although they are crudely crafted; they are dug out

with stones, sticks and bones.' The detail concerning the method of manufacturing the canoes ('dug out with stones') in Dati's poetic rendering of the Columbus 'Letter Announcing the Discover' derived from a version of that letter since lost.

51 Cf. Columbus's *Diario* (Saturday, 13 October), 69: 'They row with a paddle like that of a baker and go marvelously.'

52 A. Gerbi observes: 'The apparently classical reference is deceptive, as Pigafetta doubtless had in mind the "people covered in mud, there in the swamp, all naked and with anger in their faces," that Dante saw where the gloomy stream of Hell "forms a marsh, whose name is Styx" (Inf., VII, 106–12). Pigafetta was certainly not familiar with the Greek and Latin texts.' *Nature in the New World: From Christopher Columbus to Gonzalo Fernández de Oviedo*, trans. J. Moyle (Pittsburgh: University of Pittsburgh Press, 1985), 106.

53 Among the most vivid early explanations of cannibalism according to the revenge thesis (as opposed to the innate aggression, ritual, or materialist, i.e. consumption of protein theses). The revenge explanation, later popularized by Hans Staden's narrative (1557) of his capture by the cannibals in Staden, Hans. *Hans Staden, The True Story of his Captivity.* (London: Routledge and Sons, 1928), (151, 155–9), had already been suggested by Vespucci, who describes vengeful ritualized cannibal killing, and concludes: 'When we asked them to tell us the cause, the only reason they could give us was that this curse had begun "in olden times," and that they wish to avenge the death of their ancestors: in sum, a bestial thing; and certainly one of their men confessed to me that he had eaten the flesh of more than two hundred bodies.' Formisano, *Letters from a New World; Letters* III, 33–4. For discussion and bibliography on the truth value and ideological implications of European reports of Caribbean cannibalism, see P. Hulme, 'Columbus and the Cannibals,' in *Colonial Encounters: Europe and the Native Caribbean, 1492–1797* (London: Methuen, 1986), 14–43.

54 Smoked human flesh was by this time a commonplace of European accounts of cannibalism: 'in their houses we found human flesh hung up for smoking, a lot of it.' Vespucci, *Letters* III, 33.

55 João Lopes Carvalho was pilot of the *Concepción* upon departure and, following the fatal banquet in the island of Cebu, became pilot of the *Trinidad.* He had piloted the Portuguese ship *Bretoa* in Brazil in 1511. His four

years in Brazil seem unrecorded except by Pigafetta, who refers later to
Carvalho's son, by a Brazilian woman, who was serving in the fleet and
made prisoner in Borneo (cf. 850). Carvalho died on Tidore, 14 February 1522.

56 *Cacique* originally enters the European languages through the reports of
the Caribbean exploration and discoveries, beginning with Columbus
(glossed by Las Casas here): 'they went ahead to give the news to the
"cacique," as they call them there. Up to that time the admiral had not
been able to understand whether by this they meant "king" or "governor"
or "judge."' *Diario* (Sunday, 23 December), 271.

57 The Italian reads *gatti maimoni picoli*, as in Marco Polo and Vespucci. See
Vespucci, *Lettere*, 'Glossario': *mamoni* 242. In both Polo and Vespucci, the
term seems to refer to monkeys of large dimensions. Robertson observes
that monkeys of the genus *Cebus* are probably intended here.

58 Often identified by editors (Robertson, Skelton) as manioc or cassava,
from the root of which bread is made in Brazil. More likely, however, is
M. Masoero's identification of it as sago, derived from a kind of palm plant.

59 Tayasu or peccary (*Dicotyles torquatus*), which has quills resembling those
of the porcupine, and is generally of a whitish colour. It is tailless and very
fierce and difficult to domesticate. The flesh was eaten, and the teeth
wore worn by some of the chiefs as necklaces. See Hans Staden's *The Captivity*, 160 and note. What Pigafetta refers to as 'their navels' is a large
gland located on their backs that secretes an oily liquid.

60 The roseate spoonbill (*Ajaia ajaja*).

61 Great 'virtue' among married women and great sexual freedom with
regard to virgins is often commented upon in the travel narratives. Amoretti recalls that Cook finds the same throughout the South Sea Islands. For
these eighteenth century treatments of this topos, see Antonello Gerbi, *The
Dispute of the New World: The History of a Polemic*, trans. J. Moyle (Pittsburgh,
PA: University of Pittsburgh Press, 1973), 146–7.

62 The jealousy of Amerindian men for their women is a recurring theme,
for example, in Vespucci, *Letters* 32 and Verrazzano: 'They are very careful
with them [their womenfolk] for when they come aboard and stay a long
time, they make the women wait in the boats; and however many entreat-
ies we made or offers of various gifts, we could not persuade them to let
the women come on ship.' Giovanni da Verrazzano, *The Voyage of Giovanni*

da Verrazzano, ed. Lawrence C. Wroth (New Haven: CT: Yale University Press, 1970), 138. The natives' love for their wives is also an important theme with the Patagonian giants below (cf. 149–60), one which Montaigne would develop in his famous essay 'On the Cannibals': 'He [one of the elders] preaches two things only: bravery before their enemies and love for their wives. They never fail to stress the second duty.' *Essays of Michel de Montaigne*, trans. and ed. M.A. Screech (London: Penguin, 1991), 234.

63 Cf. Verrazzano: 'for they are easily persuaded, and they imitated everything they saw us Christians do with regard to divine worship, with the same fervor and enthusiasm we had.' *Voyages of Verrazzano*, 141.

64 The Beinecke MS interjects here: 'Which was a great simplicity.' This paragraph is generally characterized by classic Columbian motifs: the supposed Amerindian belief that the Europeans had come from heaven, as well as the classic Columbian terms of exchange, i.e., Brazil wood (resources) freely given in trade for Christian religion.

65 Another putative example of Amerindian ingenuousness. The Beinecke MS in fact introduces this sentence with the following: 'Besides the above-mentioned things (betraying their simplicity) the people of the place showed us another very simple thing.' Skelton, *Magellan's Voyage*, 45. For interesting observations regarding this particular moment of cross-cultural encounter/projection in a contemporary literary context, see H.E. Robles, 'The First Voyage around the World: From Pigafetta to García Márquez,' *History of European Ideas* 6, no. 4 (1985): 385–404, esp. 397–8.

66 The Italian reads 'per trovare alguno recapito' with *recapito* signifying hospitality or collocation, but here with sexual overtones. In fact, the *Grande dizionario della lingua italiana* (Turin: UTET, 1961–), for the word *recapito* gives under definition no. 8 (vol. 15, 623), the woman's collocation or reception in a house of prostitution, and cites A. Firenzuola, 'Io medesimo, che ho la pratica già più tempo fa di certi ruffiani, vedrò di darle [alla ragazza] buonissimo recapito' [I myself, who have frequented for some time certain pimps, will see that the girl is given an excellent reception].

67 A unique contribution to the theme of the marvellous sexual appetite of Amerindian women, a topic which elicited both great interest and anxiety in European readership. Indeed, the Amerindian woman's sexual insatiability could sometimes lead to castration, as described by Vespucci,

'Mondus Novus,' *Letters*, 49, and even death. See Gerbi, who cites episodes from Oviedo in *Nature in the New World*, 350–1.

68 This is the first of four word lists that Pigafetta provides as a part of his narrative. The lists get progressively longer, from this one of eight words to the last including 426 words. These word lists report respectively on the languages of the first four major groups of indigenous peoples encountered by the expedition, that is, the Guarani of the 'Land of Verzin' (Brazil), the Patagonian Giants or Tehuelches (cf. 231), the people of the Philippine islands (cf. 720), and those of the Moluccas (cf. 1199).

69 Brazil had been discovered twenty years by the time of Magellan's voyage: 'It is remarkable that none of the historians of the voyage mention the presence of Portuguese in Rio de Janeiro, although there is every probability that some may have been there at the time, since a trading station had been established in the bay some years before.' (Guillemard, 155).

70 Rio de la Plata. Magellan left Rio de Janeiro 26 December, proceeding to Cape Santa Maria and the river that was called St Christopher. There they remained until 2 February 1520.

71 Presumably Pigafetta refers here to Indians of the Tehuelche tribe. The name is of Arawak origin and means 'man of the south.' Pigafetta says that they are called Cannibals 'omini che se chiamano Canibali,' which could be interpreted: 'men who call themselves Cannibals.' Pigafetta does not characterize the nature of their cannibalism, other than to say – as he did with the Brazilian, whom he did not term cannibals – that they eat human flesh.

72 Mare de Sur is the name Vasco Nuñez de Balboa gave to the Pacific when he first sighted it on 25 September 1513. The name 'Pacific' was given by Magellan (see 246).

73 The commentators understand the passage to mean that 'now it is understood that it is not a promontory beyond which one finds the sea but the mouth of a river.' Antonio Pigafetta, *Relazione del primo viaggio attorno al mondo*, ed. Andrea Canova (Padua: Antenore, 1999), 177. The name Santa Maria was transferred from the cape (still so called) on which it had been bestowed by Juan de Solis in 1515, to the estuary of the Rio de la Plata. (The Genoese pilot, however, says that Magellan gave the estuary the name Rio de San Christoval, which is found in contemporary world

maps.) In any case, Pigafetta simplifies events here. Magellan spent two days sailing up the estuary and six days at anchor in it, before resuming the voyage southward on 2 February 1520.

74 Juan Diaz de Solis, born in 1470, is said to have discovered Yucatan with Pinzon in 1506. He was appointed chief pilot of Spain after the death of Amerigo Vespucci in 1512. He discovered and explored the Rio de la Plata, where he and some of his men were killed and eaten in in September 1516. Maximilian Transylvanus also recalls his death at this point in his narrative: 'Here Juan Ruy Diaz Solis had been eaten, with some of his companions, by the anthropophagi, whom the Indians call cannibals, whilst, by order of Ferdinand the Catholic, he was exploring the coast of this continent with a fleet.' In Lord Stanley of Alderly, *The First Voyage around the World by Magellan* (London: Hakluyt Society, 1874), 188. Cannibals feasting upon Europeans along these shores (with Solis and later Verrazzano the most famous victims) had become a common theme since the episode described in Vespucci's Soderini letter: 'the women were already hacking the Christian up into pieces, and in a great fire they had built, they were roasting him before our eyes.' *Letters*, 89.

75 The sea wolves were probably some species of the Otariidae or fur seals. Guillemard, 160. The 'geese' were penguins. According to Robertson, this bay where the ships were laden with seals was probably Puerto Deseado (at 47 degrees 46 minutes S).

76 St Nicholas of Bari, also known as Sant Nikolass: St Nicholas of Asia Minor (d. c. 345), venerated in the East and northern countries, where he is known by the name of Santa Claus. Among his miracles was the salvation of some sailors in a storm. St Clare of Assisi (1194–1253), St Francis's collaborator and founder of the Poor Clares, was considered a patroness of sailors due to an incident at the end of her life when she miraculously repulsed an attack of Saracens upon a monastery. For St Elmo, see note 28.

77 Pigafetta does not mention the exploration of the Gulf of San Matias, on 24 February, 'to see if there was any outlet to Molucca' (Genoese pilot).

78 Port St Julian. The Genoese pilot says that they reached it on 31 March 1520, and places it at 49 degrees 20 minutes S (in reality, at 49 degrees 30 minutes). The fleet would remain there until August 24. It was here that the mutiny, which Pigafetta touches on only briefly, broke out (cf. 176–9). For a fuller account of the mutiny, see Guillemard, *Life of Magellan*, 162–74.

79 Regarding these American giants, see note 71. Albo, who gives an account of these Indians, makes no note of their gigantic size: 'Many Indians came there, who dress in certain skins of the *anta*, which resemble camels without the hump. They have certain bows made from cane, which are very small and resemble Turkish bows. The arrows also resemble Turkish arrows, and are tipped with flint instead of iron. Those Indians are very prudent, swift-runners, and very well-built and well-appearing men.' In Stanley, *First Voyage*, 218. Maximilian Transylvanus, on the other hand, reports that they were 'ten spans tall,' that is, about seven feet six inches.

80 The guanaco (*Lama guanacoe*) is a species of llama.

81 Cf. Vespucci, 'Soderini Letter,' *Letters*, 81, note 36 for analogous description of indigenous use of this white powder, which Oviedo reports 'the Indians of Nicaragua call *yaat*, that in the jurisdiction of Venezuela is called *hado*, and in Peru *coca*.' Gonzalo Fernández de Oviedo y Valdés. *Historia general y natural* IV (New York: American Geographical Society, 1934), 179.

82 An ancient measure of length equivalent to between eighteen and twenty-one inches.

83 A Tehueleche word, which Shakespeare puts twice in Caliban's mouth (*The Tempest*, I.ii and V.i), and which he got from Richard Eden's translation of Pigafetta in *The Decades of the newe worlde* (1555).

84 Identified by Guillemard as Diego de Barrasa, man-at-arms of the *Trinidad*. *Life of Magellan*, 184.

85 'Herrera's account of the intercourse of the Spaniard and Patagonians differs widely from the above in certain points. He relates the first meeting differently, describes the death of Diego de Barrasa as occurring in a chance *recontre* with the natives, and records the dispatch of a punitive expedition of twenty men as a sequel, adding that not one of the enemy was encountered (Dec. ii., lib. ix, caps. xiii-xv). Transylvanus gives a lengthy description of a visit of seven men of the fleet to a Patagonian hut some distance onland, followed by an attempt to capture three of the savages … Neither of these accounts, it should be remembered, are first hand' (Guillemard, 185).

86 Pigafetta and Transylvanus both mention this story, and Oviedo borrows it from them. Transylvanus recounts it not as for medicinal purposes but

as part of the natives' welcoming ceremonies: 'When some of our men showed them bells and pictures painted on paper, they began a hoarse chant and an unintelligible song, dancing round our men, and, in order to astonish them, they passed arrows a cubit and a half long down their throats to the bottom of their stomachs, and without being sick. And forthwith drawing them out again, they seemed to rejoice greatly, as having shown their bravery by this exploit' (190).

87 Skelton observes that the name bestowed by Magellan exists, with the sense of 'dogs with large paws,' in various romance languages: Spanish *patacones*, Portuguese *patas de cao*, French *patauds*' (154). And the opinion that the name *Patagoni* was given by Magellan to these people because of their abnormal feet goes back to the first historians of the Spanish conquests Oviedo and Gómara. But technically speaking, the term *patagòn* for 'big foot' is not found in Spanish or Portuguese. M.R. Lida de Malkiel has suggested a literary source for the name in the anonymous Spanish chivalric poem *Primaleòn* (*princeps* at Salamanca, 1512), which was reprinted numerous times throughout Europe. In canto XXX the hero Primaleòn encounters barbarous people on an island including a particularly monstrous individual named Patagone. See M.R. Lida de Malkiel, 'Para la toponomia argentina: Patagonia,' *Hispanic Review* 20 (1952): 321–3; B. Chatwin, *In Patagonia* (New York: Summit Books, 1977), 89–91.

88 From 30 March to 24 August 1520.

89 Pigafetta addresses here directly his patron again (cf. 30) Philippe Villiers de l'Isle-Adam.

90 Padre Sanchez de la Reina.

91 Juan de Cartagena had been captain of the *S. Antonio* but had been relieved of his command for insubordination before crossing the Equator (see above, note 24). The command was initially given to Antonio de Coca, *contador* of the fleet, but at Port St Julian the latter was replaced by Alvaro de Mesquita, a Portuguese and Magellan's cousin. This seems to have sparked off the conspiracy on the night of 1–2 April when the mutineers, led by Juan de Cartagena, Juan Sebastian de Elcano, Gaspar Quesada, and Luis de Mendoza, made themselves masters of the three largest ships. On the combination of stratagem and force by which Magellan reasserted the authority, Pigafetta says nothing. The details are known from documents collected in Navarrete, vol. 4, 528–32; partial translation in

Robertson, vol. 1, 230–4: 'Magallanes, believing that boldness was more useful than meekness in the face of such actions, determined to employ craft and force together. He kept the small boat of the ship *S. Antonio* which was used for those negotiations, at his ship; and sent the alguacil, Gonzalo Gomez de Espinosa, in the skiff belonging to his ship, to the *Victoria*, with six men armed secretly and a letter for the treasurer, Luis de Mendoza, in which he told the latter to come to the flagship. While the treasurer was reading the letter and smiling as if to say "You don't catch me that way," Espinosa stabbed him in the throat, while another sailor stabbed him at the same instant on the head so that he fell dead' (Robertson, 232). For a synthetic account, see Guillemard, 162–74. It is remarkable that Pigafetta gives such a brief version of the mutiny at Port St Julian. Pigafetta's account, for Guillemard, was also 'remarkable for its extraordinary inaccuracy.' The Ambrosiana MS says that it was Cartagena who was executed and quartered while Quesada was marooned, when in fact it was the opposite. The French manuscripts get this last point right; see the Beinecke MS: 'The Gaspar Quesada had his head cut off, and then he was quartered. And the overseer Juan de Cartagena, who several days later tried to commit treachery, was banished with a priest, and put in exile on that land named *Patagoni*' (50). Peter Martyr observes: 'It was during this period that Magellan treated the captain Juan de Cartagena so severely. He was a friend of the Bishop of Burgos who had been assigned to Magellan, with royal approval, as his associate, and named second in command of the expedition. Under a pretext of a plot formed against his life, Magellan put him ashore in company with a priest, giving them only a little biscuit and a sword. He would gladly have punished their plot with death, but he feared the resentment of the Spaniards against him and did not dare to assume the responsibility. This action has been represented in different lights; but the description of other events is in agreement. According to some, Magellan was within his rights in thus acting, while according to others he was not, and the severity he showed was merely the outcome of the ancient hatred existing between the Spaniards and the Portuguese' (154).

92 The account of the shipwreck and rescue is very inadequate. See the fullest account in A. de Herrera y Tordesillas, *Historia general de los hechos de los castellanos en los islas i tierra firme del mar oceano* (Madrid: Imprento Real de Nicolas Rodriguez [sic] Franco, 1726–8). Dec. ii.,

libr. ix, cap. xiii, 295–7; Guillemard, 175–9. One man was lost, namely, the negro slave of the captain João Serrão (who had been appointed captain of the *Santiago* after the mutiny). Brito says: 'After this [i.e., the mutiny], they wintered for three months; and Magallanes again ordered the ship "Santiago" to go ahead in order to explore. The ship was wrecked but all of its crew was saved' (Navarrete, 4: 307). Like Herrera, Peter Martyr speaks of a storm as being responsible for the wreck, as do Transylvanus and Oviedo (155).

93 From the Spanish *mejillòn*, a variety of cockle, which was probably the *Mytilus* or the common mussel.

94 The *Rio de Santa Cruz*, discovered 3 May 1520 by João Serrão during the *Santiago*'s exploration.

95 Between 14 September and 18 October 1520.

96 Da Mosto identified this fish as the *Eleginus maclovinus*.

97 Cabo Virjenes, in 52 degrees 20 minutes S, marking the eastern end of the Strait of Magellan, discovered 21 October 1520.

98 *Proise*, here in the Italian, derives from an ancient Catalonian word meaning the 'bow moorings.' According to Robertson, the old Spanish word is *proís*, which signifies both the thing to which the ship is moored ashore, and the rope by which it is moored to the shore (vol. 1, 236).

99 In contrast to Pigafetta, Peter Martyr diminishes Magellan's accomplishment: 'At this point we must turn back somewhat in our history. During his childhood, Magellan had vaguely heard discussed in Portugal the existence of a strait, whose entrance was difficult to find. He was therefore ignorant of what direction to take but chance served him where his knowledge failed. There arose a tempest. While searching a shelter, one of the ships of least draught was driven by force of the waves very close to the shore. A narrow channel was discovered. The ship returned announcing the passage was found' (155). Pozzi acutely observes that Magellan probably spread the word that he knew of the strait as reported by Pigafetta in order to calm the officials and sailors: 'But Magellan certainly did not "know" and the information given by Pigafetta diminishes (involuntarily) his merits no less than they are reduced by Peter Martyr who tends to attribute everything to fortune.' Antonio Pigafetta, *Il primo viaggio intorno al mondo*, ed. Mario Pozzi (Vicenza: N. Pozza 1995), 65.

100 Martin Behaim (1459–1506) was a draper in Flanders (1477–9) after which he went to Lisbon, where he became acquainted with Columbus. In 1484 he was chosen geographer of Diego Cão's expedition to Western Africa. On his return he received the knighthood in the military order of Christ of Portugal. Later he lived on the island of Fayal in the Azores. In 1491, he returned to Germany, where he lived at Nuremberg until 1493; there he constructed his famous globe. See E.G. Ravenstein, *Martin Benhaim, His Life and His Globe* (London: G. Philip and Son, ltd. 1908). In 1493, he returned to Lisbon and in 1494 to Fayal, where he remained until 1506, when he went to Lisbon. Many myths sprung up about him, such that he visited America before Columbus and the straits of Magellan before Magellan, whom he might have known at Lisbon. See Guillemard for a discussion of knowledge about the existence of a strait prior to Magellan's discovery (189–98). Guillemard observes that 'In the *capitulacion* granted by the King to Magellan and Faleiro on 22 March, 1518, the phrase "para buscar el estrecho de aquellas mares" – to go in search of the strait – is used, and it would seem from the use of the definite article as if some actual known or rumored strait was intended' (191). On Magellan and Behaim's map see also Samuel E. Morison, *The European Discovery of America*, vol. 2 *The Southern Voyages* (New York: Oxford University Press, 1974), 381–2. Skelton writes that Behaim was unlikely to have made any map showing the antarctic strait but notes that 'On Schöner's globe of 1515 such a strait is laid down, though in 45 degrees south; but there may be significance in the fact that Schöner's source was a pamphlet (*Copia der Newen Zeytung auss Presillg Landt*) describing an expedition promoted in 1514 by the financier Cristóbal de Haro, who invested in Magellan's expedition and was related by marriage to Maximilian of Transylvania' (vol. 1, 155).

101 For Guillemard (199–200) and Skelton (155), most probably Lomas Bay, on the south side of the strait, but also possibly Possesion Bay. Andrea Da Mosto, *Il primo viaggio intorno al globo di Antonio Pigafetta*, in Raccolta Colombiana, pt. 5, vol. 3 (Rome: Ministero della pubblica istruzione, 1894) 61, note 5.

102 The 'First Narrows' or Primera Garganta, just beyond Anegada Point. Robertson translates *cantone* as 'sharp turn' while Skelton opts for 'creek.'

103 Lago de los Estrechos, St Philip's Bay, or Boucant Bay.

104 The 'Second Narrows' and Broad Reach.

105 Skelton observes: 'The first is the passage east of Dawson Island, which extends to the northeast into Useless Bay and to the southeast into Admiralty Sound. The second opening was the passage between the western side of Dawson Island and Brunswick Peninsula. Other accounts show that while the *S. Antonio* and *Concepción* reconnoitered the former channel, *Trinidad* and *Victoria* proceeded up Forward Reach, the main channel' (155).

106 Estevão Gomes, known in Spanish circles as Estebán, was an experienced Portuguese navigator and pilot with ambitions as great as those of Magellan. Pigafetta alludes here to the fact that Gomes had received a pilot's patent from the Casa de la Contratación on 10 February 1518 and had made a plan for an expedition that was forestalled by Magellan's. At a council held by Magellan on entering the Strait, Gomes seems to have argued for return to Spain. His desertion occurred probably in early November. Conspiring with Gerónimo Guerra, the captain of the *San Antonio*, he made off with that ship, and after imprisoning Alvaro de Mezquita (a nephew of Magellan's), returned to Spain, anchoring at Seville on 6 May 1521. There Gomes was imprisoned briefly after the return of the *Victoria*, but after his liberation he received honours and recognition. In 1524, Gomes proposed an expedition to discover a northwest passage. He coasted Florida and the eastern coast as far as Cape Cod, returning to Spain in 1525. Gomes participated in the 1535 expedition of Pedro de Mendoza and seems to have died while exploring the Rio de la Plata in 1538. Peter Martyr does not fail to turn the desertion of the *San Antonio* against Magellan: 'The other vessels expected it [the *San Antonio*] would follow, but it turned back and arrived in Spain some time ago, bringing the saddest accusations against Magellan. We believe that such disobedience will not remain unpunished' (156). Transylvanus records that Mezquita, upon his return to Spain, was made to stand trial 'in chains, for having, by his counsel and advice, induced his uncle to practice such harshness on the Spaniards' (195).

107 Guillemard conjectures from the records of Albo, Pigafetta, and Herrara that the river of Sardines is Port Gallant, which is located on the Brunswick Peninsula, opposite the Charles Islands: 'Port Gallant, and

Port S. Miguel. most probably correspond to the River of Sardines and
the River of Isles' (206, note 3).

108 Cabo Pilar, on the south side of the Pacific entrance of the strait.

109 João Serrão was the brother of Magellan's friend Francisco Serrão, and
a firm supporter of Magellan. Pigafetta errs in calling him a Spaniard,
though he may have become a naturalized Spaniard, since the register
speaks of him as a citizen of Seville. He was an experienced navigator
and captain and had served under Vasco da Gama, Almeida, and Albu-
querque. He fought in the battle of Cananor under Almeida (16 March
1506, a battle in which Magellan also participated). He was chief captain
of three caravels in August 1510, in the East, and was in the Java seas in
1512, but appears to have returned to Portugal soon after that. João
Serrão embarked with Magellan as captain and pilot of the *Santiago*, but
after the wreck of that vessel near Port St Julian he was given command
of the *Concepción*, in which he later explored the strait. Failing to dis-
suade Magellan from attacking the natives of Mactan, he became commander, with Duarte Barbosa, of the fleet at Magellan's death, and was
murdered by the Cebuans after the treacherous banquet given by them
to the fleet (cf. 699–714).

110 Probably the island of Santa Magdalena.

111 The little island called San Miguel. According to Guillemard the river of
Isleo (or 'of Islands') is located on Brunswick Peninsula, and is identified with the port of San Miguel, just east of the 'River of Sardines;' the
island where the cross was planted would be one of the Charles Islands.

112 The author again addresses the Grand Master of the Knights of Rhodes.

113 Tierra del Fuego.

114 Pigafetta is the only source to attribute this name to the strait. According
to the Portuguese Companion of Odoardo Barbosa (first published by
Ramusio) the strait was named 'the strait of Victoria, because the ship
Victoria was the first that had seen it; some called it the strait of
Magalhãens because our captain was named Fernando de Magalhãens'
(31). Castanheda says that Magellan gave it the name 'Bay of all Saints'
because it was discovered on 1 November, and 'Estrecho' or 'Canal de
Todos los Santos' is the name found in most subsequent Spanish charts.
This name is found in the instructions given for the expedition of
Sebastian Cabot in 1527, and in the map made that same year at Seville

by the Englishman Robert Thorne. Sarmiento de Gamboa petitioned Felipe II that it be called 'strait of the Mother of God.' In the world map of Battista Agnese showing the track of the circumnavigation, included in his manuscript atlases from 1536, the name is 'El streto de ferdinando de magellanes.'

115 Italian: *appio*, a wild celery (*Apium australe*). Amoretti recalls that Cook also found this vegetable there, as well as an abundance of scurvy grass; and owing to the availability of anti-scorbutic vegetables, deemed the passage of the strait preferable to that around Cape Horn (41).

116 The dorado is a species of *Coryphaena*, the albacore is the *Thymnus albacore*, and the bonito, *Thymnus plamys*.

117 From the Spanish *golondrina*, the sapphire gurnard or tubefish (*Trigla hirundo*).

118 Torquato Tasso based himself upon this passge for the following octave from a draft version of the *Gerusalemme liberata* (see introduction, x–xi): Spettacol quivi al nostro mondo ignoto / vider di strana, e d'incredibil caccia: / volare un pesce, un altro girne a nòto. / Fugge il volante, il notatore il caccia / e ne l'ombra ch'è in acqua osserva il moto / che quel fa in aria, e segue ognor la traccia, / fin che quel, che non vegge a volo il peso / per lungo spazio, in mare cadendo è preso.

119 The earliest recorded vocabulary of the Tehuelche of Patagonia. Da Mosto gives a list from the vocabulary of the Tehuelches compiled during the second half of the nineteenth century by the second lieutenant of the ship *Roncaglia*, parts of which correspond almost exactly with those given by Pigafetta (63, note 8).

120 The first six words are disposed in two columns at the bottom of the manuscript page and are to be read from top to bottom by column and not left to right across the columns. The same is true of the rest of the list that is disposed in two columns on the following pages, which are also to be read top to bottom. Canova's critical edition, which has been followed here, lists them all in a single column following the top to bottom by column ordering which reveals a loose organization of the vocabulary by lexical categories, for example, parts of the body (head, eye, nose) are followed by basic elements in nature (water, fire, smoke) and basic actions (to eat, to fight, to smell) intermixed with animals (fish, parrot, goose), colours (black, red, yellow).

121 Note that the position of the maps corresponds precisely to the narrative of the journey. Paragraph 40, which precedes the first two charts, concludes the Patagonian part of the voyage with the description of the author's exchanges with the giant who had been his informant for the Patagonian vocabulary, while paragraph 41 describes the beginning of the navigation of the Pacific, punctuated by the discovery of the 'Unfortunate Islands' in paragraph 42. Linking the charts is the presence of the two 'Unfortunate Islands' located in the 'Pacific Sea' on the first map of Patagonia and the strait. Thus, the pair of maps at this juncture in the manuscript present a kind of pivot around which the transition from the Atlantic to the Pacific parts of the narrative turns.

122 The passage took thirty-eight days (or thirty-six according to the Genoese pilot, who gives the date of departure as 26 November). Here Pigafetta marks a major transition in his narrative by giving the full date including the year, as he will at other important moments in the narrative (cf. 293, 696, 948, 1323)

123 This was scurvy. The official list of deaths recorded only eleven deaths between the Strait and the Ladrones (cf. Navarrete, 2: 443).

124 From 28 November to 16 December 1520, Magellan had coasted northward from Cape Deseado, before changing course to the northwest. The first island was discovered on St Paul's day, 24 January 1521, and named after St Paul according to Albo (222); although according to Transylvanus, 'They named these the Unfortunate Islands by common consent' (197). Skelton, together with most of the tradition, thinks that it was perhaps Puka Puka (19 degrees 46 minutes S, 138 degrees 48 minutes W), in the northern Tuamotu Archipelago. The second island, sighted eleven days later and named Island of the Sharks (Tiburones), would be one of the Manihiki Archipelago, perhaps Flint Island or Wostok. But for a minority opinion see also G. Nunn, 'Magellan's Route in the Pacific,' *Geographical Review* 34 (October 1935): 615–33. He argues that these islands correspond to present day Clipperton and Clarion in latitudes 10 degrees 17 minutes N and 18 degrees respectively. Nunn's theses are discussed (with bibliography) in Martin Torodash, 'Magellan Historiography,' *Hispanic American Historical Review* 51 (1971): 316–18.

125 The original, which reads: 'Ogni iorno cinquanta, sesanta e setanta leghe a la catena o a poppa,' has given rise to much discussion, since it appears, according to the revised text of Amoretti (1800: 'secondo la misura che

facevano del viaggio colla catena a poppa') to refer to the use of a log for measuring the ship's way long before the device was thought to have been in use (although the log is mentioned by Purchas as early as 1607, its use did not become general until 1620). Morison, on the other hand, observed that '*catena* in those days meant not only a chain but two important cross-beams is a vessel's hull, the first under the forecastle and the second well aft. Mariners stationed on the deck above each beam could time the seconds required for a piece of flotsam to pass between them as the ship sailed. Knowing the linear distance between these two beams and the elapsed time, anyone who knew a little mathematics could figure out the ship's speed' (*The Southern Voyage*, 420). The translation follows the proposal of A. Magnagi, 'Di una nuova interpretazione della frase "a la catena ho a popa" nella relazione di Antonio Pigafetta sul viaggio di Magellano,' *Bollettino della Società Geografica Italiana*, 6, no. 4 (1927): 458–75, who, comparing this passage with the same one in the French manuscripts concluded that the Italian text was corrupted [*a la catena* for *all'antena* (in the French manuscripts *a l'orce*)] and that Pigafetta meant 'according to when the ships experienced less favourable winds (at the windward side) or when they had the wind behind them (at the stern).'

126 Fifty years would pass before another navigator, Sir Francis Drake, circled the globe in 1578.

127 These are the Magellanic Clouds (*Nubecula major* and *Nubecula minor*). 'These Magellanic Clouds resemble portions of the Milky Way, Nubecula major being visible to the naked eye in stong moonlight and covering about two hundred times the moon's surface, while the Nubecula minor, although visible to the naked eye, disappears in full moonlight and covers an area only one-fourth of the former' (Robertson, 1: 246).

128 This refers to the practice of correcting the compass for local magnetic deviation. The Genoese pilot reports that 'we northeasted the compass box 2/4,' i.e., two points (= 22 1/2 degrees).

129 The Southern Cross. Morison, however, observes that the direction indicated ('straight toward the west') suggests instead the constellation Grus the Crane which is similar to a cross. (*The Southern Voyages*, 403–4).

130 The chart is positioned ahead of the account of the Island of Thieves in paragraphs 46–9, beginning on the facing page from the map.

131 The line of demarcation was first established following Columbus's discovery by Pope Alexander VI (cf. 325, 443, 717, 760, 772, 874, 1196,

1235, 1256). It originally ran north to south one hundred leagues to the west of the Cape Verde Islands and divided Spanish (west) from Portuguese (east) spheres of influence. With the Treaty of Tordesillas (7 June 1494) the line was moved 370 leagues west from the Cape Verde Islands.

132 To place Cipangu (Japan) twenty degrees south of the equator is far off, even for the cartography of the time. It has usually been assumed that Pigafetta derives these island names from his reading or hearsay. Cipangu goes back to Marco Polo, who told fabulous tales of the wealth of Cipangu that were later to inspire Columbus. Subdit Pradit has been taken to be a corruption of 'Septem cidades,' one of the original mythical islands of the Atlantic, but in the vicinity of Cipangu on Behaim's globe of 1492. Guillemard observes how the position Magellan found himself in 'resembled that of Columbus before sighting the new world, as day after day their despairing glances were bent westward in hopes of land' (223). Pigafetta reveals a similarly Columbian orientation by invoking two toponyms which harken back to the earlier moment of exploration history. But G. Nunn has suggested the interesting hypothesis that Sumbdit Pradit might be 'the same as the legendary islands of Khyrse and Argyre, or the islands of gold and silver. *Ptadia* (*prata* means silver in Malay). The story of the two islands was originally derived from Hindu literature. Al-Biruni (1031 AD) speaks of the islands of gold Surnendíb ... Sumbdit Pradit might well represent a combination of Surendíp and Pradit (*prada*.)' (630). More recently, Juan Gil, *Miti e utopie della scoperta. Oceano Pacifico: l'epopea dei navigatori* (Milan: Garzanti, 1992), 34, n. 18 traces in Ortelius's *Theatrum orbis terrarum* (1570) two islands near Timor called Ciempegua and Sumbdit: 'In fact, already in fra Mauro's mappamondo the islands Cianpangu and Sondai (Sonda) appear alongside Sumatra and these are surely the ones placed by Pigafetta, although imprecisely, in the middle of the Pacific Ocean.'

133 A Chinese city placed by Ptolemy in 8 1/2 degrees S, east of the Golden Chersonese, on the eastern coast of the Indian Ocean, later identified as Malacca. Vespucci, among others, sought it: 'we weighed anchor and set sail, turning our prows southward, since it was my intention to see whether I could round a cape of land which Ptolemy calls the Cape of Cattigara, which is near the Sinus Magnus' (*Letters*, I: 4).

134 The Mariana or Ladrone Islands. Herrera says they were named 'Islas de las Velas Latinas,' that is, islands of the lateen sails. The high island first sighted was probably Rota, and Guam the large island where landing was made. Transylvanus records the indigenous names Inuagana and Acaca, equated by Guillemard with Agana in Guam and Sosan in Rota (See Guillemard, 223–6). They continued to be called Ladrones and only later they took the name of Mariana in honor of the Queen D. Mariana of Austria, widow of Philip IV, and Regent during the minority of Carlos II of Spain.

135 Albo has a vivid description of this first encounter: 'then we saw a quantity of small sails coming to us, and they ran so, that they seemed to fly, and they had mat sails of a triangular shape, and they went both ways for they made of the poop the prow, and of the prow the poop, as they wished, and they came many times to us and sought us to steal whatever they could' (223).

136 An interesting testimony of European cannibalism practised by mariners in distress.

137 Da Mosto reports that these *fisolere* were small and very swift-oared vessels, used in winter on the Venetian lakes by the Venetian nobles for hunting with bows and arrows and guns (68, n. 5).

138 The apparatus described by Pigafetta as belonging to these boats is the outrigger (a projecting spar with a shaped log at the end attached to a canoe to prevent upsetting), common to many of the boats of the eastern islands.

139 The pattern of placing the chart just before the treatment of the islands depicted in the narrative, initiated with the map of the Unfortunate Islands and the Island of the Thieves, continues. By contrast, the Beinecke manuscript typically places the maps after the treatment of the islands depicted. Perhaps the anticipation of the maps represents an original authorial ordering, reflecting the experience of the journey rather than simply illustrating the account? Samar is treated in paragraphs 50–2, Suluan and Homonhom in paragraphs 53–4, and Cenalo (Dinagat), Ibusson, and Abarien (Cabalian) in paragraph 55.

140 Pigafetta again marks a major transition in his narrative, in this case, the arrival in the Philippines, by giving the full date (cf. 238).

141 Samar is an island in the Philippines, the southernmost point of which (Magellan's landfall) is in 11 degrees N. Cf. 1196, where Pigafetta describes it, accurately, from a geographical perspective, as 'the first island of the archipelago' to one arriving east to west.

142 Pigafetta later identifies this island as Homonhom (323), although Albo says it was Suluan.

143 A rare kind of fine linen. Du Cange defines it as 'Pannus subtil e gossypio vel lino.' *Glossarium mediae et infimae latinitatis* (Paris: F. Didot, 1840), 1: 744.

144 Arrack, meaning in Arabic 'ardent spirit,' is an Asian alcoholic beverage like rum. Pigafetta conserves both Portuguese forms (*ararca, uraca,* cf. 788–9) of a single Arabic word that the Europeans used generically to refer to a spirit made with fermented rice, sugar, and coconut.

145 Bananas.

146 The Yale Beinecke MS has 'By doing so they last a century.' Following L. Tormo Sanz, 'El Mundo indigena conocido por Magallanes en las Islas de San Lázaro,' in *A viagem de Fernãs de Magalhães e a questão das Molucas,* ed. A. Teixeira de Mota (Lisbon: Junta de Investigações Cientificas do Ultramar) 389–93, Canova notes that this description of the coconut tree reveals significant analogies to the descriptions of Duarte Barbosa and of Lodovico de Varthema and that 'one cannot exclude the possibility of a literary dependency' (in Pigafetta, *Relazione,* 207). For parallel passages, see Canova's 'Introduzione,' 76–80.

147 *Acquada da li buoni segnalli* in the Italian. The Spanish word *aguada* means a well or a place where water is available. Homonhon is west of Suluan and eleven miles southwest from the nearest point in Samar.

148 Passion Sunday fell on 17 March 1521. Pigafetta calls Passion Sunday the Sunday of St Lazarus according to the Ambrosian rite rather than calling it Palm Sunday in accordance with the Roman rite. The islands were called 'di San Lazaro' until 1542, when Villalobos changed the name to the Philippines in honour of Philip II. The Philippines lie between 225 and 235 degrees longitude west of Hierro in the Canaries and therefore between 195 and 205 degrees west of the line of demarcation. It is not clear whether Magellan simply miscalculated or in bad faith sought to represent their location on the Spanish side of the line, that is, as being east of 180 degrees.

149 Probably the junglefowl (*Gallus gallus bankiva*), domesticated in large numbers by the natives of the Philippines.

150 'These were presumably Negrito aborigines, not Malays' (Skelton, 159). The term *kâfir* is Arabic for 'unbeliever' and was used in the Far East to designate those people who did not worship Allah.

151 Variant form for *fiocina*, a 'harpoon' or 'eel-spear,' and hence here, a 'dart.'

152 A Venetian dialect word (*rizzagio* or *rizzagno*) for a fine thickly woven net, which when thrown into rivers by the fisherman opens, and when near the bottom closes and covers and encloses the fish (Da Mosto, 70).

153 It is difficult to identify these islands, depicted in the previous chart (IV); in any case, they would be located in the Surigao Strait, between Samar and Mindanao: possibly, Dinagat, Kabugan, Ibusson, Cabalian. The mention of these islands represented in the previous chart, located between paràgraphs 49 and 50, marks the close of a segment of the narrative of the journey that is renewed by the chart (V) that follows. In the Beinecke manuscript, the map of the Island of Good Signs, Cenalo, Hiunanghan, Ibusson, and Abarien follows, rather than introduces, the segment of the narrative corresponding to paragraphs 50 and 55.

154 Mazaua (Limasawa), depicted in the chart and treated in paragraphs 56–68, is only named in paragraph 68. The other islands depicted in the chart are Ceylon (Leyte), Bohol, Canigao, Baybay, Poro, Pacijan, and Pozon mentioned together in paragraph 69. Note that the chart includes the names of the raja Cabulen (Ceylon) and raja Malegis (Baibai) who are not mentioned in the narrative.

155 Limasawa (Mazaua), off the south end of Leyte.

156 Enrique of Malacca, a slave brought back from the East by Magellan. If, as some believe, Enrique were a native of a Philippine colony in Malacca, then he would have been the first man to circle the globe. According to Transylvanus, Enrique was originally from the Moluccas.

157 Taprobane was usually identified as Ceylon, but sometimes, as here, also Sumatra. Ludovico Varthema, the first European to speak of Sumatra, when he wrote about his 1505 visit, also took Sumatra to be Ptolemy's Taprobane.

158 A large boat used in the Philippines. From the Tagalog *balanghài*. The Italian derives from the Spanish *barangay* according to Salvatore Battaglia and Giorgio Bàrberi Squarotti, *Grande dizionario della lingua italiana* (Turin: UTET, 1961), 2:50.

159 The Ambrosiana MS reads *orade*. The doradi have already been mentioned (cf. 228). The Yale Beinecke MS provides the following gloss:
'which are fairly large fish of the kind described above.'

160 *Casi casi*, the ceremony of blood brotherhood practised among
the Malays.

161 The expression in the original, 'como uno omo d'arme,' is technical
and means 'completely armored' (Canova, in Pigafetta, *Relazione*, 214).

162 Navarrete observed that there were not more than fifty armed men in
the fleet at that time.

163 The *fusta* was a galley with eighteen or twenty rowers to a side, and with
a single lateen sail.

164 An aromatic oriental resin, used also as a perfume (cf. 730, 860).

165 A dry and brittle resinous substance obtained from Storax benzoin,
a tree of Sumatra, Java, etc. and used extensively in perfumery.

166 These names, applied to the island of Mindanao, in fact refer to two
of its regions: Butuan, in the north, and Caraga, in the north-east.

167 Colambu was Rajah of Butuan. According to Amoretti, this Rajah is the
same one Pigafetta elsewhere calls king of Mazua (Limasawa).

168 Siaiu was rajah of Cagayan.

169 *Abba* means father in Arabic and Hebrew.

170 According to Robertson, Ceylon is Leyte, anciently called Seilam (cf.
444, where Pigafetta speaks of Baybay, in central Leyte, as a separate
island); but Skelton identifies Ceylon as Panaon to the south of Leyte;
Cebu is to the west of Limasawa, and Caraga is a district of Mindanao.

171 Magellan's death is foreshadowed.

172 An Italian copper coin of the fifteenth century.

173 A Spanish coin.

174 *Doppione*, a gold coin struck by Louis XII of France during his occupation
of Milan 1500–12. Some commentators understand the expression 'uno
doppione de dui ducati' to mean instead 'a couple of two ducats,' therefore having a value of four ducats (Canova, in Pigafetta, *Relazione*, 221).

175 Pozzi notes that forty-eight hundred German knives of inferior quality
had been brought along by the expedition for trading purposes. In
Antonio Pigafetta, *Il primo viaggio intorno al mondo*, ed. Mario Pozzi
(Vicenza: N. Pozza, 1995) 256.

176 Robertson reads *Colona* for *colana* (necklace) and interprets it to refer to yet another coin of the period. The Beinecke MS reads: 'a pointed crown of massy gold for six large pieces of glass' (72).

177 Columbus also forbade such trade, but 'so that they might become Christians' ('Letter Announcing the Discovery,' 8).

178 The nut of the *Areca catechu*, which is folded in leaves of betel and chewed (cf. 788).

179 Betel was prepared with a leaf of *Piper betle*, cloves, the nut of the *Areca catechu*, lime and tobacco.

180 Cf. 323: the island of Homonhon, named in the Italian 'Acquada de li buoni segnali.'

181 Limasawa, in 9 degrees and 56 minutes N.

182 The islands of Leyte (or Panaon), Bohol (southwest of Leyte) and Canigao; the district of Baybay (in central Leyte); and perhaps the island of Apit or Himuguetan. The ships were sailing north through the Canigao Channel, along the west coast of Leyte (Skelton, 160).

183 'Flying foxes' or large fruit-eating bats (genus *Pteropus*).

184 The tabón, which are mound-building *Megapodes*, 'gallinaceous birds peculiar to the Austro-Malayan subregion' (Guillemard, 235).

185 The Camotes, west of Leyte: Poro, Pacijan, and Ponson islands.

186 These houses 'built upon logs' are schematically represented in the preceding chart.

187 Probably Cristòbal Rebelo, who is believed to have been an illegitimate son of Magellan's, also remembered in Magellan's will (Morison, *The Southern Voyages*, 423).

188 Again, the chart precedes the discussion of Cebu and the account of the death of Magellan on Mactan in the narrative. (In fact, 25 v has just the last two lines of paragraph 69 and the rest of the page blank with the chart of Cebu and Mactan on the facing page [26 r].) At this point in the Beinecke manuscript is positioned the map of Mazzaua, Bohol, Ceylon, Bohol, Canigao, Baybay, and Gatighan.

189 Siam, or modern Thailand (cf. 1268, 1275–8). Pigafetta is the first to use the word 'junk' in Italian (in the form *iunco* or *ionco*). The word derives from the Malay and Javanese word *adjong* referring to a large vessel used in war and trade (cf. 967, 1252, 1269).

190 The Portuguese had arrived as far as India and the Moluccas from the west. India Major and India Minor are differently applied by different authors. See Robertson, 1: 256.

191 The blood brotherhood of *casi casi*, mentioned earlier (cf. 354).

192 Before leaving Spain, Magellan had received the order of St James of Compostela (cf. the dedicatory letter 2–6).

193 A city in Gujarat, an Islamic realm of western India from which the Portuguese imported silk (cf. 614–15, 799, 960, 1323).

194 Ptolemy's Sinus Magnus: the Gulf of China.

195 From which 'gong.' Pigafetta, who is the first Westerner to record the term, does not elsewhere use any form of gong (which enters Italian only after 1600 via English) but rather *borchia* 'knob' or 'buckle.'

196 The first of these two men was Martin Barreta, who had sailed as a supernumerary of the *Santiago*. The other was Juan de Aroche (Guillemard, 240).

197 The ground upon which they rest serves as bottom, whereby raising them up, the merchandise remains on the ground (Amoretti, 84).

198 According to Masoero, a kind of Teleost of the Percomorph order which lives in a tropical seas and is of small dimensions. For Robertson it is a large sea snail found in the Philippines which has a shell resembling that of the *Nautilus pompilius* and is used to hold incense or as a drinking vessel.

199 'In the house that was mentioned in 528?' (Canova, 231).

200 Ferdinand I, (1503–64), House of Habsburg.

201 The Infanta Juana, 'la Loca' (1479–1555), daughter of Isabel and Ferdinand of Castile, who became queen of Castile, until declared mentally incompetent and secluded in a monastery in Tordesillas.

202 'The "tromb" or "trunk" was a kind of hand rocket-tube make of wood and hooped with iron, and was used for discharging wildfire' (Robertson, 2: 262).

203 The neighbouring island referred to here was Mactan (cf. 612). Pigafetta again foreshadows the deadly reception Magellan will receive there. The detail about Magellan destroying a village that refused to submit to the Christians is also in other sources. Canova (235) cites Peter Martyr: 'Dedit oppidum regiae sedi vicinum in praedam et combussit universum Magaglianus Domorum forte quinquaginta in Zubum regressus est cum

praeda rerum comestibilium quarum est in Zubo aliqua penuria, et sup-
pellectilium variorum' (189).

204 This Flemish statuette was recovered on 28 April 1565 by the Spanish
conquistador Miguel Lòpez de Legazpi. It is still preserved in the Basil-
ica of the Santo Niño on Cebu.

205 Not a name, but the title for one of the principal ministers of the king.
Malay *banda hara* referred to the treasurer or some other high function-
ary of the state.

206 See note 184. Again, Pigafetta, the Knight of Rhodes, emphasizes Magellan's membership in a military-religious order.

207 Idols similar to the Korawaar of New Guinea. Mariarosa Masoero, *Viaggio
attorno al mondo di Antonio Pigafetta* (Rovereto, Italy: Longo, 1987) 98.

208 Mandani is Mandaue; Lalan may be Liloan; Lubucun may be Lubú, but
Da Mosto (78, n. 3) conjectures it to be Lambusan. The list in the
French MSS is longer and includes two villages named *Cotcot* and *Puzzo*
with the names of their chiefs (Skelton, 84).

209 Mactan is a small island lying in the Bohol Strait off the port of Cebu.

210 Zula was faithful to the Sultan of Cebu Humabon while Lapu Lapu (the
Ci at the beginning of many names is an article in the Malay language
placed before the names of people) was in rebellion. Lapu Lapu will
be responsible for the defeat of the Spaniards and is today considered
the first hero of the Phillipine resistance to colonialism (Canova, in
Pigafetta, *Relazione*, 238).

211 Cf. 576, where Pigafetta first reports this incident.

212 Pigafetta addresses directly the Grand Master again (cf. 30, 177, 224).
This lengthy anthropological account represents a kind of tension-
building counterpoint to the narrative of the death of Magellan that follows. The section closes ominously with the story of the jet-black bird
that comes to the village and screeches every night at midnight (cf. 653).

213 This description is expurgated from the French MSS with the exception
of the Yale Beinecke MS The custom is called the *palang*. Amoretti notes
that Noort and Cavendish found the practice still continued when they
sailed through these seas. According to them it was an invention of the
women to prevent sodomy. See T. Harrisson, 'The "palang": its history
and proto-history in West Borneo and the Philippines,' *Journal of the
Malaysian Branch of the Royal Asiatic Society* 37, no. 2 (1964): 162–74.

214 Lapu Lapu, rajah of Mactan (cf. 612), though subject to the rajah of
Cebu, had refused to do homage to the king of Spain; and Zula, one of
his subordinate chiefs, was prevented from doing so by fear of his overlord Lapu Lapu, against whom he invoked Magellan's aid. For a full
account of the battle of Mactan and death of Magellan, see Guillemard
246–61.

215 Depending on the account, the natives were anywhere from fifteen hundred to six thousand in number.

216 According to Transylvanus, Magellan had ordered 'his men to be of
good cheer and brave hearts, and not to be alarmed at the number of
the enemy, for they had often seen, as formerly, so in quite recent times,
two hundred Spaniards in the island of Yucatan put sometimes two or
three thousand men to flight. But he pointed out to the Subuth [Cebu]
islanders that he had brought them, not to fight, but to watch their bravery and their fighting power' (200).

217 See Guillemard, 254, for various accounts of the death of Magellan.

218 This eulogy is addressed to Villiers de l'Isle-Adam, Grand Master of the
Knights of Rhodes, to whom the narrative is dedicated (cf. 30, 177,
224). As Grand Master of the Knights, Villiers de l'Isle-Adam was the
ideal defender of the fame of the sea crusader Magellan.

219 We prefer to translate *grandissima fortuna* literally rather than metaphor-
ically (Roberston has 'in the greatest of adversity'; Guillemard has 'in
the worst misfortune'; Skelton has 'in a very high hazard'). The theme
of the storm has been associated with Magellan since the beginning of
the narrative: 'a voyage through the Ocean Sea, where furious winds and
great storms are always reigning' (cf. 6). For a parallel passage see
Michel De Cuneo's praise of Columbus in his 'Letter to Hieronimo
Annari': 'But one thing I want you to know is that in my humble opinion, since Genoa was Genoa, there has never been a man so courageous
and astute in the act of navigation as the Lord Admiral; for, when sailing,
by simply observing a cloud or a star at night, he judged what was to
come. If there was bad weather, he himself commanded and stood at the
helm. When the storm had passed, he raised the sails while the others
slept.' *Prime relazioni di navigatori italiani sulla scoperta dell'America*, ed.
L. Firpo (Turin: UTET, 1966), 76.

220 For another view, see Peter Martyr: 'Magellan was killed together with seven of his companions, while twenty-two others were wounded. Thus did this brave Portuguese, Magellan, satisfy his craving for spices' (2: 159).

221 Pigafetta again marks an important point in the narrative by giving the full date (cf. 238, 293). As Masoero has observed, Magellan's death divides the narrative almost precisely in half. 'Magellano, "bon pastore" e "bon cavaliero"' in *La letteratura di viaggio dal Medioevo al Rinascimento: Generi e problemi* (Alessandria: Edizioni dell'Orso, 1989), 54.

222 Magellan's brother-in-law. In 1517 Magellan married Barbosa's sister Beatrice. Barbosa had been named captain of the *Victoria* following the mutiny at Port St Julian. He died together with João Serrão, Luís Afonso de Gòs, Enrique of Malacca, and another twenty-one men in the ambush at Cebu in 1521 (cf. 103). But according to the documentation collected by Navarrete twenty-seven men died (2: 448–9). He is not the same Duarte Barbosa that authored an important account of the Indies (1517–18), published by Ramusio (vol. 1, 1550, fols. 310–48 [see Canova, in Pigafetta, *Relazione*, 75–6]; a Hakluyt Society publication of a Portuguese manuscript of this account was published in 1928, edited by M.L Dames).

223 In reality Portuguese by birth, and brother of Magellan's friend Francisco Serrão (who lived in Ternate 1513–21 (cf. 978, 980, 984, 988, 994, 1084). João Lopes Carvalho was captain of the *Santiago*, and after that ship was lost, of the *Concepción* (cf. 218).

224 Enrique of Malacca, in the official muster, a slave brought back from the East by Magellan (cf. 340).

225 The Ambrosiana MS reads *schiavina*, a Venetian dialect word for a blanket of coarse wool.

226 According to Navarrete, Enrique was innocent, and the chiefs of Mactan and two other rajahs ordered the treachery (4: 66, n. 1, lxxxv). Guillemard cites Barros (Dec. iii. lib. v, cap. x and Herrera, Dec. iii, lib. i., cap. ix), to the effect that 'the chiefs who had made difficulties in submitting to his [the King of Cebu's] authority united to form a common cause, and sent to inform him that if he did not assist them in exterminating the Spaniards and seizing their ships, they would kill him and lay waste their country' (263). Transylvanus and Gomara are with Pigafetta

on this point, in blaming the slave. See Morison for another version according to the anonymous Portuguese (*The Southern Voyages*, 358). See also Peter Martyr for yet another motivation for the plot: 'the Spaniards think it was on account of women, for the islanders are jealous' (2: 159). See Guillemard for a critical account, 262–67.

227 The phrase *più sacente* is open to various interpretations, including 'more cunning' according to Robertson's translation.

228 The constable was Gonzalo Gòmez de Espinosa, who was left behind with the *Trinidad*, and was one of the survivors from that vessel, returning to Spain long after (Robertson, 1: 267).

229 From the Portuguese *jaqueira*, jackfruit or the tree (cf. 872, 1207). See the description at 185, where they are called *nangha*, which is an indigenous name for a variety of *Artocarpus*. 'The jack, *Artocarpus incisa*, is intensively cultivated throughout the archipelago, and its name Nangka, extends all the way to the Philippines.' John Crawfurd, *A Descriptive Dictionary of the Indian Islands and Adjacent Countries* (London: Oxford University Press, 1971), 24.

230 Most of the words in the following Bisayan vocabulary can be distinguished in the dictionaries of that language. Robertson provides a list of correspondences (1: 269–73). For commentary see G. Soravia, 'Pigafetta lessicografo dei nuovi e vecchi mondi,' in *Età delle scoperte geografiche nei suoi riflessi linguistici in Italia*. Atti del Convegno di studi, Firenze, 21–22 ottobre 1994, 66–95.

231 '*Bassag bassag* does not correspond to "shin" but to "basket for holding clothes," or "cartilage of the nose;" or possibly to *basac basac*, "the sound made by falling water"' (Robertson, 1: 269).

232 Cf. 1081.

233 '*Tahil* is found in the Tagalog dictionaries, and is the name of a specific weight, not weight in general. It is the Chinese weight called "tael," [or tail] which was introduced by the Chinese into the East Indies, whence it spread throughout the various archipelagos' (Robertson, 1: 269).

234 Cf. 533.

235 Syphilis here, although the disease of St Job commonly referred to leprosy.

236 Cf. 414.

237 Cf. 344, 348, 365, 426.

238 Cf. 339.

239 Following the massacre at Cebu, the hierarchy of command had to be reorganized. João Carvalho was named captain-general, but he would later be replaced by Gonzalo Gómez de Espinosa. Juan Sebastián de Cano would eventually assume the command of the *Victoria* (see note 278). The reduced fleet wandered from Bohol to Mindanao to Palawan, to the east coast of Borneo, then returned to the Philippines, always in search of the Moluccas. After capturing some native pilots (cf. 935) the fleet finally reached Tidore in the Moluccas on Friday, 8 November 1521.

240 Pangalo is located off the southwest coast of Bohol. The ships had sailed southwest through the Bohol Strait. The black men were Negritos.

241 According to Guillemard, the place corresponds to Caraga, in the northeast part of the island of Mindanao (234, n. 1).

242 The Malasian ceremony of *casi casi* or blood brotherhood (cf. 354). The Malay word list defines *casi casi*: 'To be one and the same thing.'

243 Cf. 387, 860. Aromatic resin used also as a perfume.

244 After visiting Borneo and Palawan (cf. 911–24).

245 Or Quipit, located on the northeast coast of Mindanao, east of Sindangan Bay, on the north coast of the Zamboanga Peninsula.

246 Earliest European mention of the island of Luzon, the largest and northernmost of the Philippines.

247 Inhabitants of the Ryukyu Islands ('Lequios'); more probably, as suggested by the Genoese pilot, they were Chinese.

248 The island of Cagayan Sulu, located to the northeast of Borneo, in 9 degrees 30 minutes N, in the Cagayan group lying in the Sulu Sea west of Mindanao (cf. 902).

249 Bananas.

250 Palawan, the most westernly of the Philippines and after Luzon and Mindanao, the largest of them, at 9 degrees 30 minutes N and 118 minutes and 30 degrees longitude. The 'Roteiro' gives a fuller account of what happened at Palawan (15–17). The natives were hostile initially but then the Europeans found another village at the port called Dyguasam, where they were able to obtain supplies. Pigafetta does not mention this place in his narrative, but it does appear in the corresponding chart (Tegozzano porto). Nor is mention made of Sundan, which also appears in the chart.

251 Cockfighting was always a great diversion among Malayan peoples. See Crawfurd. 'Most of the advanced natives of the Asiatic Islands are

gamblers, and the favorite shape which gaming takes with them is cock-fighting. This includes the people of Bali, Lomboc, Celebes, and all the Philippine Islands, the only material exception being the Javanese' (113).

252 After coasting along Palawan, they left its southern point on 21 June 1521. They passed through the Balabac Strait, between the islands of Balabac and Banggi, and south-west along the coast of Borneo to Brunei in latitude 5 degrees N.

253 Bruney Bay, in the northeast part of the island of Borneo.

254 A Spanish transliteration of Malay *parah*, which is a generic name for any vessel, whether rowing or sailing (Crawfurd, 360).

255 From Arabic *alma'dijà*: river boat. The word was common among Hispano-Portuguese navigators and already used in Italian by Cadamosto.

256 Cf. 440, and see note 171.

257 Brunei. Crawfurd cites at length from Pigafetta's account, for it represents, 'the only authentic account of a Malay court when first seen by Europeans, and before their policy or impolicy had affected Malayan society' (71).

258 Crawfurd questions this population estimate, which at five persons per hearth would bring the number to 125,000. In any case, the town 'in the time of Pigafetta was evidently a place of much more consequence than it is in ours' (71).

259 From the indigenous word *jurutulis*, 'adept in writing' (Crawfurd, 72).

260 As Crawfurd observes, 'This auspicious beginning of European intercourse had a very unlucky ending. After the reception at court, the king of Borneo sent a fleet to attack some of his heathen neighbors, and the Spaniards, fancying it came to attack themselves, opened fire on it' (72).

261 Perhaps the island of Laut Pulan, off the south-east coast of Borneo.

262 If Carvalho had not released the Moor, he might have been traded for the three Europeans.

263 The word appears to have fallen out of the manuscript; Da Mosto first restored it (88).

264 'The smallest brass, copper, tin, and zinc coins common throughout the eastern islands were called "pichis" or "pitis," which was the name of the ancient Javanese coin, now used as a frequent appellative for money in general.' (Robertson, II, 201; refers to Crawfurd, 385–8).

265 The Kati, frequently written Catty, a weight of 1 1/2 pounds avoirdupois, which contains sixteen tails (Crawfurd 196). For the *tahil* see our note 233.

266 Used in Calicut, the only weight introduced by the Arabs into the eastern archipelagos, the *bahar* varied in value in different parts of East Asia (Crawfurd, 446). Skelton calculates the *bahar* of Tidore referred to later by Pigafetta to be equivalent to about 450 pounds' weight (169).

267 Transylvanus reports: 'And to omit nothing, our men constantly affirm that the islanders of Porne told them that the king wore in his crown two pearls of the size of a goose's egg' (205). Mention of these pearls will be made again later (906–10).

268 'The Malay camphor tree is confined so far as known, to a few parts of the islands of Sumatra and Borneo, where it is very abundant. The oil (both fluid and solid) is found in the body of the tree where the sap should be, but not in all trees. The Malay name for camphor is a slight corruption of the Sanskrit one "karpura"' (Robertson, 2: 202).

269 Transylvanus gives an interesting and divergent account of the people of Borneo, among other things observing that: 'they love peace and quiet, but war they greatly detest, and they honor their king as a god whilst he is bent upon peace. But if he be too desirous of war, they rest not till he has fallen by the hand of the enemy in battle. Whenever he has determined to wage war, which is rarely done, he is placed by his subjects in the vanguard, where he is compelled to bear the whole onslaught of the enemy ... Wherefore they rarely wage war' (204).

270 The placement of the map of Burne (X) comes after mention of the island but the maps of of Mindanao (XI); and the chart of Zzolo (Jolo), Subanin, Tagima (Basilan), Cavit (Cavite) (XII) precedes their treatment in the narrative. The latter two charts are actually contiguous and continuous to one another in the Ambrosiana manuscript (46vr-47r).

271 That is, northeast along the coast of Borneo.

272 A name recorded only by Pigafetta. For Skelton, it is presumably a reef between the Balabec Strait and Brunei. Masoero identifies it as Balambangan (*Viaggio attorno al mondo*, 215).

273 Cape Sempang Mangayau is the northernmost point of Borneo, in latitude 7 degrees N. Cimbonbon is either Balambangan or Banguey, islands north of Cape Sempang Mangayau.

274 Between 15 August and 21 September 1521.

275 'The *Tridacna gigas* ... The shells sometimes attain a length of five or six feet, and weigh hundreds of pounds' (Robertson, 2: 203).

276 Masoero suggests this may have been the Port Jackson shark.

277 According to Robertson, these were the insects *Phyllium orthoptera*, known as walking leaves from their resemblance to a leaf (2: 203).

278 Carvalho was deprived of his command when the expedition departed from there; the *Trinidad* was placed under the command of Gonzalo Gomèz de Espinosa and the *Victoria* under the command of Juan Sebastian del Cano. 'At the September full moon the fleet officers, feeling that Carvalho was becoming too big for his boots as well as a menace to their future safety by acts of piracy, degraded him to his former rank of flag pilot' (Morison, *The Southern Voyages*, 444).

279 The southernmost point of Palawan in Cape Buliluyan.

280 Cagayan Sulu (cf. 767).

281 Cf. 760, 767.

282 Jolo and Basilan, in the Sulu Archipelago.

283 For the pearls of the King of Brunei, see 124. 'The true pearl oysters of the Philippine Islands are found along the coasts of Paragua, Mindanao, and in the Sulu Archipelago, especially in the last named, where many very valuable pearls are found. These fisheries are said to rank with the famous fisheries of Ceylon and the Persian Gulf' (Robertson, 2: 203).

284 Cavite and Subanin are on the west coast of the Zamboanga Peninsula, Mindanao. Skelton suggests that Monoripa may be the island of Sacoli. 'The ships then sailed ... into Moro Gulf, and eastward across it' (166).

285 According to Robertson, Pigafetta's etymology of the Malay word is correct (2: 204).

286 The principal Malay settlement in the southern part of the island Mindanao, located in the delta of the Pulangi River.

287 Magellan had passed by the north of the island in March 1521 (cf. 397, 423).

288 Cape Benuian is a promontory in northern Mindanao. Da Mosto cites an ethnologist who encountered the custom of eating the heart of slain enemies among the Manobis in eastern Mindanao (96). Tomo Sanz rejects this identification and believes the name of the tribe is a corruption of *mangian*, an indigenous term which meant 'savages' ('Mundo indigeno,' 388).

289 Ciboco, located by Albo in 6 degrees N, is perhaps Sibago off the north-east coast of the large island of Basilan; according to Albo, the course was changed to the south-east after passing this island. According to Skelton, Birahan Bartolach would be the district of Batukali in Mindanao; the island of Sarangani is south of Mindanao; Candinghar probably represents the island of Balut.

290 Islands of Kawio and Sanghihe archipelagos, extending southward from Mindanao to Celebes. Pigafetta's names are distored but some are easily recognizable, including the second and third as Kawio, the fourth as Memanuk, the fifth as Kawalusu, and the seventh as Lipang.

291 To the north of Celebes, Sanghihe is the largest island of the Sangihe group.

292 Islands of Sanghihe archipelago, extending to the south towards Celebes.

293 Skelton suggests Tahulandang, Ruang, or Biaro, which are the southernmost islands of the Sanghihe group (167). Masoero prefers Tahulandang (238).

294 This reference to the Talaud Islands appears to be out of place. The Talaud islands are two degrees north of Paghinzara, and such a route to the Moluccas is unlikely (from Siau to Talaud, far to the northeast).

295 Tifore and Maju, in the Molucca Passage, about fifty miles west of Halmahera (Gilolo).

296 Pigafetta marks the importance of the arrival in the Moluccas by giving the full date (cf. 293, 696, 1323).

297 See note 179. According to Bausani, Pigafetta refers here to the Malay *puan*, a box for holding betel (28).

298 The Portuguese had established a rigid domination since discovering the Moluccas in 1511. This explains the enthusiasm with which the Spanish expedition was welcomed at Tidore. Guillemard notes that when Francisco Serrão first discovered the Moluccas in 1511, he settled at Ternate, 'the sultan of which island was not on friendly terms with the monarch of Tidore, and for this reason the Portuguese became paramount in the former island while the Spaniards identified themselves chiefly with Tidore' (277).

299 The report of indigenous people having some foreknowledge of the coming of the Europeans is a topos of the literature of discovery and

conquest, most famously in the case of the Aztecs, but going back to Columbus's second voyage and Ramon Pane's account of the religious beliefs of the people of Haiti. See Peter Martyr, I, 166–76. Guillemard notes that Argensola gives a similar story with regard to the King of Ternate, Boleyfe, or Abuteis, when visited by Serrão and his Portuguese (277). Both Peter Martyr and Maximilian Transylvanus make note of it in their accounts of Magellan's voyage, the latter expanding upon the theme as follows: 'He [the king] having received the presents kindly, looks up to heaven and says: "I have known now for two years from the course of the stars, that you were coming to seek these lands, sent by the most mighty King of Kings. Wherefore your coming is the most pleasant and grateful to me, as I had been forewarned of it by the signification of the stars. And, as I know that nothing ever happens to any man which has not been fixed long before by the decree of fate and the stars, I will not be the one to attempt to withstand either the fates or the significa- tion of the stars, but willingly and of good cheer, will henceforth lay aside the royal pomp and will consider myself as managing the adminis- tration of this island only in the name of your king"' (206).

300 According to Bausani (29), the king was not supposed to ever find him- self in a lower posittion than his subjects.

301 As with the previous pair of maps, the two charts representing the Moluccas are contiguous and continuous in the manuscript. In the Beinecke manuscript the charts follow the account of the archipelago and the word list (see below).

302 A kind of cotton exported from India which is mentioned in the travel reports of the period in various forms. According to Bausani, the word is a Persian-Indian origin: *Bairam, bairami* (29).

303 Manzor ruled in Tidore from 1512 to 1526. He opposed the early Portu- guese colonization of the area and allied himself with the Spaniards. He was Muslim, the Islamic faith having spread throughout the area during the fifteenth century, brought by the Arabs who had taken over com- merce and trade along the coasts.

304 The cédula of 8 May 1519 (see note 11) ended 'with a long list of the quintaladas permitted to the different members of the ship's company. The quintalada was the free freight allowed to officers and crew. It was permitted to everyone, from captain to cabin-boy, and varied from 8000

to 75 pounds according to rank. It paid a duty of one-twenty-fourth to the Crown' (Guillemard, 129).

305 The northernmost of the Moluccas, and the Sultan of which had been murdered eight months earlier (see below) so that the throne was still vacant. Manzor appears to have replaced this ruler of Ternate temporarily as the overlord of the clove islands in which the latter acknowledged the sovereignty of Spain. According to Navarrete, on 10 November, Juan de Carvalho went ashore and appears to have signed a treaty with Manzor (iv, 296). For more details on the political situation in the islands of that time, see Donald F. Lach, *Asia in the Making of Europe*, vol. I, bk II (London: Methuen, 1986), 595.

306 Kolano is the common name for princes and kings of the Moluccas. Gapi was the ancient name of Ternate. According to Bausani, the name may therefore simply mean 'King of Ternate' (30).

307 The largest and southernmost island of the Moluccas, to the west of the southern coast of Halmahera (Gilolo).

308 The five original Molucca or clove islands. Given here in order from north to south, extending about one degree on either side of the equator along the west coast of Halmahera (Gilolo).

309 Calonaghapi (cf. 967).

310 Francisco Serrão, brother of João, was a Portuguese soldier or mariner who established himself in the Moluccas in 1512. Magellan and Francisco Serrão had served together in the East and had been shipmates in the expedition of Diogo Lopes de Sequeira in 1509–10 to Malacca (see Guillemard, 53–61). See Skelton for alternative versions of Serrão's death (168, n. 31).

311 While living in Ternate, Serrão had corresponded with Magellan, and by placing the Moluccas much to the east of their true position had influenced Magellan's plan and its promotion (Guillemard, 70–2).

312 Manuel I (1495–1521), king of Portugal. The *tostão* was a Portuguese silver coin.

313 See Lach's analysis of these political events in Ternate (595n30).

314 Bandan was the centre for Portuguese domination in the southern Moluccas, first reached by Antonio de Abreu in 1512. Pedro Alfonso de Lorosa had come to the Moluccas with Francisco Serrão in 1512. According to Antonio de Brito, Lorosa escaped from the ship of Tristão

de Meneses, which called at Ternate in October 1520 in order to appre-
hend Serrão (Navarrete, 4: 306). Lorosa was later executed by the Portuguese for having passed into the service of the Spaniards. According
to Bausani, his slave Manuel mentioned there may have been one of
Pigafetta's primary linguistic sources (33).

315 Now called Halmahera. Maximilian Transylvanus reports that in this
island 'they saw men with ears so long and pendulous, that they reached
to their shoulders. When our men were mightily astonished at this, they
learnt from the natives that there was another island not far off where
the men had ears not only pendulous, but so long and broad, that one of
them could cover the whole head, if they wanted. But our men, who
sought not monsters but spices, neglecting this nonsense, went straight
to the Moluccas' (205).

316 Plants that contain water, of the genus *Uncaria*.

317 Cinnabar is a red sulfide of mercury, a mineral highly esteemed in the east.

318 Cloth of the Gujerat peninsula in western India, famous throughout
Asia. Also called the cloth of Cambaya after one of the principal cities of
Gujerat (Kambayat). Cf. 505, 614, 799, 960.

319 As in the report of the shoals (cf. 947), lack of water was reported to dis-
courage expeditions to the Moluccas.

320 See note 314.

321 Diogo Lopes de Sequeira (1466–1530), Viceroy of India 1518–22.

322 The port of Mecca on the Red Sea.

323 According to Skelton, following Barros, probably Pedro de Faria, who
was sent by Lopes de Sequeira to build a fort at Molucca (169).

324 The Portuguese believed, as did the Spaniards, that the islands were on
the Spanish side of the line of demarcation.

325 Lorosa sailed with the Spanish ships in September 1521. He was in the
Trinidad when she was captured by the Portuguese squadron under
Antonio de Brito in May 1522, and was executed as a traitor.

326 The Italian reads *Li versi*: a name given to small pieces of artillery used
for the most part to fire salvoes (sp. *verso*). Cf. 1040, 1120, 1148.

327 Christmas and 24 June, corresponding to the two solstices.

328 A small island south of Tidore.

329 Sago, a dry granulated or powdered starch prepared from the pith from
a sago palm: *Sagus arenacea*, belonging to the family of the *Metroxylon*
palms. Maximilian Transylvanus reports: 'Their bread, which they call

sago, was made of the trunk or wood of a tree, rather like a palm' (198). The knowledge of bread made from the flour derived from tropical palms goes back to Marco Polo, who saw the sago palm in the island of Sumatra and described the process by which bread was made from it. 'The Sago Tree,' bk 3, chap. 16, in *The Travels of Marco Polo* (New York: Dorset Press, 1908), 345–6.

330 Crawfurd reports that *gaumedi* is a word used for cloves by the natives of the Moluccas, meaning 'cow's marrow' (102). The chart which pictures the clove tree call them *Cavi gomode*, apparently a combination of the Portuguese *cravo* ('nails,' for the resemblance to iron nails) and the native word *gaumedi*.

331 Bausani reports that *Tjengkih* (which Pigafetta transcribes as *chianche*) is the most common Malay-Indonesian word for the clove tree (41).

332 Buru is the largest island to the west of Ceram. The father of the king was probably Tjiliati, the first Muslim king of Tidore, who took the Muslim name Djamaluddin (1495–1512), but the dates are not certain. Pigafetta appears to be the only source that speaks of his violent death. A. Bausani, *L'Indonesia nella relazione di viaggio di A. Pigafetta* (Rome: Centro di cultura Italiana Djakarta, 1972), 41–2.

333 The one that had cost Duarte Barbosa and João Serrão their lives at Cebu. This episode of the mens' suspicions is narrated in greater detail by the 'Roteiro,' 163.

334 *Sembahjang* indicates in Malay-Indonesian the canonical Islamic prayer (Bausani, 42).

335 The island of Makian was half under the domination of Tidore and half under the domination of Ternate.

336 The patron saint of gunners whose feast is celebrated 4 December.

337 A small Venetian coin struck by the Doge Niccolò Marcello in 1473.

338 The *quintalada* mentioned above (cf. 967), a percentage that each member of the crew received on the ship's earnings.

339 According to Bausani, Pigafetta here translates literally an expression typical of the Indonesian langagues (44).

340 A term of South Indian origin referring to silk produced in India and highly esteemed at Malacca and in Indonesia during the period.

341 The Italian reads *oggi* ('today'), and therefore presents a trace of the original diary upon which Pigafetta elaborated his account.

342 Santiago de Compostela.

343 A small island to the south of Tidore (cf. 1061).

344 Again, the Italian reads *oggi*.

345 This is the earliest European description of the birds of paradise, Malay *burung dewata*, 'bird of the gods.' Maximilian Transylvanus reports: 'The kings of Marmin began to believe that souls were immortal a few years ago, introduced by no other argument than that they saw a certain most beautiful small bird never rested upon the ground nor upon anything that grew upon it; but sometimes saw it fall dead upon the ground from the sky. And as the Mahometans, who traveled to those parts for commercial purposes, told them that this bird was born in Paradise, and that Paradise was the abode of the souls of those who had died, these kings embraced the sect of Mahomet, because it promised wonderful things concerning the abode of the souls. But they call the bird Mamuco Diata, and they hold it in such reverence and religious esteem, that they believe that by it their kings are safe in war, even though they, according to custom, are placed in the fore front of battle' (206).

346 The passage has usually been taken to refer to the practice of sodomy: 'as Svetonius refers regarding Caesar and Nicomede' (Amoretti, 157), although Canova notes that the sources do not present any other other record of sodomitic practices of this type.

347 Robertson translates 'headless' but the phrase 'e parenno siano senza capo' probably means 'they seem to have no leader.' Otherwise, how could they be hanged as described below.

348 The seasonal shift of the trade winds from the west to the east normally occurs in November–December. Periodic winds from the west begin typically in May. See the Genoese pilot for an account of the misfortunes of the *Trinidad* under the command of Gonzalo Gomez de Espinosa. She sailed 6 April 1522, reached the Marianas, continued as far as 43 degrees N, and then turned back in August. Reaching Molucca in November, Espinosa surrendered to Antonio de Brito.

349 Pigafetta does not say when or why he changed ships from the *Trinidad* to the *Victoria*. It was perhaps because of disagreements with the commander of the *Trinidad*, Espinosa, whom Pigafetta never mentions.

350 Carvalho had already been succeeded in command of the fleet in September 1521 by Espinosa, who also remained behind at Tidore with the

fifty-three men. Carvalho died there on 14 February 1522, before the *Trinidad* sailed. Pigafetta never mentions Espinosa or Elcano, commander of the *Victoria*.

351 According to Bausani, Pigafetta here refers to the Muslim *quædï* or canonical judge who was a figure second in importance only to the king (50).

352 For Bausani this corresponds to the Malay-Indonesian *kemendikai*, a dialect variant of *mendikai* (a form that is given in Pigafetta's Malaysian vocabulary: *mandikai sucui*): a kind of melon (*Citrullus edulis*). But for Skelton and Robertson, it is most probably mango (*Mangifera indica*) (51).

353 Fruit of the guava, a myrtaceous tree of Arawaken origin: this tropical American shrub was brought by the Portuguese from Brazil, spread rapidly throughout tropical regions of Asia, and was widely cultivated for its sweet and yellow fruit.

354 According to Bausani, *nori/nuri* is the common Malayan-Indonesian term for a kind of parrot, and Pigafetta's *Cathara* is a deformation of *Kakatua* (51).

355 Actual latitudes: Ternate: 40 degrees S; Tidore: 50 degrees S; Motir: 26 degrees N; Makian 20 degrees N; Batjan: between 30 and 31 degrees S.

356 This 'wonderfully accurate' (Crawfurd, 352) list of 450 words is of considerable interest 'since it is accurate and one of the oldest extant specimens of the Malay language, the earliest surviving Malay manuscripts being dated from around 1500–1550' (Lach, 1: bk 1, 176). For a summary of scholarship, see C.C.F.M. Le Roux, 'Nogmaals Pigafetta's Maleische woorden,' *Tijdschrift voor Indische taal~, land~ en volkenkunde* 79 (1939): 446–51; and more recently, Bausani's list of correspondences and annotations to his list (74–84).

357 'The original was probably *rumio*. All Islamic languages use rumi in the sense of "from the territories of the ex-Eastern Roman Empire," especially Anatolia hence "Turk"' (Bausani, 74).

358 'These are Tagalog words that mean "this is your brother" (*Kapatid~mo jari*)' (Bausani, 75).

359 '*Cenin* means eyelashes and not eyelids while *quilai* was moved to correspond to eyelashes. But *quilai* (Tagalog and Bisayan *kilay*, Brunei dialect *kirai*) means eyelashes … There is missing therefore a correct translation for eyelids' (Bausani, 75).

360 'Pipi is more precisely "cheek"' (Bausani, 75). Many of these impressions are due to Pigafetta's method of gathering information by pointing and gestures.

361 '*Belankang* means "behind" or "back;" the shoulders are more properly *bahu*' (Bausani, 75).

362 'an interesting combination of words (*telur kaki*) meaning "the egg of the leg," a very efficacious expression but unknown to modern use' (Bausani, 76).

363 Crawfurd reports that the Javanese name is *bàras*, and that this 'with various corruptions is to be found in at least twenty different languages' (368). It appears in the word list of the Philippines (53).

364 Crawfurd notes that the two most frequent names for coconut are the Malay *nùr* and the Malay *Kàlapa* corresponding to Pigafetta's *mor* and *calambil* respectively.

365 Crawfurd reports the Malay name to be *pisang* (31) Cfr. 282.

366 'The cane is called in Malay and Javanese *tàbu* … This name is universal' (Crawfurd, 409).

367 See note 229.

368 Crawfurd notes that the only cucurbitaceous cultivated plants that thrive well in the Indian and Philippine archipelagos are the cucumber and gourd, known by these names in all the islands of the archipelagos (273).

369 '*Sabungan* means "combat" and not "cock" (*ajam*). Yet one often encounters the expression *ajam sabunganin* the sense of "fighting cock"' (Bausani, 77).

370 In reality, the word means 'tiger.'

371 Italian MS *Al canne*. Translated by Robertson and Skelton: 'For reeds.' But note Pigafetta spells *canne* meaning dog (cf. 1287), and the masculine article also argues in favour of this interpretation. Crawfurd notes that the word for dog is *kuyo* among the Rejangs and Lampungs (121). Bausani says that Pigafetta gives a local form here: '*kujuk* means dog in the Malay of Brunei and in some other Indonesian dialects' (77).

372 'Another interesting misunderstanding which gives some indication, perhaps, of the method Pigafetta used to obtain his linguistic information. *Air madu* means "honey." "Bee" is *lebah*. *Gula* means "sugar"' (Bausani, 77).

373 Seems to be the same word as 103 above, meaning 'smoke.' Canova notes that Pigafetta's understanding might derive from expressions like daging asap ('smoked meat').

374 Cf. 520 and note.

375 'The correct form of silver was given earlier (*pirac* = pèrak). The strange expression *soliman danas* probably ... was given the name of a local silver coin' (Bausani, 77).

376 Cf. 1081 and note.

377 *Sukat* is a unit of measure used for grains and sometimes liquids, more or less equivalent to three kilograms.

378 *Bukit* means 'hill' or ' mountain.' 'Perhaps the misunderstanding derives from the fact that the land of the Indonesian islands looks like a hill viewed from the sea' (Canova, in Pigafetta, *Relazione*, 314).

379 '*apa* = "what," *nama* = "name," *itu* = "that"' (Bausani, 78).

380 'Musk is obtained from a species of beaver (*kesturi*)' (Bausani, 78).

381 'Baik means "well," "good" in general' (Bausani, 78).

382 'I believe that the only solution is to accept Gonda's suggestion and hold that "case" here means "casse." Thus we have the Malay *peti*, meaning chest or box, and the Minangkabau *alvang* its synonym' (Bausani, 79).

383 'It is curious that petang means the opposite, that is, not "morning" but "evening"' (Bausani, 79).

384 Italian MS.: *magalda*, from the German *magoald*, 'bad' put together with *maga*, 'witch.' The first attestation in the dictionaries of Italian is from Aretino (Canova, 317).

385 '*Tuan diam* means more precisely "Sir, be quiet!" or "be still"' (Bausani, 80).

386 'The meanings corresponding to the two Malay expressions should be reversed: *pintal benang* means "to sew" while *benang* means "sewing thread"' (Bausani, 80).

387 'Pigafetta's expression *ebarasai* seems the result of a misunderstanding. Probably when he heard someone sneeze he asked an Indonesian friend what they were used to saying when someone sneezed. His question was misunderstood and he was answered something like *la bersin* ("he sneezes" or "he sneezed") or perhaps *hai, bersin!* ("oh, a sneeze")' (Bausani, 80).

388 'Literally translated the expression means "come here, sir, eat!"' (Bausani, 81).

389 The Italian MS reads *disdissiare*, which is an old Vicentine dialect term
for 'to wake.' 'The Malay form closest to that given by Pigafetta could
be *bangukan* "to raise" or "to straighten"' (Bausani, 81).

390 '*Sabah alchair* means exactly the opposite, that is, "good morning"'
(Bausani, 81).

391 Cf. 837.

392 A Malay word of Chinese origin that entered the European languages
through Malay. The exoticism is already found in Varthema and in
Giovanni da Empoli (Canova).

393 Cf. 1323.

394 Malay for crocodile.

395 '*Sedap* and *manis* are synonyms which mean "sweet," "delicate." There
is no trace of Pigafetta's "kiss"' (Bausani, 82).

396 According to Sanvisenti, the 'essere agrizato' of the manuscript is old Vicentine for the violent sensation of fright or fear (478). Bausani, however,
reports that the corresponding Malay *amarah* means 'to be angry' (83).

397 '*Apa djadi* means more precisely "What's happening"' (Bausani, 83).

398 'The names of the numbers given by Pigafetta are singularly exact and
complete' (Bausani, 84).

399 The place is highlighted by a caption in the corresponding chart.
Bausani notes that the report is confirmed by the *Trattato delle Molucche*,
which speaks of dwarves kept at court by the kings of Ternate and
Tidore, perhaps taken from this island (52).

400 Islands of the archipelago between Makian and Batjan. Modern names:
Kajoa, Laigoma, Gumorga, Gafi, and Siko. Giogi is perhaps Goraitji,
south of Makian. Laboan must be Labuha, a port on the west side of
Batjan. But the *Trattato delle Molucche* speaks also of a separate island,
called Kaisiruta, which would correspond to Kasirota, very near to the
north-west of Batjan. Tolimau is Tolimao, an island which is part of
another small archipelago to the south-west of the archipelago of Kajoa.
In this archipelago, the largest island is Pigafetta's Titameto (today
Tameti), Latalata, Tabobi (Tappi), Maga (Lumang), and Batutiga (Obi)
must be islands to the north-east of Kasiruta.

401 Sula Besi, in the Sula group (Sula Taliabu, Sula Mangole, and Sula Besi),
south-east of Obi, and much farther than 'five leagues from Molucca'
(Skelton, 177).

402 As before, the chart precedes the islands that are about to be encountered and described.

403 Skelton notes that these island names are very confused; some appear to belong to the Sula group, others to the waters round Ambon (Skelton, 177). Tenetum, now Tenado, is part of the Ceram group of islands. Lamatola ought to be Lifamatola, the westernmost of the Sula group. Masoero identifies Atulabaou as Taliabu, Biga as Banggai, Pailarurun as Cailaruri.

404 Earlier (see note 229) Pigafetta speaks of the comilicaias a type of melon. In the Malay vocabulary *chiacare* is translated as *mendikai* while here they are called *nangka*. Bausani idenitifies the *nangka* as *ortocarpus integrifolia*, the jackfruit. *Chanali* has not been identified but may be the *Champada*, 'a smaller fruit than the jack, but more delicate in flavour, and far more esteemed. It is exclusively a native of the Archipelago, and chiefly of Sumatra and the peninsula' (Crawfurd, 24).

405 Pigafetta has already spoken of this fruit (the mango) in more or less the same terms (cf. 1193).

406 Buru is to the west of Ceram.

407 It is strange that he says Amboina is bounded by Halmahera (Gilolo). Pigafetta may have meant 'bounded by Ceram,' which is very near.

408 Benaia is probably Boano, in the strait of Manipa: the other two islands are perhaps Manipa and Kelang.

409 The island of Ambelou is in 3 degrees 15 minutes S.

410 The Banda group; in fact, ESE of Buru, and in 4 degrees S. A few of the names that follow in the text are identifiable. *Pulae* = Ai, *ulurun* = Rhun, *Rosoghin* = Rosengain. The island of Manuk, which may correspond to Pigafetta's Manucan, is however far to the south of the archipelago of Bandan. Samianapi is identified by Masoero as Gunong Api.

411 Solor, Nobokamor Rusa, and Lomblen. The ship had crossed the Banda Sea (in fact traversing no more than 4 degrees of latitude, half of Pigafetta's reckoning) and came to the island chain of the Sundas extending from Sumatra to Timor. The passage taken by the *Victoria* was Boleng Strait or Flores Strait, to the east or west of Solor; and thence they sailed east to Alor, reaching it on 10 January 1522 (Skelton, 178).

412 Nostra Signora de la Guida. But Pigafetta tells of making a pilgrimage to Santa Maria de la Antigua at the end of his narrative.

413 Malua, today Alor, at about 8 degrees 20 minutes S latitude.

414 Pigafetta distinguishes between long red pepper (Malay-Indonesian *tja-bai*) and black 'round' pepper (*lada*) in his Malay vocabulary. In the list he calls the latter *sabi* (*tjabai*) instead of *luli* as here.

415 An unidentified island of the Alor group, possibly Haruku, to the east of Amboina (Masoero). According to Bausani, it would be another island of the Alor group between Lomblen (Galiau) and Pantar (56).

416 Canova notes that many of the *mirabilia* recounted by Pigafetta in the last part of the narrative find parallels and/or possible sources in prior (Marco Polo) and nearly contemporary tradition of travel writers, for example, in the *Itinerario de Ludovico de Vartema Bolognese* (Rome, 1510); the *Viaggio* of Niccolò Conti; P. Bracciolini, 'Historiae de varietate fortunae,' in *Opera omnia*, II, ed. R. Fubini, Torino, 1966), 625–54; the *Suma Oriental* by Tomé Pires (A. Cortesão, *A Suma Oriental de Tomé Pires e o livro de Francisco Rodrigues*, Coimbra, 1978) and Duarte Barbosa's *Livro* (*Além-Mar: códice casanatense 1889 com o Livro do Oriente de Duarte Barbosa*, introdução de F. Braudel, textos de G. Guadalupi, C.R. Boxer, R. Barchiesi, Milan-Lisbon: Franco Maria Ricci, 1984. Tomé Pires also speaks of pygmy islanders, but locates them in Papua (*Suma*, 349). For further discussion and sample parallel passages, see Canova's introduction to his edition (in Pigafetta, *Relazione*, 80–92).

417 Note that Pigafetta gives the full date here to mark yet another important transition in the narrative (cf. 238, 293, 696, 948, 1323).

418 Timor.

419 Ambeno is on the north-west coast of Timor in 9 degrees 15 minutes S.

420 Silabão.

421 Sandalwood (*Santalum album*) is a native of several of the islands of the Malay archipelago, but more especially of Timor and Sandalwood Island (Sumba).

422 Places on the south side of Timor according to Skelton but Bausani identifies Lichsana as Liquicá on the north coast near Deli.

423 More than three thousand kilometres from Timor. Elsewhere Pigafetta speaks of Luzon and its commercial contacts with China and Borneo (cf. 763, 843–4).

424 Syphilis (although the 'disease of St Job' was usually referred to leprosy in Europe). The report picked up by Pigafetta in Timor implies that the

Portuguese had brought it to the East, but it appears to have been known and recorded much earlier in India and China. According to Skelton, there is a possible confusion with yaws, also endemic in the Pacific islands before European discovery (178–9).

425 Flores. Ende is on the southern coast of Flores, an island of the Sunda archipelago, between Sumbawa and Timor, between 7 and 9 degrees S and 120 and 123 degrees E.

426 The first seven of these names, collected by Pigafetta from the Javanese pilot, probably represent islands of the Sunda chain westward from Flores (Ende) to Sumbawa (Zumbava), Lombok (Lomboch), Bali (Chorum), and Java.

427 These are small islands of the Sunda archipelago, but they are not all recognizable and Pigafetta is referring second-hand information. Canova notes that Pigafetta's attention to the pronounciation of Java reflects his attention to indigenous languages.

428 The cities or districts of Java and the adjacent islands named in this paragraph are Majapahit (the capital), Sunda (probably western Java, inhabited by Sudanese), Daha (in eastern Java), Demak, followed by two unidentified places: Gaghiamada and Minutaranghan (but Bausani reports [58] Gaghiamada as the name of the famous minister of Majapahit, Gadjah Mada [1331–64]), Japara, Tuban, Geresik, Surabaya, Bali. Patih Yunus was one of the first Muslim sovereigns of Japara (north-east Java). After conquering Japara in 1511 he became the first sultan of Demak.

429 A topos of European travel literature to the Orient, Niccolò de' Conti observed this Hindu custom (Satí) in Birmania, at Ava (Ramusio, I, 340 r.), and Duarte Barbosa describes it among the people of Pegu (Ramusio, I, 335 r.), as did Varthem and Pires (for parallel passages, see Canova, in Pigafetta, *Relazione*, 82–6).

430 Perhaps Enggano, off the south-west coast of Sumatra, with which legends of an island of women like those in other parts of the world were associated. Pigafetta's mention of the island and the legends associated with it is significant in that it predates by many years the discovery of the island by the Portuguese (1593) and the Dutch (1596). An Italian traveller of the nineteenth century, E. Modigliani, wrote an interesting book on the island: *L'isola delle donne: un viaggio a Enggano* (Milan: U. Hoepli, 1894).

431 According to Bausani, this is perhaps the first time a European text mentions this Indonesian legendary cycle (60). Together with Indian (the bird *garuda*, the horseback ride of Visnu) and universal (the cosmic tree) motifs, there are also Indonesian elements (the centre of the waters). Indonesian are the names of the objects in this myth: Pigafetta's *puzathaer* is *pusat air,* 'the centre of waters;' *paughanghi* is the mythical tree *pauh djanggi,* literally, 'mango of the negroes.' The *pauh djanggi* is a legendary tree that grows in a sunken sandbar in the centre of the ocean (*pusat tasik*). A version of the legend is contained in Walter William Skeat's *Malay Magic: An Introduction to the Folklore and Popular Religion of the Malay Peninsulae* (London: Cass, 1965), 8–10.

432 A mistake for 'Arctic Pole,' if the southern extremity of the Malay Peninsula in 1 1/2 degree N latitude is intended.

433 Bangkok.

434 Yuthia or Ayutthaya, the ancient capital of Siam.

435 These places, most of which are easily recognizable in the modern forms, lie along the east side of the Malay Peninsula or in the Gulf of Siam.

436 Cambodia.

437 Champa is a Hindu and Buddhist kingdom between Cambodia and Cochinchina, on the east side of the Gulf of Siam.

438 Cochinchina.

439 The emperor Chitsong, of the Ming dynasty, reigned 1519–64. Skelton suggests that Pigafetta's account of China which follows leans heavily on Marco Polo (179). However, we have not identified any direct correspondences, and Pigafetta himself informs us that he gathered his information about China from 'a Moor who said that he had seen them' (cf. 1303).

440 Canton.

441 Nanking and Cambaluc (Peking).

442 The dragon, emblem of China.

443 Naga is the Sanskrit name of the mythical dragon, and appears in all the dialects of the Indian archipelago (Crawfurd, 290).

444 Details about musk and its collection are also reported in Pires, Tomé. *The Suma oriental of Tomé Pires.* London: Hakluyt Society, 1944, 228) and Duarte Barbosa, *Além-mar. Códice Casanatense 1889 com o Livro do*

Oriente de Duarte Barbosa (Milan: Franco Maria Ricci, 1984), 102. For parallel passages see Canova, in Pigafetta, *Relazione*, 345.

445 Chincheo, in Fukien; Marco Polo's Zayton, the great port of Cambay.

446 The name is that given in the sixteenth century to the Legions of Ryukyu Islands, but Pigafetta locates it on the mainlands. Robertson suggests that Pigafetta refers here to the city of Linching, in Shantung, north of the Yellow River (2: 234).

447 Moni may have been the name of a kingdom, not of the king, perhaps an echo of Mangi, the southern port of China, south of the Yellow River.

448 Probably Hainan.

449 Names already applied by Pigafetta to Pacific islands in 15 degrees S (cf. 262 and note).

450 The full date marks the beginning of the return trip. *Laut chidol* are Javanese words (*Laut Kidul* or *Loro Kidul*) meaning 'South Sea,' i.e., the Indian Ocean.

451 Cf. note 152.

452 Identifications: Pegu, Bengal, Orissa, Quilon in Malabar, Calicut, Cambay and Gujarat, Cananor, Goa, Ormuz.

453 The cries of the *polea* in order to avoid contact with members of the superior castes is recounted by other travellers, including Vartema and Barbosa (cfr. Canova, in Pigafetta, *Relazione*, 349).

454 The *Victoria* left behind the coasts of Timor on 13 February 1522, and a course was laid west-south-west, 40 to 41 degrees S latitude, to take them well to the south of the Cape of Good Hope for the westing. The Cape was not in fact rounded until 6 May according to Pigafetta (cf. 1334).

455 Peter Martyr concludes his account of the circumnavigation with a passage treating this phenomenon: 'It only remains for me to mention a fact which will astonish my readers, especially those who suppose they have a perfect knowledge of celestial phenomena. When the *Victoria* reached the Cape Verde islands, the sailors believed the day to be Wednesday, whereas it was Thursday. They had consequently lost one day on their voyage, and during their three years' absence. I said: "Your priests must have deceived you, since they have forgotten this day in their ceremonies and the recitation of their office." They answered: "Of what are you thinking? Do you suppose that all of us, including wise and experienced men, could have made such a mistake? It often happens

that an exact account is kept of the days and months, and moreover many of the men had office books and knew perfectly what had to be recited each day. There could be no mistake, especially about the office of the Blessed Virgin, at whose feet we prostrate ourselves each moment, imploring her assistance. Many passed their time reciting her office and that of the dead. You must, therefore, look elsewhere for an explanation, for it is certain that we have lost one day." Some gave one reason and some gave another, but all agreed upon one point, they had lost a day. I added: "My friends, remember that the year following your departure, that is to say, the year 1520, was a bissextile year, and this fact may have led you in error." They affirmed that they had taken account of the twenty-nine days in the month of February that year, which is usually shorter, and that they did not forget the bissextile of the calends of March of the same year. The eighteen men who returned from the expedition are mostly ignorant, but when questioned, one after another, they did not vary in their replies. Much surprised by this agreement, I sought Gaspar Contarino, ambassador of the illustrious republic of Venice at the court of the Emperor. He is a great sage in many subjects. We discussed in many ways this hithero unobserved fact, and we decided that perhaps the cause was as follows: The Spanish fleet, leaving the Gorgades Islands, proceeded straight to the west, that is to say, it followed the sun, and each day was a little longer than the preceding, according to the distance covered. Consequently, when the tour of the world was finished – which the sun makes in twenty-four hours from its rising to its setting – the ship had gained an entire day; that is to say, one less than those who remain all that time in the same place. Had a Portuguese fleet, sailing towards the east, continued in the same direction, following the same route first discovered, it is positive that when it got back to the Gorgades in would have lost a little time each day, in making the circuit of the world; it would have consequently have to count one day more. If on the same day a Spanish fleet and a Portuguese fleet left the Gorgades, each in the opposite direction, that is to say one towards the west and the other towards the east, and at the end of the same period and by different routes they had arrived at the Gorgades, let us suppose on a Thursday, the Spaniards who would have gained an entire day, would call it Wednesday, and the Portuguese, who would have lost a day, would declare it to be Friday. Philosophers may discuss the matter with more profound arguments, but for the moment I give my opinion and nothing more' (2: 169–71). See also Ramusio's 'Discorso sopra il viaggio fatto da gli Spangoli intorno al mondo' for another version of the same story, which evidently had a great appeal for humanists (I, 346).

456 The thirteen men left at Santiago were soon after repatriated in a Portuguese ship from India.

457 Again, the reference to the 'giorno presente' reveals a trace of Pigafetta's original diary.

458 The emperor Charles V.

459 King John III of Portugal (1502–57) ascended to the throne in 1521.

460 Louise of Savoy, mother of Francis I (1476–1531). Her designation here as 'Regent' can only refer to the period between February 1525 (Battle of Pavia) and January 1526 (Treaty of Madrid) when her son was prisoner of the Spanish. These chronological parameters, combined with the fact that the Grand Master was at Viterbo only until 25 June 1525, would appear to date this passage and the presentation of the work to sometime between February and June of 1525.

Bibliography

Albo, Francisco. *Diario o derrotero*. In Stanley, *First Voyage*, 211–36. (Original in Navarrete, *Colección*, vol. 4, 209–47.)

Amat di S. Filippo, P. *Gli illustri viaggiatori italiani con una antologia dei loro scritti*. Rome: Stablimento tipografico dell' Opinione, 1885.

Amoretti, Carlo. *Primo viaggio intorno al globo terracqueo*. Milan: G. Galeazzi, 1800.

Anonimo Portoghese. *Narrazione di un Portoghese compagno di Odoardo Barbosa, qual fu sopra la nave Vittoria dell'anno 1519*. In Ramusio, *Navigazioni*, 953–5.

Arditi, P. *Viaggio all'isola di Madera e alle Azzorre, 1567*. In Luzzana Caraci and Pozzi, *Scopritori e viaggiatori*, 741–63.

Atkinson, Geoffroy. *La littérature géographique française de la renaissance, repertoire bibliographique (avec 300 reproductions photographiques)*. Paris: A. Picard, 1927.

– *Les Nouveaux Horizons de la Renaissance française*. Paris: Droz, 1935.

– *Supplément au répertoire bibliographique se rapportant à la Littérature géographique française*. Paris: A. Picard, 1936.

– *The extraordinary voyage in French literature before 1700*. New York: AMS Press, 1966.

– *Les relations de voyages du XVIIe siècle et l'évolution des idées*. New York: B. Franklin, 1971.

Avonto, L. *I compagni italiani del Magellano con un'appendice sul 'Roteiro' di un pilota genovese*. Montevideo: Ediciones El Galeón, 1992.

Bandello, Matteo. *Novelle di Matteo Bandello*. Edited by G.G. Ferrero. Turin: UTET, 1974.

Barbosa, Duarte. *Além-Mar. Códice Casanatense 1889 com o Livro do Oriente de Duarte Barbosa*. Introduction by F. Braudel, annotation by G. Guadalupi, C.R. Boxer, and R. Barchiesi. Milan: Franco Maria Ricci, 1984.

Barros, J. de. *Asia de João de Barros. Dos feitos que os portugueses fizeram no descobrimento e conquista dos mares e terras do Oriente.* Edited by H. Cidade and M. Murias. Lisbon: Divisão de Publicações e Biblioteca, Agência Geral das Colonias, 1946.

Battaglia, Salvatore, and Giorgio Barberi Squaretti. *Grande dizionario della lingua italiana.* Turin: UTET, 1961.

Bausani, A. *L'Indonesia nella relazione di viaggio di A. Pigafetta.* Rome: Centro di cultura italiana Djakarta, 1972.

Beccaria, G.L., *Spagnolo e spagnoli in Italia. Riflessi ispanici sulla lingua italiana del Cinque e del Seicento.* Turin: Giappichelli, 1968.

Benso, Silvia. *Letteratura di viaggio dal Medioevo al Rinascimento. Generi e problemi.* Alessandria: Edizioni Dell' Orso, 1989.

Berchet, G., *Fonti italiane per la storia della scoperta del nuovo mondo, Raccolta Colombiana,* pt. 3, vols. 1–2. Rome: Ministero della Pubblica Istruzione, 1892.

Busnelli, M.D., 'Per una lettura del *Primo viaggio intorno al mondo* di Antonio Pigafetta,' *Studi di lessicografia italiana* 4 (1982): 5–45.

Cachey, Theodore, Jr, 'Tasso's *Navigazione del mondo nuovo* and the Origins of Colombus Encomium (GL, XV, 31–2).' *Italica* 69, no. 3 (1992): 326–44.

– 'Dal Nuovo Mondo alle isole Fortunate.' In *Le Isole Fortunate: appunti di storia letteraria italiana,* 203–62. Rome: L'Erma di Bretschneider, 1995.

Canova, Andrea. 'Proposte per l'edizione critica della "Relazione" di Antonio Pigafetta e la letteratura di viaggio nel Cinquecento.' *Studi di filologia italiana* 55 (1997): 87–105.

– 'Esperienza e letteratura nella "Relazione del viaggio attorno al mondo" di Antonio Pigafetta: la descrizione del Brasile.' *Annali di storia moderna e contemporanea* 4 (1998): 459–76.

Cardona, G.R. 'L'elemento di origine o di trafila portoghese nella lingua dei viaggiatori italiani del '500.' *Bollettino dell'Atlante Linguistico Mediterraneo* 13–15 (1971–3): 162–219.

– 'I viaggi e le scoperte.' In *Letteratura italiana,* vol. 5, *Le Questioni,* 687–716. Turin: Einaudi, 1986.

Castanheda, F. Lopes de. *Historia do descobrimento e conquista da India pelos Portugueses.* Edited by P. de Azevedo and P.M. Laranjo Coelho. Coimbra: Impr. da Universidade, 1924–33.

Ciscato, Antonio. *Antonio Pigafetta viaggiatore vicentino del secolo XVI.* Vicenza: Fratelli Giuliam, 1898.

Chatwin, Bruce. *In Patagonia.* New York: Summit Books, 1977.

Bibliography

Clairis, C. 'Indigenous Languages of Tierra del Fuego.' In *South American Indian Languages: Retrospect and Prospect.* Edited by E.M. Klein and L.R. Stark, 753–64. Austin: University of Texas Press, 1985.

Cocco, F. *Malo e il suo Monte.* Malo: Amministrazione Comunale, 1979.

Colón, C. *Textos y documentos completos. Relaciones de viajes, cartas y memoriales.* Edited by C. Varela. Madrid: Alianza, 1989.

Columbus, Christopher. 'The Letter Announcing the Discovery.' In Cecil Jane, ed., *The Four Voyages of Columbus,* 2–19. New York: Dover, 1988.

– *The* Diario *of Christopher Columbus's First Voyage to America.* Edited by O. Dunn and J.E. Kelley Jr. Norman: University of Oklahoma Press, 1989.

Crawfurd, John. *A Descriptive Dictionary of the Indian Islands and Adjacent Countries.* London: Oxford University Press, 1971 (reprint of London, 1856).

Da Mosto, Andrea. *Il primo viaggio intorno al globo di Antonio Pigafetta, Raccolta Colombiana,* pt. 5, vol. 3, 49–112. Rome: Ministero della Pubblica Istruzione, 1894.

Dati, Giuliano. *L'invenzione delle nuove insule di Channaria indiane.* Edited by T.J. Cachey Jr and L. Formisano. Chicago: Newberry Library, 1989.

de Herrera y Tordesillas, A. *Historia general de los hechos de los castellanos en las islas y tierra firme del Mar Oceano.* Madrid: Imprento Real de Nicolas Rodriguez [*sic*] Franco, 1726–8.

Díaz-Trechuelo, L. 'La organización del viaje magallánico: financiación, enganches, acopios y preparativos!' In *Viagem de Fernão de Magalhães,* 265–314.

Dionisotti, Carlo. *Geografia e storia della letteratura italiana.* Turin: Einaudi, 1967.

Età delle scoperte geografiche nei suoi riflessi linguistici in Italia. Atti del Convegno di Studi, Florence, 21–22 October 1992. Florence: Accademia della Crusca, 1994.

Fernández de Oviedo y Valdéz. *Historia general y natural,* vol. 4. New York: American Geographical Society, 1934.

Foa, A. *Dizionario biografico degli italiani.* Rome: Istituto della Enciclopedia Italiana, 1960.

Folena, G. 'Le prime immagini dell'America nel vocabolario Italiano.' *Bollettino dell'Atlante Linguistico Mediterraneo* 13–15 (1971–3); 673–92; republished as 'Prime immagini colombiane dell'America nel lessico italiano,' in *Il linguaggio del caos. Studi sul plurilinguismo rinascimentale,* 99–118. Turin: Einaudi, 1991.

Formisano, L. 'Appunti sullo stile narrativo di Colombo.' *Rivista di letterature moderne e comparate* 42 (1989): 223–33.

– 'Linee di ricerca sul tema: "il viaggio alle Indie Occidentali."' In Benso, *Letteratura di viaggio dal Medioevo al Rinascimento,* 85–94.

– 'La ricezione del Nuovo Mondo nelle scritture di viaggio.' In *Età delle scoperte geografiche,* 129–47.

Gerbi, Antonello. *The Dispute of the New World: The History of a Polemic.* Translated by J. Moyle. Pittsburgh: University of Pittsburgh Press, 1973.

– *Nature in the New World: From Christopher Columbus to Gonzalo Fernández de Oviedo.* Translated by J. Moyle. Pittsburgh: University of Pittsburgh Press, 1985. Original: *La natura delle Indie Nove: Cristoforo Colombo a Gonzalo Fernández de Oviedo.* Milan: Ricciardi, 1975.

Gil, Juan. *Miti e utopie della scoperta. Oceano Pacifico: l'epopea dei navigatori.* Milan: Garzanti, 1992.

Greenblatt, Stephen. *Marvelous Possessions. The Wonder of the New World.* Chicago: University of Chicago Press, 1991.

Guglielminetti, M. 'Il Messico a Venezia nel 1528: Benedetto Bordon e Hernán Cortés.' In A.C. Aricò, ed., *L'impatto della scoperta dell'America nella cultura veneziana,* 108–9. Rome: Bulzoni, 1990.

– 'Per un sottogenere della letteratura del viaggio: gl'isolari fra Quattro e Cinquecento.' In Benso, *La letteratura di viaggio dal Medioevo al Rinascimento,* 107–17.

Guillemard, F.H.H. *The Life of Ferdinand Magellan and the First Circumnavigation of the Globe.* London: George Philip & Son, 1890.

Hakluyt, Richard. *The Principal Navigations, voyages, traffiques …* Glasgow: J. MacLehose and Sons, 1903–5.

Harrisson, T. 'The "Palang": Its History and Proto-History in West Borneo and the Philippines.' *Journal of the Malaysian Branch of the Royal Asiatic Society* 37, no. 2 (1964): 162–74.

Hulme, P. *Colonial Encounters: Europe and the Native Caribbean, 1492–1793.* London: Methuen, 1986.

Lach, Donald F. *Asia in the Making of Europe.* Chicago: University of Chicago Press, 1965.

Leed, Eric J., *The Mind of the Traveler: From Gilgamesh to Global Tourism.* New York: Basic Books, 1991.

Leite de Faria, F. 'As primeiras relaes impressas sobre a viagem de Ferno de Magalhes e a questo das Molucas.' In *Viagem de Fernão de Magalhães*, 512–18.

Lida, De Malkiel, M.R. 'Para la toponimía argentina: Patagonia.' *Hispanic Review* 20 (1952): 321–3. Republished in *El cuento popular y otros ensayos*, 93–7. Buenos Aires: Editorial Losada, 1976.

Lestringant, Frank. *Arts et légendes d'espace. Figures du voyage et rhétoriques du monde.* Paris: Presses de l'École normale supérieure, 1981.

– *André Thevet, cosmographe des derniers Valois.* Geneva: Droz, 1991.

– *L'atelier du cosmographe ou l'image du monde à la Renaissance.* Paris: Albin Michel, 1991.

– *Écrire le monde à la Renaissance. Quinze études sur Rabelais, Postel, Bodin et la littérature géographique.* Caen: Éditions Paradigme, 1993.

– *Cannibals: The Discovery and Representation of the Cannibal from Columbus to Jules Verne.* Translated by Rosemary Morris. Berkeley and Los Angeles: University of California Press, 1997.

– *Le Livre des isles, atlas et récits insulaires de la Genése à Jules Verne.* Geneva: Droz, 2002.

L'umanista aronese Pietro Martire d'Angheria primo storico del 'Nuovo Mondo.' Atti del Convegno di Arona, 28 October 1990. Edited by L. Stoppa and R. Cicala. Novara: Associazione di storia della Chiesa novarese: Interlinea, 1992.

Luzzana Caraci, I., and Pozzi, M. 'Notizie del Mondo Nuovo con le figure de paesi scoperti descritte da Antonio Pigafetta vicentino cavaglier di Rodi.' In I. Luzzana Caraci and M. Pozzi, eds., *Scopritori e viaggiatori del Cinquecento,*' 509–71. Milan: R. Ricciardi, 1996.

Magnagi, A. 'Di una nuova interpretazione della frase "a la catena ho a popa" nella relazione di Antonio Pigafetta sul viaggio di Magellano.' *Bollettino della Societá Geografica Italiana* 6, no. 4 (1927): 458–75.

Mahaffy, J.P. 'Two Early Tours in Ireland.' *Hermathena* 40 (1914).

Manfroni, Camillo. *Relazione del primo viaggio intorno al mondo, di Antonio Pigafetta seguita del Roteiro d'un pilota Genovese.* Milan: Edizioni Alpes, 1928.

– *A. Pigafetta. Il primo viaggio intorno al mondo.* Edited by C. Manfroni. Milan: Istituto editoriale italiano, 1956.

Mantese, G. 'I genitori di Antonio Pigafetta.' *Archivio Veneto* 67 (1960): 26–41.

– *Memorie storiche della chiesa vicentina*, pt. 3, vol. 2: *1404–1563*. Vicenza: N. Pozza, 1964.

– 'La Pieve di Santa Maria di Caltrano e la sfuggente ombra di Antonio Pigafetta.' *La Voce dei Berici*, 29 May 1966. Republished in *Scritti scelti di storia vicentina*, 376–78. Vicenza: Istituto per le ricerche di storia sociale e di storia religiosa, 1982.

Márquez, Gabriel García. 'Fantasía y creacíon artística en América Latina y el Caribe.' *Texto Crítico* 14 (1979) 122–8.

– 'The Solitude of América.' *New York Times*, section 4 (6 February 1983).

Martyr, Peter. *De Orbe Novo: The Eight Decades of Peter Martyr*. Translated by F.A. MacNutt. 2 vols. New York: G.P. Putnam's Sons, 1912.

Masoero, Mariarosa. *Viaggio attorno al mondo di Antonio Pigafetta*. Rovereto, Italy: Longo, 1987.

– 'Magellano, "bon pastore" e "bon cavaliero".' In Benso, *La letteratura di viaggio dal Medioevo al Rinascimento*, 51–62.

Medina, J.T. *El describimiento del Océano Pacífico. Hernando de Magallanes y sus compañeros. Documento (Anexo a la memoria Universitaria)*. Santiago, Chile: Imprenta Universitaria, 1920.

Modigliani, E. *L'isola delle donne: un viaggio a Enggano*. Milan: V. Hoepli, 1894.

Morison, Samuel E. *Admiral of the Ocean Sea*. Boston: Little, Brown, 1942.

– *The European Discovery of America*, vol. 2, *The Southern Voyages*. New York: Oxford University Press, 1974.

Navarrete, Martín Fernández de. *Colección de los viajes y descubrimientos que hicieron por mar los españoles*, vol. 4. Madrid: De Orden de S.M. en la Impr. Nacional, 1837.

Nowell, Charles E. *Magellan's Voyage Round the World: Three Contemporary Accounts*. Evanston, IL: Northwestern University Press. 1962.

Nuovo Mondo. Gli Italiani. 1492–1565. Edited by P. Collo and P.L. Crovetto. Turin: Einaudi 1991.

Nunn, G. 'Magellan's Route to the Pacific.' *Geographical Review* 34 (October 1935): 615–33.

Olschki, L. *Storia letteraria delle scoperte geografiche*. Florence: Olschki, 1937.

Pasini, C. 'Antichi cataloghi manoscritti dei codici della Biblioteca Ambrosiana.' *Aevum* 69 (1995): 665–95.

Pancaldo, L. 'Navegaçam e voyagem que fez Fernando de Magalhaes de Sevilha pera Maluco no anno de 1519.' In Avonto, *Compagni*, 313–35.

Patagonia. Natural History, Prehistory and Ethnography at the Uttermost End of the Earth. Edited by C. McEwan, L.A. Borrero, and A. Prieto. London: British Museum Press, 1997.

Pelletier, M. *Géographie du monde au Moyen Âge et à la Renaissance.* Paris: Éd. du CTHS, 1989.

– *Couleurs de la Terre.* Paris: Bibliothèque nationale de France, 1998.

– *Les îles, du mythe à la réalité.* Paris: Éd. du CTHS, 2002.

Penrose, B. *Travel and Discovery in the Renaissance, 1420–1620.* Cambridge, MA: Harvard University Press, 1952.

Pfister, M. 'Riflessi nel lessico italiano dei viaggi di Colombo, di Vespucci e di Magellano.' In *Età delle scoperte geografiche*, 9–22.

Pigafelta, Antoni. *Relation du premier voyage autour du monde par Magellan. 1519–1522.* Edited by J. Denucé. Paris: E. Leroux; Anvers: G. Janssens, 1923.

– *The First Voyage around the World: An Account of Magellan's Expedition.* Edited by T.J. Cachey Jr. New York: Marsilio, 1995.

– *Il primo viaggio intorno al mondo.* Edited by Mario Pozzi. Vicenza: N. Pozza, 1995.

– *Relazione del primo viaggio attorno al mondo.* Edited by Andrea Canova. Padua: Antenore, 1999.

Pires, Tomé. *The Suma Oriental of Tomé Pires.* London: Kakluyt Society, 1944.

Pizzorusso, Valeria Bertolucci. 'Uno spettacolo per il Re: l'infanzia di Adamo nella 'Carta" di Pero Vaz de Caminha.' *Quaderni Portoghesi* 4 (1978): 49–81.

Polo, M. *Milione.* Edited by V. Bertolucci Pizzorusso. Milan: Adelphi, 1994.

Pregliasco, M. 'Tipologia di un viaggio minimo.' In Benso, *Letteratura di viaggio dal Medioevo al Rinascimento*, 63–84.

Quint, David. 'The Boat of Romance and Renaissance Epic.' In K. and M. Brownlee, eds., *Romance: Generic Transformation from Chrétien de Troyes to Cervantes*, 178–202. Hanover, NH: University Press of New England, 1985.

Quirino, C. *Philippine Cartography (1320–1899).* Amsterdam: N. Israel, 1963.

– *First Voyage around the World by Antonio Pigafetta and De Moluccis Insulis by Maximilianus Transylvanus.* Introduction by C. Quirino. Manila: Filipiniana Book Guild, 1969.

Raccolta Colombiana: Raccolta dei documenti e studi pubblicati dalla R. Commissione Colombiana pel Quarto Centenario dalla scoperta dell'America. Rome: Ministero della pubblica istruzione, 1892–1896.

Ramusio, Gian Battista. *Navigazioni et Viaggi: Venice 1563–1606*. 3 vols. Introduction by R.A. Skelton and analysis by G.B. Parks. Amsterdam: Theatrum Orbis Terrarum Ltd., 1970.

Ravenstein, E.G. *Martin Benhaim, His Life and His Globe*. London: G. Philip and Son, Ltd. 1908.

Robertson, James Alexander. *Magellan's Voyage around the World by Antonio Pigafetta: The Original Text of the Ambrosian MS*. Translation, notes, bibliography, and index by J.A. Robertson. Cleveland: Arthur H. Clark Co., 1906.

Robles, H.E. 'The First Voyage around the World: From Pigafetta to García Márquez.' *History of European Ideas* 6, no. 4 (1985): 385–404.

Said, Edward. *Orientalism*. New York: Pantheon, 1978.

Sanudo, Marin. *I Diarii (1496–1533): pagine scelte*. Edited by Paolo Margarol. Vicenza: N. Pozza, 1997.

Sanvisenti, D. 'Studi sulla lingua di Antonio Pigafetta.' *Archivio glottologico italiano* 30 (1938): 149–71.

– 'Il lessico del Pigafetta.' *Rendiconti del R. Istituto Lombardo di Scienze e Lettere. Classe di lettere e scienze morali e storiche* 75 (1941–2), 469–504, and 76 (1942–3), 3–33.

Schurhammer Georg. 'Una ipotesi sulla fine di Antonio Pigafetta.' In *Orientalia*. Lisbon: Centro de Estudos Históricos Ultramarinos, 1963.

– *Scopritori e viaggiatori del Cinquecento*. Edited by I. Luzzana Caraci and M. Pozzi. Milan and Naples: Ricciardi, 1996.

Silva, C.R. de. 'The Portuguese and the Trade in Cloves in Asia during the Sixteenth Century.' *Studia* 46 (1987): 133–56.

Skeat, W.W. *Malay Magic: An Introduction to the Folklore and Popular Religion of the Malay Peninsula*. London: Cass, 1965.

Skelton, R.A. *Magellan's Voyage: A Narrative Account of the First Circumnavigation by Antonio Pigafetta*. 2 vols. New Haven, CT: Yale University Press, 1969.

Soravia, G. 'Di alcune parole indonesiane e filippine in viaggiatori italiani.' *Archivio glottologico italiano* 68 (1983): 86–98.

– 'Pigafetta lessicografo dei nuovi e vecchi mondi.' In *Età delle scoperte geografiche*.

Stanley, Edward John, Lord of Alderly. *The First Voyage around the World by Magellan*. London: Hakluyt Society, 1874.

Tiraboschi, Girolamo. *Storia della letteratura italiana*. Florence: Molini, Laudi, 1809.

Tormo Sanz, L. 'El mundo indígena conocido por Magellanes en las Islas de San Lázaro.' In *Viagem de Fernão de Magalhães*, 379–409.

Torodash, Martin. 'Magellan Historiography.' *Hispanic American Historical Review* 51 (1971): 313–35.

– 'Magellan Historiography: Some Twenty Years Later.' In Proceedings of the International Colloquium on the Portuguese and the Pacific. Edited by Francis A. Dutra and João Camil dos Santos, 11–16, Center for Portuguese Studies, University of California Santa Barbara, 1995.

Transylvanus, Maximilian. *De Moluccis insulis*. Rome, 1523. In Stanley, *First Voyage*, 179–210.

– *The Travels of Marco Polo*. New York: Dorset Press, 1908.

A Treatise on the Moluccas (c. 1544). Probably the Preliminary Version of António Galvão's Lost 'História das Molucas.' Edited, annotated, and translated into English from the Portuguese manuscript in the Archivo General de Indias, Seville by H. Jacobs, SJ. Rome and St Louis: Jesuit Historical Institute, 1971.

Trovato, P. *Il primo Cinquecento*. Bologna: Il Mulino, 1994.

Verrazzano, Giovanni da. *The Voyages of Giovanni de Verrazzano*. Edited by Lawrence C. Wroth. New Haven, CT: Yale University Press, 1970.

Vespucci, Amerigo. *Lettere di viaggio*. Edited by L. Formisano. Milan: Mondadori, 1985.

– *Letters from a New World*. Edited by Luciano Formisano. New York: Marsilio, 1992.

A Viagem de Fernão de Magalhães e a Questão das Molucas. Actas do II Colóquio luso-espanhol de história ultramarina. Edited by A. Texeira da Mota. Lisbon: Junta de Investigações Científicas do Ultramar, 1975.

Vidos, B.E. 'Saggio sugli iberismi in Pigafetta.' In *Actas del V Congresso internacional de estudios lingüísticos del Mediterráneo*. Málaga: Diputación de Málaga, Instituto de Cultura, 1977.

Voyage of Magellan: The Journal of Antonio Pigafetta. Translated by Paula Spurlin Paige from the edition in the William L. Clements Library. Englewood Cliffs, NJ: Prentice Hall, 1969.

Index

Persons

Places